Oscar and Bosie

Oscar and Bosie

A Fatal Passion

Trevor Fisher

SUTTON PUBLISHING

First published in 2002 by
Sutton Publishing Limited · Phoenix Mill
Thrupp · Stroud · Gloucestershire · GL5 2BU

British Library Cataloguing in Publication Data
A catalogue record for this book is available from the British Library

ISBN 0 7509 2459 4

Typeset in 10/13pt New Baskerville.
Typesetting and origination by
Sutton Publishing Limited.
Printed and bound in England by
J.H. Haynes & Co. Ltd, Sparkford.

To Sarah,
who has had to live with
Oscar and Bosie
for far too long

Contents

List of Plates

Acknowledgements

The Author wishes to express his deep indebtedness to the late Mrs Sheila Colman for her encouragement in this project, and for her great generosity in allowing him to have sight of papers and other material belonging to Lord Alfred Douglas, and for granting permission to use copyright material in her possession. The author also wishes to warmly thank Merlin Holland for permission to use material copyright to his family.

Additional thanks are owed to Ellmann Properties for permission to quote extracts from *Oscar Wilde*, the seminal biography by Richard Ellmann; to the Marquis of Queensberry for permission to make use of and quote material connected with the Queensberry family; to Jean Graham Hall and Gordon D. Smith for permission to quote from *Oscar Wilde – The Tragedy of Being Earnest*, Barry Rose 2000; to Messrs Constable & Co. for permission to quote from *Aspects of Wilde* by Vincent O'Sullivan, 1936; to London Management for permission to quote from *Letters to Reggie Turner* by Max Beerbohm, © The Estate of Max Beerbohm; to Donald Sinden, for permission to quote from *A Touch of the Memoirs*, published by Hodder & Stoughton 1982; to The Society of Authors on behalf of the Bernard Shaw Estate for permission to quote from Shaw's correspondence with Lord Alfred Douglas; and to Sheridan Morley for permission to quote from *Oscar Wilde*, 2nd Edition published by Pavilion Books 1997. Background sources are referred to in the end notes and Bibliography.

Any errors, omissions or misattributions relating to Copyright matters are entirely the Author's responsibility and, if brought to his attention, he would be glad to correct them in future editions. Thanks are also owed to the editorial staff at Sutton Publishing for their patience and fortitude in coping with what has, right up until the final deadline, been a rather long and complicated project dogged, one sometimes felt, by the quarrelsome shades of its main protagonists.

TF

Terminology

The terms "homosexuality" and "homosexual" are used throughout this book to denote same sex love between men. The alternative "gay" has come into use only in the latter part of the last century; and would have meant, to a Victorian, merely happy or lighthearted. At the time of the affair between Oscar Wilde and Bosie Douglas, sex between persons of the same gender was illegal: the practice was unknown to most people and "homosexual" was a medical term that had not yet entered popular usage. Several contemporary terms existed: one, "Uranian love", was used by Wilde himself (*Letters 2000*, p.1019). "Queer" was a common euphemism among the clandestine homosexual community until the 1960s, but is nowadays considered pejorative. To avoid causing confusion or offence, I shall stick to the scientific "homosexual". "Sodomy", although nowadays sounding rather high-minded, was virtually the only contemporary word to describe the sex act between men, and I have retained it throughout.

The spelling of Marquis/Marquess is contentious. I have retained Marquis as being Queensberry's own preferred style, although the latter is nowadays more common.

PROLOGUE

Destructive Passions

In the Summer of 1891, Oscar Wilde was at the peak of a delicious notoriety. A decade of public posing and literary activity had scandalised respectable folk, delighted the *avant garde* and established an enormously visible public persona. That Spring he had created a sensation with his novella, *The Picture of Dorian Gray*, published to critical acclaim and widespread public disapproval. The bookseller W.H. Smith underlined his family reputation by refusing to sell it, claiming it was "filthy". Radicals and aesthetes applauded Wilde for his daring, few more enthusiastically than Wilde's young friend, the poet Lionel Johnson. Only recently down from Oxford, Johnson revelled in the decadence Wilde displayed, sharing his delight with an even younger friend still studying at Wilde's old college, Magdalen. This was Lord Alfred Bruce Douglas, known to friends and family by his childhood nickname of "Bosie". Johnson suggested that he introduce his undergraduate friend to Oscar Wilde.[1] Oscar was 36 and, though married with two children, cultivated the company of aesthetic young men. Johnson, himself a young Aesthete,[2] believed Bosie and Wilde would enjoy each other's company. Both were intrigued, and so Johnson made the introductions for a meeting.

It was a wholly decorous affair. Johnson arranged date and place, picked up Bosie from his mother's London house in Cadogan Street, and the two travelled by cab to Wilde's house in Tite Street, Chelsea. At the end of his life, Bosie was to claim that Oscar Wilde took a violent fancy to him on sight, but this is unlikely.[3] Wilde flattered all the young men he met, and the inscription in the copy of *The Picture of Dorian Gray* which he gave to Bosie at their second meeting merely read: "For Alfred Douglas, from his friend who wrote this book, July 1891".[4] The flowery inscriptions that followed, and the passionate emotions they betrayed, did not emerge until the following Summer.

Nevertheless, a seed was sown which grew into the most famous love affair between two men, possibly since David and Jonathan. The story is well rehearsed: how Bosie's father, the pugnacious Marquis of Queensberry, was consumed by hatred of the relationship and set out to destroy it. How he picked a public quarrel, aiming to provoke Wilde into challenging him, hounding the writer and finally leaving an ambiguously worded calling card at his club. How Wilde rashly initiated a prosecution for libel, an act that (as so often happens in libel cases) rebounded on him. How, on the basis of the evidence that emerged, Wilde was charged in two subsequent criminal trials with committing illegal acts, imprisoned and died in exile. And how the subsequent explosion of public outrage triggered by the revelations at the Wilde trials ended the Aesthetic movement and brought decadent experiments like the *Yellow Book* and *Savoy* magazine to an end.

The private consequences for Wilde and his circle were disastrous. After his release, Wilde spent his remaining years in exile in Paris, unable to write and crippled by financial worries. He died in 1900, aged only 46, never having recaptured the literary genius which had made him the most successful playwright of his time. His wife Constance died in exile, aged only 40, living under an assumed name, struggling to bring up her children without a father. Bosie Douglas had been protected from prosecution but made himself publicly notorious by openly associating with Wilde and defending him in public – behaviour that nevertheless did not prevent him being unjustly blamed for Wilde's downfall. Afterwards, he was to turn proselyte for far-right-wing nationalist causes, and campaigned publicly against decadence and corruption. Only in his declining years could he admit to himself the true nature of his sexual relationship with Wilde. In the meantime, he had destroyed Wilde's friend, one-time lover and literary executor, Robert Ross, the darling of the literary *demi monde*, in a campaign of rabid vituperation and pursuit startlingly reminiscent of that waged by his father against Wilde twenty years earlier. Douglas, too, was to meet his nemesis in court.

The fall of Oscar Wilde from literary prominence to social disgrace has an Icarus-like quality, adding to the enormous interest in his life and literature which clearly now makes him one of the most written about authors in English literature. The Gay Rights movement, emergent since the 1970s, has naturally focussed attention on Wilde and played up the extent of his "martyrdom" by "respectable" Victorian society. There is an enormous body of work on the life of Oscar Wilde, and, indeed, a substantial body of writing on the troubled life of Lord Alfred Douglas; but no attempt has been made to explore the relationship in its own right.

The lives of both men have been exhaustively dealt with by biographers, their relationship outlined in books and PhD theses, explored in films and television documentaries and portrayed on the stage. The story has become legendary without a truly satisfactory account having emerged. False leads abound, notably in the writings of both men. In his books *Oscar Wilde and Myself* (1914), the *Autobiography* of 1929, *Without Apology* in 1938 and *Oscar Wilde; A Summing Up* of 1940, Douglas presented a shifting vision of his friendship with Wilde, moving from open hostility to warm sympathy, without ever fully addressing the reality of the relationship, particularly their sex life together and with others. Wilde left no overtly autobiographical study; but his letters, among the most abundant correspondence in literature, give only a partial and misleading account, particularly in relation to Bosie Douglas. Often written brilliantly for effect, they provide a body of information that is simultaneously essential for any study of Wilde, and a potent seedbed for many of the myths and misstatements about the relationship which have grown over the intervening century. But the sentiments, emotions and even the "facts" they contain are scarcely to be trusted.

This is particularly so where Wilde's long and bitter prison letter to Bosie Douglas known as *De Profundis* (From Out of the Depths) is concerned. The letter has attained iconic status[5] but, despite its abundance of evidence and sharp insights into the relationship, it provides many pitfalls for the unwary. Wilde transfers responsibility for his downfall to the conflict between Bosie Douglas and his father, painting himself as the innocent victim "in the mad, bad line from which you come". The image which Wilde projects, of a brilliant man driven to imprisonment and exile by the Oedipal conflict of a father and son, captures an important part of the dramatic truth of his downfall. But it was not the whole truth about his relationship with Douglas, and comes nowhere near to explaining his folly in suing Queensberry, thus triggering one of the great "what if. . .?" arguments of literary debate. Two interesting points about *De Profundis* merely add to the confusion: first, that Bosie Douglas almost certainly never even read the letter; and, secondly, that despite everything in it, and behind it, they remained lovers and friends until the final curtain. Nothing, it seemed, no bitterness or quarrel, could dent the essential solidity of the relationship itself.

Nevertheless, Wilde's polemic laid the foundation of the immensely powerful myth that Bosie Douglas drove the great man to his ruin and then abandoned him – an impression reinforced by the letters he wrote from Naples in 1898 asserting that Douglas had played the role of Judas, deserting his friend when he was most needed. Once these letters became public, Wilde's supporters and most neutral observers could only see Bosie Douglas as the Dark Angel who destroyed a glittering personality. This view has dominated most commentaries on Douglas's relationship with Wilde. It remains the most potent of the myths that have come to surround the relationship. But it wasn't true.

Douglas spent most of the latter part of his life defending himself against this charge in polemics of his own that were rarely effective. He and his defenders produced persuasive evidence that he did not betray Wilde and had in fact supported him throughout his final years. However, Douglas destroyed his credibility by manic behaviour that reinforced the image Wilde had created of him in *De Profundis*.

There is the opposing view to consider: that the tormented father who hounded Wilde into the dock at the Old Bailey in order to save his son, was not seeking to persecute Wilde *per se*, but primarily aimed to destroy Bosie Douglas and his beloved mother, Queensberry's divorced and much put-upon wife, Sybil.[6] Bosie himself was dominated by this view, seeing conflict with his father as no more than a conventional aspect of the bitter quarrel that had led to his parents' divorce. However, he could never argue this heterodox case effectively because of the savage temper that habitually broke through at the slightest criticism. A small number of supporters have nevertheless fought his corner over the years, tenaciously swimming against the tide created by Oscar Wilde's enormous personal and literary stature. The Douglas case, while demanding attention, has always failed to do more than keep alive the bitter factional disputes that the relationship sadly created.

Few of those who were caught in the maelstrom could avoid poisonous emotions that have endured long since those who experienced them at first hand have passed away. Understanding the all-consuming passion that bound these two men together so completely calls for a more objective approach. Bosie Douglas and the Marquis of Queensberry, Oscar Wilde and his loyal friend Robert Ross, Sybil Queensberry, Constance and the boys have become characters in a drama of romance, betrayal and obsession. Yet the fatal passions that consumed them were neither romance nor myth. Their human frailties and follies were more complex than the legends allow, and deserve to be revealed in their own terms. In *The Ballad of Reading Gaol*, written in France after his release, Wilde, who had been confronted in prison perhaps for the first time by the reality, as opposed to the manufactured image, of his life, repeats over and again in various ways, the haunting refrain: "Each man kills the thing he loves". This was no mere poetic contrivance, but a lament for a life lost – perhaps, too, a dreadful accusation that will stand for as long as the affair is remembered.

ONE

The Douglases and the Wildes

At two o'clock in the afternoon of 6 August 1858, Archibald William Douglas, 7th Marquis of Queensberry,[1] took himself off to shoot rabbits on his Scottish estate in Dumfriesshire. The Marquis was forty, possessed a fortune worth some £780,000 at contemporary values, had a wife and six children, of whom his son and heir John Sholto was fourteen years old and training for the navy as a midshipman. To outward appearances the family was settled and content. Queensberry had suffered heavy betting losses that week at Goodwood, but they were not calamitous for a man of his great wealth. He invited his oldest child, Gertrude, to join in him the shoot but, when she declined, went off alone.

About an hour later, men working in the grounds of the estate saw Douglas shoot a crow and move off into a nearby field. Shots were heard, but from 3.30 there was silence. Around 4 p.m., two cousins went looking for him. They were directed to the field from which the shots had been heard and were "overwhelmed with horror on discovering the body of his Lordship prostrate on the earth and covered with blood. Life was found to be extinct, and the limbs were beginning to stiffen".[2] Queensberry had been killed by a single shot from his double-barrelled gun. The charge had entered his chest at an angle, penetrated his heart, and lodged in his back.

Four labourers were called and the body was placed on an improvised litter. The men then carried the remains back to the ancestral home, Kinmount House, weeping servants following in a ragged line. When they arrived at the house, the Marquis's children watched uncomprehendingly. A crowd blocked the doorway, their mother stood tense and dazed. One of the brothers lay face down on the sofa, sobbing. Another brother stood trembling beside him, while Gertrude hovered in the background, weeping bitterly. Four men shuffled into the hall carrying the body covered in a cloak and took it in to the library. Word was sent to Portsmouth to tell John Sholto of his father's death.

Fatal gunshots were not uncommon in the world of field sports in which Archibald Douglas lived his life. Such a tragedy normally evoked shock and sympathy, but there was very little lamenting over the

Marquis's sudden demise. Press comment in fact was remarkably sharp: the local paper carried an obituary the day before the funeral, remarking: "Sudden and sad has been the end of the 7th Marquis of Queensberry. Born in high rank . . . he has perished in a moment. Faults he had not a few. That passion for the turf, and kindred pursuits still more questionable, absorbed much of his time and energies, brought clouds about his otherwise radiant path. . . . What might he not have become had he avoided the vortex in which he was involved? We entertained high expectations of the deceased nobleman, and it was because we did so and were disappointed that we speak thus."[3] This carping obituary, with its veiled references to "questionable" pursuits, was reprinted in *The Times*.

The death of the 7th Marquis brought his son and heir, John Sholto Douglas, to the title. His premature inheritance was far more, unfortunately, than the title and wealth of a Victorian aristocrat. The Douglases possessed a decidedly eccentric temperament. It was marked in the late Archibald William, passed on to his eldest son John Sholto and, as it would be, through him, to his third son, Alfred Bruce "Bosie" Douglas. John Sholto, the 8th Marquis, and Bosie were to make the famous "Douglas temperament" a national disgrace.

For, Archibald Douglas had been an impetuous, pig-headed, irresponsible man, incapable of holding down a job, and a reckless gambler. He tried to make a career in the army, but, lacking discipline, resigned his commission. He entered politics in 1847 as the local MP, but an obsession with his lack of an English peerage ruined a promising career. Having risen to become a Privy Councillor in relatively short order, he agreed to serve in Palmerston's government in 1855. However, he quarrelled with the Prime Minister when Palmerston refused to add an English title to his Scottish peerage, and resigned from national politics in a fit of pique. Moreover, he was perceived to have abandoned his fellow countrymen by also resigning his office as Lord Lieutenant of Dumfries. This explosive reaction to anything that prevented them from getting their own way would be echoed in the behaviour of both John Sholto and his son, Bosie Douglas.

Archibald William compensated for his political failure by immersing himself in the life of the turf, where he displayed a stunning lack of judgement. His crowning folly was a disastrous wager on the Goodwood Cup of 1858. He took a bet of "20 monkeys to one" (a "monkey" being £500) against James Merry's horse, Saunterer. He accepted the bet despite being advised by experts that Saunterer was unbeatable. The horse won in a canter, and the Marquis lost £10,000.[4] This was a considerable sum, but it was less important to a wealthy man than the humiliation he suffered in having taking such a ridiculous risk. He had lost face in the only social circles that mattered to him. Worse, he had to return to Kinmount to face his wife. The stresses Douglas experienced following his humiliation at Goodwood impacted on a temperament that was both impetuous and dangerously rigid. Whatever private torments he was going through were never recorded, but Archibald William left Goodwood not to travel to Scotland, but to head south to Portsmouth to pay a paternal visit to John Sholto at the naval training school HMS *Britannia*. He then turned north again on the long journey back to Dumfriesshire. Two days later, he was dead. Whatever words had passed between them, John Sholto did not see his father alive again.

The shock of the tragedy for the 14-year-old was no doubt tempered by succeeding to both the title of 8th Marquis and the wealth that went with it. At Kinmount, he inherited an imposing mansion on a large country estate with the Solway Firth glinting in the distance. The title carried an automatic place at the head of County society. It was a heady brew for an adolescent. It certainly did nothing to limit his bounding belief in his own judgement and self-importance. Rigid, quarrelsome, self-opinionated and capable of reckless and destructive acts, John Sholto Douglas would cut a controversial path through Victorian society until, in 1895, he faced Oscar Wilde at the Old Bailey in the most sensational libel action of the era.

* * *

At the time John Sholto Douglas was coming into his title, Oscar Fingal O'Flahertie Wills Wilde was already four years old. He enjoyed an upbringing very different to the life of the aristocratic milieu of the Douglases, but with a family background similarly at odds with convention. Wilde was the second son of two of the leading professional figures of mid-century Dublin, the nationalist poet Jane Francesca Wilde and her husband, William Robert Wilde, surgeon and writer. It was an outstandingly successful family. Oscar's father was at the top of his profession, having founded Dublin's St Mark's Hospital in 1844, ten years before Wilde's birth. Oscar enjoyed a contented and secure childhood, surrounded by prosperity and stimulated by a rich intellectual environment. The house in Merrion Square hosted dinner parties and receptions that were a major feature of Dublin's literary life. When newly wed, Jane Wilde described her husband as "the best conversationalist in the metropolis".[5] William Wilde liked to dominate the dinner table, and Oscar learnt from his father the art of talking well.

When William married Jane Elgee on 14 November 1851, he was 36 and already the foremost medical specialist on the ear and eye in Ireland. His textbooks on eye complaints (1851) and surgery on the ear (1853) brought him a Europe-wide reputation. He was chosen to be the Commissioner for Medical Information in Ireland during the 1851 census, and his outstanding skills earned him the position of Surgeon Oculist in Ordinary to the Queen. He was knighted in 1864 for services to medicine; yet, he was not merely a conventional medical specialist. He wrote a book on Swift's last illness, based on the skull of the writer, which had come into his possession. His abundant energies extended outside medical matters to the archaeology and folklore of Ireland.

Wilde *père* was also a man of intense sexuality and curious personal habits. He was much shorter than his very large wife, portraits showing a man with a curiously simian appearance. He was said to have a strong animal smell emanating from his body and, in his autobiography, W.B. Yeats told several stories about him that he had learnt from his family – his grandfather having known William Wilde. One was a "horrible folk story", that Wilde had taken out the eyes of a man who had come to consult him as an oculist and put them on a plate, intending to replace them. A cat passed by and ate them. This is of course an impossible story to believe: its significance is that Yeats felt it was worth retelling. Similarly, it was rumoured, Wilde had an unwashed quality to his skin that led to the crude Dublin joke: "Why are Sir William Wilde's nails so black? Because he has scratched himself".[6] It is impossible to believe an eminent surgeon would tolerate dirt, the evidence pointing to a physical condition rather than deficiencies in personal hygiene, but it is a fact that Wilde and his Bohemian household were regarded as slovenly.

This did not lessen Wilde's attractiveness to women. He had fathered three illegitimate children before his marriage, and acknowledged all three as his own. Oscar's parents possessed unconventional attitudes to relationships. As Sir William lay dying his wife demonstrated her indifference to convention by allowing a mysterious black-veiled woman to enter the house every day and sit silently by the bedside. Oscar told his friend and biographer Robert Sherard:

> She was aware of my father's constant infidelities, but simply ignored them. Before my father died, in 1876, he lay ill in bed for many days. And every morning a woman dressed in black and closely veiled used to come to our house in Merrion Square and unhindered either by my mother or anyone else, used to walk straight upstairs . . . and sit there all day, without ever speaking a word or once raising her veil. . . . Not one woman in a thousand would have tolerated her presence, but my mother allowed it because she knew my father loved this woman and felt it must be a joy and comfort to have her beside his dying bed.[7]

When the couple met, Jane Elgee (probably born in 1821) was as well known as her husband. Under the pen name Speranza she had written nationalist poetry supporting Young Ireland in the rebellion following the potato famine of the 1840s. After the editor of the *Nation* was put on trial by the British for sedition, Speranza took over as editor and wrote inflammatory editorials, which the British authorities added to the indictment against him. When the trial reached the point of discussing these editorials, she rose in the courtroom and declared herself to be the author. The sensation caused by Speranza's melodramatic *denouement* echoed across Ireland and Irish America. Young Ireland was defeated, however, and Jane Wilde reconciled herself to marriage and domesticity. She was not jealous of her husband's pre-marital affairs, having herself once been caught enjoying the company of the noted Dublin lawyer Isaac Butt in circumstances "which were not doubtful". Oscar Wilde's parents were devoted to the marriage, however, and Jane bore her husband three children – William, born September 1852, Oscar on 16 October 1854, and a girl, Isola, in April 1857.

Oscar therefore grew up as part of a secure Anglo-Irish provincial world which appeared to offer a career for those talents who could avail themselves of its privileges. He was to rebel against this world, but never in a sense that Irish Fenians or Home Rulers would understand. His childhood offered nothing to suggest that a challenge to British Imperial hegemony was desirable. School and home in Dublin were pleasurable and uneventful. Holidays on the coast or in the Irish countryside were enjoyable recreational outings. On one occasion, legend has it, Oscar spent a childhood holiday making sandcastles on the beach with another talented boy, the young Edward Carson. In 1895, Carson would confront Oscar as an implacable destroyer across the courtroom of the Old Bailey in London. William Wilde used these holidays to pursue his interests in Irish folklore and archaeology. From this, Oscar, the ultimate sophisticate, privately imbibed a rustic spiritualism and belief in omens that would be lifelong. He told Vincent O'Sullivan shortly before his death that, one night as a child, he had woken to hear the cry of the banshee and sobbed "Why are they beating that dog? Tell them to stop beating that dog!". The following day, one of the family died. He claimed also to have heard the banshee cry from his prison cell, the night his mother passed away.[8]

This tranquil upbringing was disturbed only slightly in 1864 when Oscar's mother appeared in court. In January 1864, William Wilde was awarded a knighthood for services to medicine, prompting one of his patients, Mary Travers, to claim that, while treating her, Wilde had administered chloroform and raped her. The case was not strong, the alleged rape having taken place in 1862. Travers had remained Wilde's patient, and even received money from him to go abroad the same year, which she had failed to do. The award of the knighthood infuriated Travers, and she began to circulate scurrilous rumours about Sir William. These reached Jane Wilde, who promptly wrote a letter of protest to Travers's father claiming his daughter was making unfounded allegations about her husband. In May 1864, Travers discovered the letter and sued Lady Wilde for libel.

The case came to court just after Oscar Wilde's tenth birthday, by which time he had been packed off to boarding school. Mary Travers was dismissed by Dublin opinion as an hysteric, and, although she won the case on a technicality, Sir William was exonerated when the jury awarded Travers the insulting damages of one farthing. Wilde continued to practise successfully as a medical man, and received the highest award in professional life in April 1873 when the Royal Academy of Ireland awarded him the Cunningham Gold Medal. By the time his two sons had reached Trinity College (Willie in 1869, Oscar in 1871) they would have heard the students singing a ribald ballad, starting:

> An eminent oculist lives in the square,
> His skill is unrivalled, his talent is rare,
> And if you will listen, I'll certainly try,
> To tell you how he opened Miss Travers's eye.[9]

This was amusing rather than damaging. The libel action had no obvious impact on Oscar, for, while the case may have sown the seeds of later cynicism about relations between the sexes, he gave no sign of cynicism in his youth. In fact, he gave no sign at all of the outrageous celebrity he was later to become. He entered adolescence as the promising child of talented parents, displaying few emotional traits which might throw light on his later unorthodox behaviour and sexuality. Perhaps he saw how a certain harmless notoriety could be won by swimming against the currents of provincial respectability. His mother's challenge to Mary Travers and the subsequent libel action marked 1864 as a year to remember, and certainly set a family precedent; but, for Oscar, starting his boarding school career at Portora School at Enniskillen was far more important than the goings on in a remote Dublin courtroom.

* * *

By 1864, John Sholto Douglas was restlessly seeking a direction for his life. After inheriting his title in 1858 he had continued the training of a midshipman which he had begun at the age of twelve. His inheritance ended any chance of his accepting naval discipline or any other kind of restraint. He was enormously popular with his shipmates, who found that naval leave at the Douglas seat of Kinmount was immensely entertaining, with little punctilio. Nor did the navy, then still a notoriously brutal institution, attempt much in the way of suppressing Queensberry's taste for vigorous physical conflict. After completing his midshipman's course he was promoted to lieutenant and posted with his ship HMS *Forte* to the West Africa station. On arriving at Madeira, Queensberry and four other officers defied orders by galloping through the town and inciting a riot. Arrested by the local police, they spent several hours in the lock-up until bailed by the captain of the *Forte*. Queensberry no doubt expected to be disciplined on returning to the ship, instead he and his companions were warmly congratulated by the captain, presumably for acting in the best traditions of the navy.

Queensberry had escaped with his reputation intact, but, like his father, he could not hold down a career. On returning to England in 1864, just short of his twentieth birthday, he resigned his commission. Curiously, he then enrolled at Magdalene College, Cambridge, although he was barely literate and had no interest in intellectual affairs at all. He went up at the start of the 1864 academic year and matriculated at the end of the Michaelmas term. He appears to have done little work in the year he spent at university. Bosie said later, of his own academic failure, that his father had always denied that a degree had any value.[10] Cambridge did however have a major impact on Queensberry's place in sporting legend, for it was there that he became involved in formulating the rules of boxing.

Apart from the destruction of Oscar Wilde, the Queensberry Rules are possibly the only lasting achievement of John Sholto Douglas. But, though the Rules bear his name, he did little personally to formulate them. By nature a bare-knuckle brawler, Douglas was neither temperamentally nor intellectually fitted to formulate rules. At Cambridge, he was one of a hearty group of student athletes, who taught him the finer points of cricket and long-distance running. Above all, he struck up a friendship with the idol of the Cambridge games playing set, John Graham Chambers. Chambers was an exemplary product of the playing fields of the Victorian public school and university. A champion walker, outstanding oarsman and superb swimmer, Chambers was President of the University Boat Club, rowed twice against Oxford in the boat race, and won the Colquhoun sculls in 1863. Throughout his life, Queensberry venerated successful sportsmen. He fell under Chambers's spell, although he was not himself a successful athlete. Queensberry threw himself wholeheartedly into the interests of his new friend, and, when he left Cambridge, kept up the friendship.

Chambers was interested in codifying and upgrading the practice of sport and, after founding the Amateur Athletic Club, turned his attention to boxing. He enlisted his friend Queensberry's assistance and, in 1866, the two men visited America. In both Britain and the USA fighting took place under the London Prize Rules of 1839, which did little more than regulate barroom brawling. Chambers and Queensberry formulated the basic rules of the belted glove and the three-minute round which still govern boxing today. Chambers did most of the work, but insisted that the rules be known as the Queensberry Rules. He knew that a code defined by a commoner would wither on the vine but, with aristocratic patronage, the rules stood a good chance of being accepted. Queensberry was somewhat embarrassed by this turn of events, but his name opened doors and the code spread across the world. Indirectly, Cambridge had given Queensberry his most lasting success.

It is not clear why Queensberry abandoned university life so quickly. However, by early 1865, he was approaching his twenty-first birthday and his inheritance of an estate worth over three-quarters of a million pounds. Perhaps more importantly, he had fallen madly in love and was determined to wed. Marriage was both the most decisive step Queensberry ever took, and probably the most inept. The 8th Marquis was almost a caricature of the "huntin', shootin', fishin'" breed of blue-blooded aristocrat. His life centred around sport and physical endeavour. Yet he fell in love with a cultured, anaemic and highly bred woman, Sybil Montgomery, who was in almost every aspect his opposite. "Her delicate features and creamy complexion", according to Queensberry's sister Gertrude, "were more suggestive of high breeding than robust health. She looked, indeed, as fragile as a beautiful piece of porcelain, with her pretty turquoise-blue eyes and her lovely little mouth, small as a rosebud and quite as bewitching".[11]

John Sholto was certainly bewitched by Sybil Montgomery and they married on 22 February 1866. It was a marriage that was stormy from the first and it ended, uncommonly for the period, in divorce. But, in the person of their third son, Alfred Bruce, it created the child who would rebel against everything his father stood for.

* * *

Between the ages of nine and 17, Wilde was a student at Portora School, sometimes pretentiously called "the Eton of Ireland". It prepared students for Trinity College Dublin, priding itself on its high academic standards. At Portora, Oscar discovered the Ancient Greeks, overtaking his older brother in classical studies. By the time Willie was in his last year at Portora he was only thirteenth in Classics, while Oscar was fourth. Oscar had fallen in love with the Greeks, particularly the *Agamemnon* of Aeschylus, beginning the intellectual love affair that led to the seductive attractions of Plato and Greek Love. This does not seem to have been evident at his boarding school, however, where his reputation was that only of a brilliant scholar. In 1870 he won the Carpenter Prize for Greek Testament, crowning his school career in 1871 by being one of three pupils awarded a Royal scholarship to Trinity College. His name was inscribed in gilt letters on the College's notice board. Twenty-five years later, it would be surreptitiously erased.

Until arriving at Trinity, Wilde had developed quite conventionally. But his deviation from orthodox "respectability" can be dated to the time he began to study under the Revd J.P. Mahaffy. Mahaffy was an outstanding Classics scholar who made a lasting impression on Wilde through his academic incisiveness and willingness to explore controversial aspects of the Greek legacy. The relationship was much closer than usual between an undergraduate and his teacher. In the preface to the first edition of his book *Social Life in Greece,* published in 1874, Mahaffy thanked "Mr Oscar Wilde of Magdalen College" and another student, H.B. Leech, for "having made improvements and corrections throughout the book". The first edition touched on homosexual love and, in considering the charge that it was unnatural, commented: "As to the epithet 'unnatural', the Greeks would answer, probably, that all civilisation was unnatural".[12] This was a dangerous philosophy and, when Mahaffy produced a second edition the following year, all references to Greek Love had been removed, as had the acknowledgements to Wilde and Leech.

Oscar's outstanding academic career at Trinity culminated in his winning the Berkeley Gold Medal for a classical essay, opening the door to the decisive move of his intellectual life. He won a scholarship to Magdalen College, Oxford, going up on 17 October 1874, the day after his twentieth birthday. Wilde was older than the average undergraduate and possessed with boundless self-confidence. For Oscar, entering Oxford was a profoundly significant event. Looking back on his life from his prison cell, Wilde wrote: "The two great turning points of my life were when my father sent me to Oxford, and when society sent me to prison".[13] The move opened up endless vistas for the new undergraduate. Without Oxford, Wilde might only have developed as a brilliant classical scholar with an interest in Greek Love. Oxford turned him into an Aesthete.

On arriving at Magdalen, Oscar Wilde immersed himself in an intense cultural world of aestheticism. The Pre-Raphaelite movement of the mid-Victorian period had created a current that ran directly counter to the utilitarianism of conventional Victorian society. In the visual arts the Pre-Raphaelite leaders, notably Edward Burne Jones and Dante Gabriel Rossetti, blazed a path which outraged the Philistines. Oxford was the intellectual centre of the aesthetic movement, which attracted influential followers. By the time Wilde arrived there was a small but influential coterie pursuing aesthetic ideas between the contrasting polarities of John Ruskin, Slade Professor of Art, and Walter Pater, fellow of Brasenose College. Both men were Aesthetes, but had very different views on what aesthetics were. For Ruskin, it meant a moral approach to art. He saw culture as reaching a high point in the Medieval period then declining as the Renaissance moved artistic sources from the religious to the pagan. Pater saw the development of paganism as valuable, praising the Italians for what he regarded as a refined decadence. Wilde appreciated that this was a fundamental divide. After a brief flirtation with Ruskin, he moved firmly into Pater's camp.

The attraction of Pater for Wilde was Pater's view that beauty was the supreme virtue and, even more crucially, that art was morally neutral. Pater was in the mainstream of the movement crudely dubbed "art for art's sake", but more accurately summarised as the rejection of morality in favour of the sensual. In his *Studies in the History of the Renaissance* (1873) – which Wilde described in prison as "that book which has had such a strange influence over my life"[14] – Pater elevated not just the pursuit of beauty, but the pursuit of experience, to the primary status as the rationale of life. Pater argued: "Not the fruit of experience, but the experience itself, is the end. . . . What we have to do is to be forever curiously testing new opinions and courting impressions, and never acquiescing in a facile orthodoxy . . . to burn always with a hard, gemlike flame, to maintain this ecstasy, is success in life".[15] Wilde was never to deviate from this philosophy.

He was intellectually attracted to aestheticism, but an equally potent reason to embrace the doctrine was the heady discovery that, through Aesthetics, Oscar could become a noted figure. This was not an immediate discovery – pictures of him in his first two years as an undergraduate show him wearing distinctly unaesthetic tweeds and bowler hat – but Wilde began to see possibilities for self-promotion in the Aesthetic cult. During the craze for Japanese porcelain, he was widely credited for a remark that "I am finding it harder and harder every day to live up to my blue china".[16] This precocious quip reverberated around Oxford. It was picked up by George du Maurier in a notable cartoon of 30 April 1880, when he had begun to satirise the Aesthetes in *Punch.* The aesthetic movement was steadily becoming a national phenomenon, and Wilde was in the vanguard. But it was also a movement with a distinctly ambiguous sexual agenda, and Du Maurier acutely sensed the sexual dimension, portraying the figure in the "blue china" cartoon as a long-haired fop, albeit a heterosexual one. The Wilde figure is portrayed as an overdressed bridegroom, showing a piece of Chinese porcelain to a Pre-Raphaelite woman dressed like a Rossetti portrait and exclaiming, "It is quite exquisite, is it not?" To which his bride gives the riposte "It is indeed. Oh Algernon, let us live up to it!"

This was harmless enough, and suggested nothing about Wilde's sexuality which could contradict his public image, for Wilde squired women about and was indeed only four years away from his own marriage. Yet Du Maurier touched on a different possibility with his effeminate character Maudle, also based on Wilde. On 12 February 1881, Du Maurier portrayed Maudle, coiled intently on a sofa, commenting to a mother, "How consummately lovely your son is, Mrs Brown", a caption whose overtones might have bypassed most of Punch's audience. Overtly, the cartoon was about whether the son should choose a career or become what the pugnacious Queensberry might have described as a "Belgravian loafer". But for an element of the Victorian public who were aware of the doctrines being discussed at Oxford under Platonism, for whom Boy Love was not about choosing a career, this was a distinctly double-edged cartoon. With eerie prescience, while in the 1880 cartoon the Wilde figure was slim and elegant, in the 1881 cartoon he was fleshy, double chinned and overweight. As the Saroni pictures in New York show, Wilde in the early 1880s was slim and carried his well-muscled body with elegance. Fifteen years later, he had become corpulent, heavy and with every sign of overindulgence in good food and wine.

Du Maurier's cartoons were sophisticated and, for a Victorian audience, when even the well-educated were barely aware of homosexuality and the homoerotic implications of Greek classicism, the references would have been obscure. The nineteenth century was a period in social history when the fierce controversies over male love had barely begun, and Wilde could not be seen as anything but a foppish but otherwise conventional literary figure in the Pre-Raphaelite tradition. This had never been linked to male love in any serious way – despite the attacks of the critic Robert Buchanan.

Buchanan's attacks on the "Fleshly School of Poetry" were not aimed at the sexual habits of the poets. Yet in 1883, after Wilde had returned triumphantly from America as a lecturer on "The House Beautiful", the popular journal *Illustrated Sporting and Dramatic News* carried a crude but threatening cartoon. Three frames showed a Wildean figure first disporting near a sunflower, then turning into a convict, wearing the characteristic arrowed uniform of the prisoner. It carried no caption, and the message would have been obscure to many. Nothing untoward was shown in the cartoon, but it was suggestive. The only crime of which Wilde could have been thought guilty was sexual. Homosexuality was illegal, the maximum penalty being twenty years' penal servitude. The notorious Labouchère Amendment of 1885 created the new misdemeanour of gross indecency, a charge requiring a lesser burden of proof but still carrying a maximum sentence of two years' hard labour. Henceforth, it became a blackmailers' charter. This suggests Wilde's notoriety was beginning to imply to cynical minds that his challenging of straitlaced Victorian mores might go beyond the harmless championing of Japanese porcelain and the interior designs of William Morris and his circle.

Wilde had deliberately put himself in this exposed position at the opening of the Grosvenor Gallery, on 30 April 1877. He chose the venue to make his London début. Lampooned by Gilbert and Sullivan in *Patience* as "the greenery-yallery Grosvenor Gallery", the gallery was intended to be a leading centre for the Aesthetic movement. On the big occasion, Wilde was determined to be noticed. He wore what became known as his "'cello" coat – bronze-coloured in some lights, red in others, and with the back cut in the outline of a 'cello. Wilde attended with his artistic friends Frank Miles and Lord Ronald Gower – the latter flamboyantly homosexual – and upstaged a mighty trio, the Prince of Wales, Gladstone and John Ruskin. Once he had the attention of the audience, Oscar stole the show with his wit and brio.

Unlike Gower, at this stage Wilde was only flirting with homosexuality in obscure poetic references. Publicly, he squired young women about with relish. Those who believe Wilde later suffered from syphilis often postulate that he contracted this from a female prostitute he met while at Oxford. He also flirted with Catholicism, seeking instruction from Father Bowden at the Brompton Oratory. However, on the day he was due to be inducted into the Church, Wilde did not turn up. Instead, he sent a bunch of white lilies.

Wilde was under family pressure not to abandon his Irish Protestant roots, but an equally important factor in his decision ultimately not to convert was prudence. Wilde was still uncertain of his career path; so, while cultivating the image of a dilettante, in practice he dedicated himself wholeheartedly to his studies. Bosie Douglas, a dozen years later, would emulate the aestheticism without the hard work. Wilde's dedication was rewarded with high honours. While he awaited the results of his finals, he entered the Newdigate Poetry competition and, on 10 June 1878, carried off the prize. Speranza was ecstatic and, two weeks later, had even more cause for maternal celebration when Wilde received a first class Honours degree in his final exams to add to the First of two years earlier.

On receiving his double First in Greats in 1878, Wilde appeared to have the academic world at his feet; but, with his growing sense of self-importance, saw little merit in a life of scholarship. He applied for a

Classics fellowship at Trinity, but was not offered it. Even had he been, he might not have accepted it. Asked by his friend "Bouncer" Ward what his ambition was, he looked into the future and replied: "God knows. I won't be a dried up Oxford don. I'll be a poet, a writer, a dramatist. Somehow I'll be famous, and if not, I'll be notorious".[17]

Oscar had proved himself academically with his double First, but his failure to become an academic left him in limbo. Graduation marked the end of adolescence. He had now to meet the challenges of adult life. He would do this by creating and recreating his public image, to develop a career as a celebrity and wit. But, for the next decade, while he lived by his wits with remarkable success, Oscar had little to show for it save a growing confidence that he could create and wear any number of masks with impunity.

* * *

To Oscar Wilde, for whom he became "the screaming, Scarlet Marquis", the Marquis of Queensberry was nothing but a malevolent threat and probably as some have mistakenly seen him, mad. Usually portrayed as a crude, cunning and unfeeling brute, nevertheless John Sholto Douglas was certainly not mad: he was entirely sane throughout his dealings with his family and with Oscar Wilde. However, he was so thoroughly selfish and insensitive that he could never empathise with or acknowledge the views of anyone else. In his relationships with his wife and children he always assumed that his orders, however bizarre, would be met with loyal obedience. When this proved not to be the case, his reaction was invariably to lash out in impotent rage against those who had dared to repudiate him. As he grew up, Bosie would deliberately thwart him to stoke up the fires of that rage.

John Sholto Douglas was in essence a throwback to feudal society, and had he stayed in his house and estate and married a countrywoman happy to Love, Honour and Obey, and to provide sons, he might have enjoyed a reasonably successful family life, but Queensberry married against type. His bride came from a family with a cultured but impoverished background. Both partners were 21 when they wed in 1866. It was a marriage of choice, but passion lay more on Queensberry's side than Sybil's. Their grandson, the 10th Marquis, later wrote that "My grandfather was madly in love with her, and there is no doubt that the response on her side was very much less ardent".[18] But, whatever

Queensberry's passion for Sybil, it was not enough to compensate for a fundamental clash of temperament. The partners had totally contrasting characters. Queensberry was anti-intellectual and addicted to the outdoor life. Sybil, on the other hand, was a woman educated to shine in the drawing rooms of literary society.

Sybil Montgomery was a refined and delicate woman of great beauty. Bosie Douglas, who adored his mother, rhapsodised in his autobiography that "My mother was something I despair of describing. She was so beautiful that just after her marriage, when she and her sister . . . went driving in London in the Park, people stood on chairs to see them. . . . She had angel's beauty, a gentle, sad, proud, tiny, flower-like face and head, with a slim figure like a Tanagra statuette. She was, and is, the most unselfish, the most good and sweet and kind and patient . . . woman that every drew the breath of life."[19]

Sybil was undoubtedly beautiful, and was to prove an excellent mother, but she was entirely the wrong wife for Queensberry. Sybil had no interest in sport or hunting, and no skill in running a large household. Sybil had been educated to appreciate poetry, music and fashionable novels. She was an accomplished artist and spoke both French and Italian. There was little call for either in Dumfriesshire. Instead, Kinmount had an almost feudal structure of tenants and servants needing a mistress with a firm hand. Sybil preferred to stay in bed until midday, and, when Queensberry returned from the hunt, he would often find lunch not ordered. Quarrels were inevitable; while, in the first year of marriage, making-up usually followed, after the birth of the son and heir Francis – who was given the honorary title of Viscount Drumlanrig, a title often cursed – reconciliations became fewer. The marriage began to break down after the birth of a second son, Percy Sholto, in October 1868. According to Queensberry's grandson, it was after Percy's birth that Sybil's attitude to her husband turned from indifference to active dislike; yet three more children were born to the marriage – Alfred in 1870, Sholto in 1872 and Edith in 1874. The birth of Alfred was the turning point in the marriage.

At the end of 1869, Queensberry had removed his family wholesale from Scotland to become master of the Worcester foxhounds. He was largely an absent husband, boasting that he never missed a day in the field. Nevertheless, Sybil became pregnant again and her third son, Alfred Bruce, was born on 22 October 1870. From the start, the new arrival was an exceptionally beautiful child with a special hold on his mother. Sybil gave her new son the nickname "Boysie". Shortened to Bosie, it remained with him all his life. Queensberry did not object to Sybil naming the new arrival Alfred, after her beloved father, although Queensberry disliked his father-in-law, but the birth did not bring the parents closer together, and Sybil had to seek solace in the new arrival. For Sybil, the new baby had arrived at a time of special loneliness, when she was deprived of affection, almost deserted in a rented house and living among strangers. He was therefore a very special child, on whom Sybil lavished exceptional devotion. Bosie knew he was spoilt by his mother, but, looking back, blamed this, as he blamed everything, on his hated father:

> What was lacking in my home was a father. My mother's spoiling would not have harmed me if my father had been a real father, and had ever taken half as much interest in his children as he did in his dogs and his horses. As it was, I scarcely ever saw him; and when, for the first time in his life, he suddenly tried to exert his authority over me in a very ruthless and violent way (I am referring to the occasion when he suddenly ordered me to give up my friendship with Oscar Wilde), I defied him, and he ruthlessly and deliberately ruined my life.[20]

Bosie Douglas was brought up by his mother, and her influence in shaping his character was crucial. Queensberry later complained that Bosie was "no son of his", but he could hardly complain. Sybil was left to bring up her children virtually alone, as her husband spent most of his time hunting in England with the Cottesmore and the Quorn. The family unit centred on Sybil became close-knit and affectionate, and within it Bosie had a special focus as the centre of his mother's attention. "After Bosie's birth", Queensberry and Colson suggest, "virtually no one else mattered to her. . . . He was a very beautiful child; he had inherited from his mother not only her lovely face, but also her wit and intelligence. From this time onwards her husband no longer counted in her life and her other children took second place".[21] Nevertheless, he was his father's son, and Queensberry's place in his life remained important, albeit too remote from his childhood to have any practical influence.

During the first decade of Bosie's life, that influence was relatively benign. The legend that Queensberry conducted a running battle with his children during their childhood is false – his neglect was virtually absolute.

Bosie wrote in his autobiography that: “All through my childhood and youth the shadow of my father lay over me, for though I loved him, and had indeed a quite absurd admiration for his supposed heroic qualities, I could not be blind to his infamous treatment of my mother”.[22] In fact, in his childhood, when the family lived at Kinmount and the Marquis was based in London, that infamous treatment was limited and the hatred of Bosie for his father did not develop until adolescence. Queensberry’s visits to Kinmount were infrequent, but he was generous with money. Bosie, for instance, regretted that, while his father bought him a pony, he left it to the servants to teach him how to ride. Bosie had a lifelong respect for his father’s sporting achievements particularly as a horseman: Queensberry was a steeplechaser of Grand National standard. But, as Bosie approached adolescence, developments in his father’s life began to bring home to him that his parents’ relations were strained.

The Queensberry marriage disintegrated during the 1870s. After the birth of Edith in 1874, sexual relations between husband and wife ceased and the couple took to living apart. Bosie recalled in his autobiography that: “Between the time when I was five years old and time when the Wilde–Queensberry conflict began, I can truthfully say that I could count on the fingers of both hands the number of occasions when I had been under the same roof as him. He did not live with us. He had rooms in London, and he hardly every turned up at our house in London or the country except for one or two nights at the most. I have been as much as two or three years when I was a boy without seeing him at all”.[23] If Bosie’s memory was correct, this means that the marriage had broken down by 1875.

Queensberry seems to have assumed that his desertion of the family and neglect of his children had no effect on his paternal authority over them. He was mistaken, for while Sybil earned the love and respect of her children by her constant presence in their lives, Queensberry was as remote as the North Star. Nevertheless, the desertion had no immediate consequences for Bosie and the other children; while they were in Scotland, they romped in the woods around Kinmount, carefree and developing a deep affection for each other and their beloved mother. Their father simply did not enter their horizons. Sybil did not attempt to embitter her children against her husband, however, and Bosie developed the hero worship of his absent father which lasted until he went to Winchester.

* * *

Queensberry took rooms at 24 James Street in London, where valets were later to testify that he entertained young women in the bedroom. Sybil ignored her husband's mistresses while she was five hundred miles to the north. She devoted herself to bringing up her children, seeking to ignore the controversies about Queensberry's controversial religious views that began to reach her ears in the late 1870s. She became aware that Queensberry was abandoning the Christian beliefs which dominated Victorian society, but she could hardly have seen any danger to herself or her family in the atheist views her husband had turned to. Nor did the children register much awareness of their father's new attitudes: Bosie never regarded his father's religious views as an issue in themselves. But his religious views were, like all his views, obsessive and carried to lengths that were dangerously ill-judged.

Queensberry revealed that he had abandoned orthodox Christianity in 1876, after the collapse of his marriage, by writing a long poem called "The Spirit of the Matterhorn". That he was driven to write a poem indicates he was undergoing a severe personal crisis, for he was not an intellectual man. The ideas of the poem veer towards pantheism or a curious spiritual materialism, worshipping the body. They were definitely anti-Christian. Queensberry had long been friendly with the secularist leader, George Jacob Holyoake; in May 1877, Queensberry became President of Holyoake's British Secular Union. Sybil saw this as little more than publicity seeking, embarrassing but having no practical consequences. She underestimated him. Queensberry saw it as his duty to proselytise his new faith as enthusiastically as if he had been engaging in a foxhunt. Predictably, running against the grain of the religious beliefs of Victorian society had serious consequences.

One of the peculiarities of the British constitution was that Scottish peers who did not have an English title could only sit in the House of Lords if they were elected, by their peers, as one of 16 Representative Peers. The Queensberry title is the only one of its rank in Scotland that does not have a lesser British title allowing its holder into the Lords as of right. Queensberry, like his father, felt his lack of an automatic place in the Lords as a personal slight that became a deeply festering wound. However, he was somewhat assuaged when his fellow peers elected him a Scottish Representative Peer in 1872. Their Lordships might have turned a blind eye to his embrace of secularism had Queensberry behaved with discretion, but discretion was not in his nature. His position in the House of Lords allowed him to spread pamphlets around the Palace of Westminster, which he did without any sense that he would anger other peers. Bishops in the House were particularly outraged by his activities, but by 1880 all the Scottish peers were fully aware that Queensberry was no longer professing the Christian faith of a Victorian parliamentarian. They met at Holyrood, unanimously passed a resolution that Queensberry "held as a negation all that his brother peers held as most sacred", and voted that he should be removed as a Representative Peer. Queensberry was humiliated.

His reaction to this public dressing down was explosive. The Marquis turned his back on Scotland and, in an act that effectively punished his family for his own mistakes, he abandoned Kinmount and took Sybil and the children to live in London. Transposed from the glens of Dumfriesshire to a rented house in the Cromwell Road, the children were devastated, particularly Bosie. At ten years old he lost his idyllic country surroundings and his governesses, and was forced to live in a city he hardly knew existed. He never forgave his father and experienced the first sense that his father was less than heroic. His loss of Kinmount was more than just the loss of a rural idyll; it was for Bosie the loss of childhood and the loss of innocence. In a real sense, Bosie Douglas spent the rest of his life trying to return to the joy and security he had known with his mother on the family estate.

The upheaval, moreover, made the children cruelly aware of their father's public humiliation, and their mother's distress. Any chance Sybil might have had of shielding her family from her husband's desertion was destroyed. While Queensberry insisted his family live in London, he maintained his pied à terre in James Street and the family still did not see him. His mother meanwhile found an escape from London and her marital unhappiness by renting a summer house near Bracknell, prosaically called The Hut. It could take 25 at a pinch, and allowed her to recreate Kinmount with her beloved children during the summer holidays. Sadly, it was also near Ascot, and Queensberry took to imposing himself on his unhappy wife during the races. Bosie witnessed the ensuing rows at first hand and experienced them as intolerable attacks on a mother he was helpless to defend. His rage at his father grew.

The Marquis was not the only member of the family to make headlines. Queensberry's unmarried sister Gertrude, who was 40, ran off and married a baker's lad called Tom Stock, who claimed to be 21 but was probably 17. The *Whitehall Review* commented that: "The mutations of opinion in the Queensberry family are, indeed, somewhat singular. . . . This is a strange passage in the history of the peerage".[24] The

Queensberry family was becoming a laughing stock, but for Sybil and her children, the behaviour of her husband was far from funny. As he aged – he was forty in 1884 – Queensberry was becoming more irascible and his infrequent visits to The Hut were marked by terrible rages. Sybil was a conventional Victorian who regarded divorce as anathema – Sir Charles Dilke had seen his political career ruined merely by being named co-respondent in the Crawford divorce case of 1886 – but, by the end of the same year, Sybil came to the end of her tether. According to Bosie, "The final straw that broke the back of my mother's angelic patience was that my father wanted to bring his mistress to my mother's house, and proposed that they should all live under one roof".[25] Whether this actually happened or not is unclear – Bosie always embroidered stories about his father – but there is no doubt that Sybil had reached the limit of her endurance, and wanted an end to the marriage.

The divorce was granted in Edinburgh on 22 January 1887. Sybil found servants to prove her husband's adultery, suggesting collusion by Queensberry. The court heard that he had entertained women in his bedroom, and took only an hour to grant the decree. That should have been the end of the marriage, which would have allowed Bosie, then 16, to establish civilized relations with his father. Up to this point he still hero worshipped his father, and later recorded that at Winchester "one of my favourite occupations was looking up the old numbers of the Field newspaper, of which there was a bound set in our house library, for records of the races ridden by my father in the sixties and seventies. As a boy I adored my father, and looked up to him as a wonderful man of almost legendary prowess as a sportsman and a fighter".[26]

But civilised relations proved impossible as Queensberry continued to abuse his wife. He refused to pay her the money due under the divorce settlement, forcing her to go to law repeatedly to obtain her rights. From this point, Bosie's view of his father turned sour. While Queensberry had been an absent father, his marriage was not a problem for the children. Paradoxically, once it had ended, the abysmal treatment of Sybil became an open wound. This was made worse because the situation was no longer a private matter. The treatment of Sybil by Queensberry had become a public scandal and outside the raffish world of the turf, he was ostracised. By 1889, Queensberry was a social pariah, and he knew it.

His children could not escape his company entirely. Bosie dreaded the occasional visits to him at school and university, complaining later that Queensberry's moods could change from affability to towering rage for no apparent reason, and that "he would often disconcertingly refuse to listen to, and indeed completely ignore, what was said to him. He would habitually fail to understand a point of view which did not coincide with his own".[27] Bosie was describing faults which, unfortunately, were to became very much his own. Until going up to university in October 1889 and for some time thereafter, Bosie maintained sensible relations with his father, who supplied the money for his education and was always financially generous – Bosie had more pocket money than most boys at his schools. But he was drifting away rapidly from his father from the time of the divorce, becoming attracted by a decadent sub-culture that stood in diametric opposition to everything that Queensberry stood for.

Queensberry took little notice of what his son was thinking, for he was preoccupied with a family problem centred on his younger brother. Jim had been married in 1888 at the age of 33. The family heaved a sigh of relief, for Jim had been a worry to them as he had failed to make a living at anything. Moreover, in marrying Martha Lucy Hennessy, of the Cognac brandy family, he had married into wealth. Alas, Jim lacked the strength of character to cope with marriage, particularly when this involved playing the role of stepfather, and he rapidly began exhibiting signs of mental instability. He drank heavily, fell into violent rages, and had to be sedated by the family doctor. Queensberry put his brother's problems down to drink, failing to detect anything more serious. His wife and the doctor were more perceptive, fearing that Lord Jim "might one day commit a rash act", a prediction which came true at the start of 1891. The ninth ten-yearly census was carried out at the start of the year, and the heads of households throughout the country had to fill in the required forms. In London, only two men fell foul of the authorities for failing to fill in the form correctly. One was a man who refused to give full information. The other was Lord James Douglas.

Douglas had returned the form in pencil giving his full name – James Edward Sholto Douglas – but describing his wife as a "cross sweep" and a "lunatic", and his stepson as a "shoeblack born in darkest Africa". The Registrar General promptly summoned Lord James to appear in court. Martha took the blame on herself, claiming her husband had been too ill to fill the form in properly, and a deal was struck with the local magistrate. James wrote a letter of apology, paid costs to the authorities, and filled in a new form correctly. The papers barely reported the incident, but Martha knew that her husband's bizarre behaviour had come close to causing a major scandal.

Martha was desperate and turned to the head of the Douglas family for advice. Queensberry could only suggest that James take a holiday, fishing in Ireland. He did not offer to go along to support his brother, so the poor unfortunate man was left to fend for himself without help or advice miles from home. As he was on the verge of a serious breakdown, a period of solitude in the country was the last thing this tortured man needed. In the ten days that Douglas spent on his own, his mind became unhinged. By the time he returned to Dublin, his behaviour was so strange that a railway inspector was detailed to accompany him to England. Shortly after leaving Holyhead, his behaviour became erratic and he paced up and down the corridor beset by worry. At Stafford he dashed off the train and sent a wire to the editor of the *Globe* newspaper: "Facts, lies – Lord Douglas", the product of a mind now wholly disordered. On arrival at Euston late that evening, Jim booked in at the station hotel. The doctor and Queensberry agreed to fetch him the following morning but, when they arrived at the hotel, they discovered pandemonium. Jim's room had been entered by a maid half an hour earlier. Having received no reply to polite knocking at the door, she tiptoed into the room, then fled screaming. Jim was lying in a pool of blood between the bed and the dressing table. His throat was cut from ear to ear.[28]

The Queensberry family was now front page news. When the inquest opened on 6 May 1891, Queensberry was the first witness. He created a sensation by refusing to take the oath. Not until he was allowed to make a simple affirmation would he say a word, then brusquely testified to his brother's depression and mood swings. The doctor confirmed this, opining that Jim had probably cut his throat with the razor found lying by his side, and had been dead for ten hours when found. The coroner had no hesitation in bringing in a verdict of 'suicide whilst of unsound mind'. Three days later, Queensberry accompanied his brother's body to Kinmount, where another brother, Lord Archibald Douglas, who had converted to Catholicism and become a priest, blithely read the full Roman Catholic burial service over the coffin despite the verdict of the court that his brother was a suicide.

* * *

The reputation of the Queensberry family for eccentricity had been reinforced, this time in the most tragic of circumstances. Though

Queensberry still enjoyed the companionship of his sporting friends, he could hardly have been unaware that the wider public regarded both himself and his family as bizarre. Brooding on the slights which had blighted his life, John Sholto Douglas was far from content with his lot. His temper was however to be tried far more violently by the activities of his sons, who were now growing to manhood and were showing signs of independent behaviour very different to what Queensberry regarded as dutiful behaviour. Yet there was little sign in 1891 that Bosie would become the most troublesome of the Douglas children. He appeared to be a conventional young man who had passed respectably through Winchester and was pursuing academic studies at Magdalen College Oxford. Had Queensberry followed Bosie's career with more attention, however, his son's activities would have appeared anything but respectable.

* * *

Queensberry had very little opportunity to find out what Bosie was thinking or doing. His desertion of his family gave Sybil an easy victory where the love of her children was concerned. But the relationship with his third son was markedly worse than with any of the others as Bosie adored his mother as much as she did him, and he consequently loathed his father. From adolescence, Bosie moved further and further away from anything his father might have considered suitable behaviour from a child bearing the Douglas name. At the age of 14, Bosie was sent to Winchester. He had wanted to go to Eton to follow a schoolfriend, but his father had made one of his random interventions in his son's life, refusing to allow his son to go to a school which produced what he called "Belgravian loafers". "My father was like that", Bosie later wrote, "he knew nothing about Eton, or any public school, having been on the *Britannia* and in the Navy himself; but his prejudices once formed were as utterly insurmountable as they were often unreasonable".[29] Although Queensberry probably never realised what was happening, Eton could have had little worse effect on Bosie than Winchester where turning his son into a loafer was concerned.

When Bosie arrived at the school, Winchester was a rough place with much of the casual bullying of the late-Victorian public school. Bosie loathed the first eighteen months he was there, comparing it to the Rugby of *Tom Brown's Schooldays.* He arrived very much his mother's son, claiming later to have been "a sensitive, dreamy child . . . passionately pure and devoted in my heart to every noble ideal".[30] This was knocked out of him by Winchester, though this in itself testifies to an inner toughness. Bosie was a beautiful child throughout his time at Winchester – photographs of him show a boy markedly younger and more delicate than his contemporaries – but he was never effete, and became a popular member of the school, with a taste for cross country running. Winchester reinforced his taste for high living. He recalled: "I had a natural taste for the best in everything . . . . I had been accustomed all my life to be in houses where my eyes rested on beautiful pictures, glorious tapestries, and the harmony of everything that is connoted by perfect taste. I left Winchester neither better nor worse than my contemporaries – that is to say, a finished young blackguard, ripe for any kind of wickedness."[31]

The worst of Winchester was that it accustomed Bosie to a life of pleasure and self indulgence, partly sexual and partly conventionally hedonistic. Bosie hints that, at Winchester, he acquired a taste for homosexuality, but only of the juvenile kind indulged in by most boys at a single-sex boarding school. He recalled: "I had many fine friendships, perfectly normal . . . I had others again which were neither pure nor innocent. But if it is to be assumed from this that I was 'abnormal' or 'degenerate' or exceptionally wicked, then it must also be assumed that at least ninety per cent of my contemporaries at Winchester and Oxford were the same".[32] Yet, for most of his contemporaries, the juvenile fumblings of an all-male environment were a passing phase forgotten when women became an issue. Where Bosie and friends such as Lionel Johnson were concerned, they remained much more.

Bosie gained a sense from his experience as an aristocratic public schoolboy with no social responsibilities, that he was privileged to do whatever he liked, with neither consequence nor cost. Looking back later on the course of his life, Bosie recalled this phase in his life as a beautiful fantasy:

> Life in those days of boyhood at Winchester and Oxford was pretty well rose coloured all through, once the first two nightmare years of Winchester were over – a wild "rag" at school and the University, and a constant succession of amusement, sport, luxury and pleasure at home. I think I have put it concisely in one of the sonnets in my poem "In Excelsis", written more than thirty years later in my cell at Wormwood Scrubs Prison:

"For I was of the world's top, born to bask
In its preferment where the augurs sit,
And where the Devils' grace, to counterfeit,
Is all the tribute that the augurs ask."[33]

For most of his life, Bosie's sense that being at the world's top, basking in its preferment, was without cost and unquestionable. It was one of the attractions Bosie had for Wilde. Like his father, Bosie hunted with the Cottesmore from his uncle George Finch's "glorious" house, Burley-on-the-Hill. During vacations from 1886 to 1895, before the Wilde scandal closed the gilded doors of the upper classes to both men, he claims that he "frequently met and consorted with the late King Edward (then Prince of Wales), the Duke of Cambridge, and other Royalties. I spent two seasons at Homburg, while I was an undergraduate, with my mother and my grandfather, Alfred Montgomery, who was on very intimate terms with the Prince. My grandfather also introduced me to the Duke of Cambridge at Homburg, and afterwards used to take me to his house in Piccadilly".[34] Fortunately, this ultra-privileged existence did not depend on scholastic achievement, for Bosie did not exert himself at Winchester, taking from school life only that which appealed to him. Though Bosie disliked team sports, running appealed to his individualistic nature and he won the school steeplechase – two and a half miles across country – in 1887, when he was 16. At Oxford he won the two-mile race at Magdalen sports and the mile handicap, and tried to get his Blue by running the three-mile 'Varsity race with a plaster bandage around his knee. Characteristically, when he failed to overcome this minor handicap, he gave up running in disgust.[35]

A more lasting effect of Winchester was that his family nickname became public knowledge. When he had been at the school for a year, his brother Percy sent him a farewell telegram as he was about to sail as a naval midshipman for the Pacific. It ended with the words "Goodbye darling Bosie"; all the members of Sybil's close-knit family called each other "darling" as a matter of course. Bosie was out when the telegram arrived, inquisitive boys opened it, and when he came in he was hailed with derisory shouts of "Hullo, darling Bosie". The name stuck, even his housemaster using it and, when he went to Oxford, it followed him and became permanent.[36] It is symbolic of his life's character, which never lost much of its boyish immaturity.

Despite Bosie's apparent scholastic idleness, Winchester gave him his first and, probably, his greatest literary success. In his last year at the school, in the summer of 1888, he edited a weekly paper called the *Pentagram*, with two friends. A dozen weekly copies appeared, and it was bought by so many old boys of the school that its circulation exceeded the school population at that time. This gave Bosie a taste for more, and editing became a lifelong addiction. Lionel Johnson contributed two poems to the *Pentagram* – he had already gone up to Oxford – in this way affirming the connection with Douglas which was to bring Bosie into Wilde's circle.

Bosie left Winchester at Christmas 1888, just past his eighteenth birthday. His academic achievement was so limited that he was sent to the continent with a tutor, not the last time his family had to employ a tutor to repair Bosie's educational failings. While abroad he claims an affair with a woman, a "celebrated beauty at least twelve years older than myself, and the divorced wife of an earl". According to Bosie, he was hauled out of the lady's bedroom by his tutor dressed in one of her beribboned nightgowns, while matrons in the hotel attacked the lady for having seduced the innocent lamb. Though the story sounds implausible, that Bosie names his tutor gives the story credibility. He also claims sexual promiscuity with prostitutes on the notorious promenade of the Empire Theatre, and outside the aristocratic Corinthian Club. Though Bosie protests a little too much over his heterosexual early tastes, there is no reason to believe he was being "economical with the truth".[37]

By the time Bosie reached Magdalen College, Oxford, in October 1889, he was idle, pleasure loving and breathtakingly insolent. His energies were not devoted to academic study. Bosie's academic career was indifferent and he was lucky to be able to progress beyond the second year. He failed maths in the exams known as Responsions, was sent down for a term and was coached by a parson in Herefordshire called Lambert. This tutor succeeded in keeping Bosie on the academic path. Bosie was also "gated" – confined to quarters – for going to the Derby.

To all outward appearances, Bosie's career at Oxford was notable only for some modest progress as a poet and editor. He put real effort into poetic writing, and during his second year at Magdalen contributed a poem to the *Oxford Magazine*, the first writing he had produced that showed real quality. It was called "Autumn Days" and the college President, (later Sir) Herbert Warren wrote Bosie an effusive letter of congratulation. Bosie recalled bitterly in his autobiography that when, shortly after the Wilde trials, he published, anonymously, a volume of poetry called *The City of the Soul*, featuring the same poem, he sent a copy to Warren who returned it with the comment "I regret that I cannot accept this book from you".[38]

But in the summer of 1891, the future seemed bright. While Bosie had no intention of a literary career – or indeed any career at all – he had literary leanings and contributed to an undergraduate magazine called the *Spirit Lamp*. During his third year he was approached by the owner who, on graduating, offered it to Bosie. He took it on, and edition number IV, May 1892, contained the brief announcement that "The present number of the *Spirit Lamp* appears, and all future numbers will appear, under the sole editorship of Lord Alfred Douglas."[39] This was a significant move for Bosie. Whatever indolence he displayed in his studies, he took his editorial role seriously and became a figure of some stature in the aesthetic world. Queensberry did not take umbrage at this – he dabbled in poetry himself, and Bosie even published one of his father's poems in the magazine. Nevertheless, Bosie Douglas was moving towards an involvement with the aesthetic world which would have turned the "Scarlet Marquis" purple with rage had he known about it.

The *Spirit Lamp* made the first public connection between Bosie Douglas and Oscar Wilde. Bosie published Wilde and other decadents and made the magazine a journal of the Aesthetic movement. Wilde's poem "The New Remorse" was published ("The sin was mine, I did not know") along with other decadent pieces. Yet the *Spirit Lamp* overall was not conspicuously decadent and there was little evidence of it being the mouthpiece of a movement. While there can be little doubt that there was a homosexual underworld at the university in 1892, how far Bosie was involved in it remains obscure. It is reasonable to assume that he was associating with renters and that, when he took over editing the *Spirit Lamp*, he was taking over from a like spirit whose name he preferred to forget. There is no clear evidence of what the homosexual underworld at Oxford was like while Bosie was an undergraduate, but little doubt that it was established, and that Bosie was part of it. When Wilde in *De Profundis* recalled: "the origin of our friendship was you in your undergraduate days at Oxford coming to beg me to help you in very serious trouble of a very particular nature",[40] he provided an important clue to what Bosie was doing at Oxford. The "trouble" took place in the spring of 1892 and, immediately after Wilde had rushed to Oxford to organise Bosie's rescue, the affair began. Oscar Wilde had already become a magnet for Aesthetic young men who could penetrate beneath the masks Wilde habitually wore. Bosie Douglas looked beneath the masks of decadent charm and wit and was enthralled.

TWO

A Long and Lovely Suicide

At the time Wilde moved to London in early 1879, lack of money was a serious problem and, to earn some, he seriously contemplated becoming an Inspector of Schools. A year later his finances were so precarious that he actually made an application and, although he was turned down, the thought recurred. Yet Wilde cannot have been fully committed to this somewhat unlikely ambition, for he was well on his way to inventing himself as the Oscar of the First Period, namely the "Professor of Aesthetics".

Wilde had developed a reputation at Oxford; while, at the Grosvenor Gallery in 1877, he had for the first time commanded a public audience; and a royal one at that. After graduation, he intended to use his reputation to make his fortune. Wilde came down from Oxford with £2,800 inherited from his father – too small a sum for a life of leisure, but enough to live on while making an impact. He found lodgings with the artist Frank Miles, while he exploited the notoriety of the Aesthetes. He resorted to gimmicks, on one occasion greeting a hostess with a snake draped around his neck. He paid court flamboyantly to the leading women of the day, the courtesan Lillie Langtry and the actresses Ellen Terry and Sarah Bernhardt. Famous more for just being famous than anything else, Oscar was in the public eye. But publicity alone would not translate into financial success.

His book of poetry, published in 1881, was received badly by reviewers, who criticised it as derivative. He had to finance it himself and gave away copies of the first edition to create a market. The Aesthetes were still little more than the butt of lighthearted humour and dramatists put them on to the stage only to make fun of them. Gilbert and Sullivan's *Patience* was the best of a series of skits on the movement that appeared at this time. The show premièred on the London stage in April 1881. The two central characters, Bunthorne and Grosvenor, were based on a number of "Aesthetic" characters including Swinburne, Rossetti and Whistler; but, while Wilde was the most obvious target, the barbs against Mediaevalism were aimed more at Ruskin than at him. "Bunthorne's song" was thought to refer to Wilde, as he was widely believed to have "walked down

Piccadilly with a poppy or a lily", but when an American journalist asked him about it, he made the acute remark that: "To have done it was nothing, but to make people think one had done it was a triumph".[1] His ability to appear to be doing things while not doing them fed his conceit that his critics could not discern between the image and the reality of his life. And, until the Marquis of Queensberry was charged with libel in April 1895, no one was sufficiently moved to look beneath the surface.

In 1881 image was all, and the image of Oscar Wilde as the Professor of Aesthetics was brilliantly spun by its owner. When *Patience* transferred to New York in the Autumn, producer Richard D'Oyly Carte needed to explain the Aesthetes to the Americans, and Wilde was invited over to lecture. He accepted, and in January 1882 arrived in the New World at the height of his epigrammatic form, flouncing through customs with the famous line: "I have nothing to declare but my genius". Wilde's tour was a *succès d'estime.* It allowed him to develop his lecturing skills, revealing hidden talent in dealing with hecklers who sought to make fun of him and his "Aesthetic" clothing, particularly his silk knee breeches! He delivered 141 lectures on "The English Renaissance", "The House Beautiful" (later adopted as a magazine title) and "The Decorative Arts", on both seaboards and from the deep South to the far North. The extensive reports arriving back in Britain kept him in the public eye, particularly as baiting the philistine English middle class was a constant theme. As the tour progressed, English press comment began to take on a sharper edge. Walter Hamilton, who devoted a separate chapter to discussing Wilde in his book, *The Aesthetic Movement in England,* published in 1882, thought the reaction to him excessive, both for and against. "Nothing can excuse the gross personal abuse which some journals, but more particularly *Punch,* have showered upon him. The ridicule that has been lavished upon his actions and dress is as unreasonable as the excessive adulation which his poems have earned from some of the more intense Aesthetes. . .".[2]

The growing press abuse of Wilde in fact created a groundswell of sympathy amongst those who knew him. Fifty years later, in *Summing Up,* Bosie Douglas was still driven to fury recalling the attacks of *Punch* on Wilde from the early eighties onward. Yet Oscar's baiting of the Philistines was deliberate, and designed to create a reaction. In his first lecture in New York, Oscar slung epithets at the British public, asserting that: "To know nothing about their great men is one of the necessary elements of English education. The pre-Raphaelites . . . had three things which the English public never forgive – youth, power and enthusiasm."

"To disagree with three fourths of all England on all points is one of the first elements of sanity. . ."[3] and so on. "Three fourths" of England was a large group of people to dismiss out of hand. Yet Wilde suffered no personal reaction and his ability to ride out the storm reinforced his conviction that he lived a charmed life.

Oscar returned from the USA at the end of 1882 still regarded as more eccentric than dangerous. He was in funds after the American trip and went to France to polish up the language, work on his play *The Duchess of Padua*, and ponder his next move. It was clear that his image as the Professor of Aesthetics had now outlived its usefulness, and he decided on the next change of image in a coolly calculating manner. He lived in Paris while deciding how to re-invent himself, meeting and cultivating Robert Harborough Sherard, the young man who became Wilde's longest lasting friend. Sherard watched Wilde begin his transformation from the aesthete who had postured in silk and long hair in America. Wilde met Sherard at the end of February and so dazzled the young man that he kept copious notes of their conversations. Wilde was cynical about marriage and fornication. One night he patronised the well-known prostitute, Marie Aguetant. The following morning, he commented to Sherard "What animals we all are, Robert". There was little at this stage to suggest to anyone that, beneath the practised languor, Wilde was anything but "normal".

"The Oscar of the first period is dead! We are now concerned with the Oscar of the second period!"[4] Sherard recorded this theatrical declamation as Wilde was having his hair cropped into Neronian curls and investing in a new wardrobe. *Punch* noticed too, and, in the edition of 31 March 1883, carried a mock advertisement for: "the whole of the Stock-in-trade, Appliances, and Inventions of a Successful Aesthete, who is retiring from business". Oscar Wilde had begun the skilful transformation of his public image into what, unknowingly, would in 1895 prove his Achilles heel. Had he lived a century later, he would undoubtedly have got away with it; indeed, nowadays his behaviour and affectations would scarcely have earned him a minor celebrity. In the last decade of the nineteenth century, however, they were beyond the Pale.

* * *

Wilde was now making strenuous attempts to build a career as a dramatist, but his initial steps in the theatre were unsuccessful. *Vera* was finally produced in New York in 1883 but failed. His second play, *The Duchess of Padua*, completed in Paris while Wilde was making the acquaintance of Robert Sherard, did not make its stage appearance until 1891, when it too failed. Wilde depended for a slender income on lecturing and reviewing, notably for the *Pall Mall Gazette*. When, in November 1883, he became engaged to Constance Lloyd, his decision could be viewed as a cynical attempt to escape from a financial cul-de-sac. Constance, daughter of a wealthy Anglo-Irish family, brought a considerable dowry to the marriage. The marriage has also been seen as a homosexual blind, something that may well have been true by the time Wilde met Bosie Douglas, but was not in 1884. Constance was undoubtedly in love, seeing Wilde as "My hero and my God",[5] the man who would save her from unhappiness – she had been cruelly treated by her nearest relatives. Wilde responded to Constance with genuine feeling and he entered into matrimony in high spirits. Money was undoubtedly very welcome, but he appears to have been genuinely affectionate towards his wife at the start of the marriage.

Constance and Oscar married on 29 May 1884. Wilde was 29, and took his bride straight off to Paris. There he met Robert Sherard, who clearly resented the radiant happiness of the couple and Wilde's cheerful demeanour. When Wilde began to describe the pleasures of the nuptial bed, beginning "It's so wonderful when a young virgin. . ." Sherard rapidly changed the subject. Wilde clearly enjoyed heterosexual love at this time, and Sherard never doubted that Wilde was heterosexual.[6] Sherard was obtuse and may have been misled; but then even the worldly Frank Harris was equally blind to the reality of Wilde's sexuality, until the trials disabused him. In the honeymoon period at least there is no reason at all to doubt that it was a marriage in the fullest sense of the word.

The Wildes settled at 16 Tite Street, in Chelsea, where Oscar rose brilliantly to the challenge of producing "The House Beautiful" for real, using £5,000 of Constance's dowry and the designs of E.N. Godwin, architect and theatrical designer. When Yeats came to Christmas dinner, having heard the Dublin gossip about the slovenliness of the paternal home, he was staggered by the immaculate white décor: walls, furniture and carpets; the elegance of the dinner arrangements, and felt himself to be dishevelled. Wilde's triumph in interior design seemed, however, to be strangely artificial. Yeats thought the family, with the beautiful wife and the two charming children, suggested some deliberate artistic composition.[7] Wilde could well have been posing: it is hardly surprising that The House Beautiful contained The Family Beautiful. But Wilde's obsessive pursuit of beauty exacted a heavy price, a price paid by Constance Wilde and her hopes of happiness.

Constance first became pregnant in September 1884, giving birth to Cyril on 5 June 1885. She does not seem to have appreciated that her swollen condition alienated her husband. He wrote lovingly to his wife while lecturing in Edinburgh in mid-December, lyrically penning: "The air is full of the music of your voice, my soul and body seem no longer mine, but mingled in some exquisite ecstasy with yours. I feel incomplete without you".[8] Nevertheless, he appears to have reacted badly to the inevitable consequences. Pregnancy disgusted Wilde and he began to drift away from Constance, though Constance became pregnant again within eight months of the birth of Cyril. Wilde's second son, Vyvyan, was born on 6 November 1886. Perhaps the birth of a second son was a deep disappointment for both parents, who had wanted a daughter. The Wildes seem to have been far more casual about Vyvyan's birth, for while Cyril's was recorded to the minute, Vyvyan's was scarcely noted; when, after the maximum period of six weeks, it was registered, the parents could only recall the date vaguely to within five days of the beginning of November.[9]

Whether this disappointment ended Wilde's sexual relations with his wife is unknown, but Wilde's passion certainly cooled.[10] Oscar had already begun his pursuit of beautiful young men, who could better fulfil his Platonic ideal of physical perfection.

The first was Henry Marillier, a Cambridge undergraduate. He invited Wilde to visit in November 1885. Wilde went, saw a performance of the *Eumenides* and wrote some passionate letters with characteristic flamboyance. It was in one of his letters to Marillier, written in December 1885, that Wilde uttered one of his most eerily prophetic lines. Discussing art, he suggested: "I would go to the stake for a sensation and be a sceptic to the last! Only one thing remains infinitely fascinating to me, the mystery of moods. To be a master of moods is exquisite, to be mastered by them more exquisite still. *Sometimes I think that the artistic life is a long and lovely suicide, and I am not sorry that it is so*".[11] [*Author's emphasis*]

Marillier was probably not a lover, but around this time Wilde began the secret involvement in the homosexual underworld whose dangers were so much a part of its attraction. In 1886, while his wife was pregnant with Vyvyan, he met Robert Ross, a Canadian youth who was an admirer of his poetry. The homosexual Ross was determined to seduce Wilde, and both men later claimed he was Oscar's first male lover. Oscar, the great believer in "experience", had no objections to exploring other aspects of love, and in this manner he opened the door to the homosexual subculture whose forbidden wall he had long peeped over. Sexual relations with Constance seem to have ceased anyway after the birth of Vyvyan. What passed between man and wife is unknown, but Constance seems to have accepted this: Ellmann, a recent biographer, and others believe that Wilde had contracted syphilis at Oxford, and told his wife that a recurrence now made sex impossible. We cannot know. Whether Wilde had syphilis remains disputed, the medical evidence is ambiguous at best, but it is a suggestive theory.

The affair with Robert Ross did not last, probably ending when Ross went up to Cambridge in the Autumn of 1888, but Ross remained a devoted friend. He certainly knew Wilde's innermost secret. Wilde wrote to him that he had been lecturing in Stratford – he had actually visited for the unveiling of a statue of Shakespeare executed by Ronald Gower. He concluded: "My reception was semi-royal, and the volunteers played 'God Save the Queen' in my honour".[12] It was a secret joke between members of a secret fraternity. By 1890, Wilde was constantly surrounded by a circle of admiring young men, a situation tolerated by Constance, who clearly had no idea that this was more than a literary gathering. André Raffalovich, initially a friend of Wilde, satirised the Wildes and their circle in a passage of his 1890 novel *A Willing Exile*: Oscar and Constance were represented as Cyprian and Daisy Brome: "Mrs Brome, of course, knew many men. Cyprian was, or seemed to be, intimate with countless young or youngish men; they were all curiously alike. Their voices, the cut of their clothes, the curl of their hair, the brims of their hats, the parties they went to, Daisy could not see much difference between them. Affectation characterised all these men, and the same sort of affectation. They were all gushers, professional gushers . . . married (some were married) or unmarried, they gushed alike, only some were ruder than others, and some were duller than others. . .".[13]

Wilde's relationships with young men were indeed gushing. In December 1890, for example, he wrote to the poet Richard Le Galliene: "I want so much to see you: when can that be? Friendship and love like ours need not meetings, but they are delightful. I hope the laurels are not too thick across your brow for me to kiss your eyelids".[14] The language suggested more than was the case – Le Galliene was not homosexual. Oscar was, however, regularly trawling around Oxford. In mid-February 1890 he encountered the undergraduate poet Lionel Johnson, whom he roused from bed where he was reading T.H. Green and entertained with witticisms. Both these relationships were platonic; but, through Johnson, the fatal introduction to Bosie Douglas was about to be made.

Wilde's habitual posing and his overblown rhetoric convinced many that he was a married man with little more than a taste for outrageous behaviour. Yet, though Wilde continued writing charming children's fables, he also developed a taste for critical essays, which came to be seen as decadent. The first of these, "The Decay of Lying" and the deeply antinomian study of the poisoner Wainwright, "Pen, Pencil and Poison", emerged without overt comment and Frank Harris published the latter in his *Fortnightly Review.* Despite his friendship with Wilde, however, Harris could not stomach the "Portrait of Mr W.H.", which posited a homosexual Shakespeare, and it was published in *Blackwood's Edinburgh Magazine.* Wilde was now writing with astonishing fecundity. In 1891, he published two volumes of stories, one volume of critical essays, wrote the long essay "The Soul of Man Under Socialism", completed his first successful play, *Lady Windermere's Fan,* and wrote much of *Salomé.* Yet none of this had the impact of the novella which he had published the previous year, *The Picture of Dorian Gray.* The initial version was published in *Lippincott's* magazine on 20 June 1890. Both its hinted-at homosexuality and its stated hedonism were repugnant to "respectable" Victorian opinion. If the homosexuality was understated, the hedonism was clear. The character of Lord Henry preached his gospel – widely believed to be Wilde's own – with unmistakeable clarity: "The aim of life is self- development. To realise one's nature perfectly, that is what each of us is here for. Return to the Hellenic ideal. The only way to get rid of a temptation is to yield to it. A new Hedonism – that is what our century wants. Youth! Youth! There is nothing in the world but youth!"[15]

Respectable Victorians had only a hazy idea of the Hellenic ideal, but the philosophy of hedonism was far from obscure. The press was savage, notably the *St James' Gazette* and, more pointedly, W.E. Henley's *Scot's Observer.* Henley knew Wilde well, he had been one of Wilde's proposers when Wilde had applied to join the Savile Club in 1888. But the friendship did not survive *Dorian Gray.* The editorial commented that the story was "false art . . . it is not made sufficiently clear that the writer does not prefer a course of unnatural iniquity to a life of cleanliness, health and sanity. Mr Wilde has brains, and art, and style, but if he can write for none but outlawed noblemen and perverted telegraph boys. . ."[16] – the latter being a reference to the Cleveland Street scandal, in which Lord Arthur Somerset had escaped abroad to avoid prosecution for involvement in a homosexual brothel involving post boys. The meaning was clear.

W.H. Smith removed that edition of *Lippincott's* from his stalls, and the publishers asked Wilde to tone down the text for book publication. He did so, but left in a passage which formed the basis of his most eloquent speech at the trials defending something that he later called "Uranian love": "The love that he bore him – for it was really love – had nothing in it that was not noble and intellectual. It was not that mere physical admiration for beauty that was born of the senses, and that dies when the senses tire. It was such love as Michael Angelo had known, and Montaigne, and Winckelman and Shakespeare himself".[17]

Passages such as this drew down the fiercest criticism. Wilde defended his work in print. He persuaded a sympathetic editor, his friend Frank Harris, to let him publish a defence in his paper the *Fortnightly Review*, and the article appeared in March 1891. Though Harris knew Wilde very well, he again assumed Wilde was merely posing. Ward and Lock had agreed to publish a book version and the book reached booksellers in April. It was a telling moment, for Wilde could no longer be seen as merely one member of the Aesthetic movement. Henceforth, he was to be seen as the leader of the Decadents. The young men who would come to be regarded as Decadent by "respectable" Victorian opinion now looked to him for inspiration.

Among them was Bosie Douglas, whose close friendship with Lionel Johnson was based on their similar tastes. When Johnson lent him a copy of *Dorian Gray*, Bosie read it over and over again. More than anything else, *Dorian Gray* turned Oscar Wilde into an intellectual hero for the young undergraduate. When Johnson suggested that Douglas might wish to meet the author of this controversial volume, Douglas was delighted. For Johnson, this was no more than bringing another attractive young man into Wilde's circle of attractive young men. It was an entirely innocent move for all the parties concerned. Its consequences were earth-shattering, however.

* * *

When Oscar Wilde met Bosie Douglas in the summer of 1891, Wilde was 36 and Bosie 20 years old. Neither of them could ever remember precisely how they had first met, and Wilde clouded the record by writing in 1897 that "our friendship really begins" with Bosie writing to him to ask for help over a blackmail attempt,[18] but by this he almost certainly meant the affair proper. He claimed hardly to have known Bosie before this, he had been acquainted with him for eighteen months in which he met him only four times and with little real intimacy. This contradicts Bosie's view that Oscar took a violent fancy to him on sight, being infatuated from the first. He did not reciprocate immediately, but was flattered that a man as distinguished as Wilde should pay close attention to him and his views.[19] Bosie almost certainly exaggerated the attention Wilde paid to him: Wilde paid close attention to the views, preferences and whims of all the young men of a certain type who came into his circle at that time. It was how he flattered them into becoming members of the affected group described by Raffalovich in 1890. Bosie was initially no more than one of Oscar Wilde's undergraduate "friends", charmed but not especially intimate.

Whatever the date, Bosie was drawn willingly into Wilde's orbit and held fast. Wilde's intriguingly faceted personality, with its heavy flavour of decadence and wilful contradiction, fascinated him deeply. Bosie was a petulant, idle undergraduate, but he had a real interest in Aesthetics. And both he and his undergraduate circle had dipped knowingly into the decadent end of the aesthetic pool, seeing Wilde as their standard bearer. They welcomed *The Picture of Dorian Gray* with knowing delight. Of no one was this more so than the man who introduced him to Wilde, Lionel Johnson. When *Dorian Gray* appeared, Johnson was ecstatic, and wrote Wilde a poem in the safety of Latin verse entitled "In Honorem Doriani Creatoresque" in honour of Wilde. It contained the lines:

"*Hic sunt poma Sodomorum:*	Here are apples of Sodom,
Hic sunt corda vitiorum:	Here are the very hearts of vices
Et peccata dulcia.	And tender sins.
In excelsis et infernis,	In heaven and hell be glory
Tibi sit, qui tanta cernis,	Of glory be to you,
Gloriarum gloria.	Who perceive so much."[20]

Johnson had lent Bosie his copy of *Dorian Gray*, and Bosie had devoured it. Wilde's decadence was the whole point of the fascination that the writer had for him. But Bosie could draw on more than Wilde's public persona as a literary figure with a talent for sensational writing. Oscar's decadence was certainly a subject for discussion in the highly privileged adult circles in which Bosie moved, devouring salacious gossip. In that Summer of 1891, Wilde was invited to join the Crabbett Club. This was no gentleman's club like the Savile, which had blackballed Wilde in 1888, but an informal circle organised by one of Bosie's older cousins on his mother's side, the poet Wilfrid Scawen Blunt. The club met once a year at Blunt's country house, Crabbett Park, for the purpose of playing lawn tennis and reading poems composed by members for a prize. It was an élite gathering of the rich and distinguished. Members included George Curzon (later Viceroy of India and Foreign Secretary), George Wyndham (Conservative MP, Under-Secretary for War during the Boer War and yet another of Bosie's cousins), George Leveson Gower, Comptroller of the Queen's Household, Lord Houghton, and Lewis "Lulu" Harcourt, the son of the Liberal Chancellor Sir William Harcourt. Bosie Douglas was, so he claimed, the last member to be invited to join, in 1892, as the club was later wound up when two of the members (Lords Curzon and Houghton) became Viceroys and a third, Oscar Wilde, was sent to prison.[21]

Crabbett was one of those curious gatherings, half country house party and half poetic convention, which attracted the upwardly mobile leaders of later Victorian society.[22] The Souls, which included two future Prime Ministers in Balfour and Asquith, both of whom knew Wilde, and the Apostles at Cambridge, later the home of another notorious affair involving not only homosexuality but also treason, were even more élitist societies, but Wilde was not invited to join either of these. His position savoured more of notoriety than prominence. It did not guarantee acceptance in the very highest Establishment circles, but Scawen Blunt was not Establishment either, and invited whomever he liked to his club. It was the practice that any new member should be proposed in a speech at the dinner on the first night of the meeting, and opposed by someone else. Wilde was opposed by George Curzon, who chose to make a deadly attack on him. Scawen Blunt wrote in his diary:

> He (Curzon) had been at Oxford with Wilde and knew all his little weaknesses and did not spare him, playing with astonishing audacity and skill upon his reputation for sodomy and his treatment of the subject in *Dorian Gray*. Poor Oscar sat helplessly smiling, a fat mass, in his chair . . . (he was sitting on my left and when he rose to reply I felt sorry for him – it seemed hardly fair.) But he pulled himself together as he went on and gradually warmed into an amusing and excellent speech . . . the discussion went a long time between them, and I doubt if anything better was ever heard, even from Disraeli in his best days.[23]

This diary entry was for 4 July 1891, and Blunt later noted that he had played down the ferocity of the exchange between Wilde and Curzon. The injured Wilde never returned to the Crabbett Club, and Blunt noted later that "the indictment was too home a thrust for Oscar not to feel it, and I think that it was for this reason that he did not come to our Club parties again. . . . What is really memorable about it all is that, when two years later he was arraigned in a real Court of Justice, Oscar's line of defence was precisely the same as that made in his impromptu speech that evening at the Crabbett."[24]

This was little more than gossip, but gossip in such a circle was likely to reach Bosie's ears. He did not join the Crabbett himself until the Summer of 1892, when the affair had begun, and never discussed whether he knew – or suspected – Wilde's sexual secrets in the Summer of 1891 when they met. Given what Lionel Johnson had written and Curzon had said in Scawen Blunt's hearing, it would have been remarkable if Bosie had not heard the gossip. However, such suspicions were not entertained by everyone who knew Wilde; not even his closest friends. Robert Sherard did not suspect, nor Frank Harris and others who knew Wilde. When Bosie's mother wrote to Sir Herbert Warren that she was worried by her son's friendship with an older man, Warren gave Wilde a glowing reference. Remarkably but unsurprisingly, that dutiful Victorian wife Constance Wilde had no suspicions; she probably did not even know what homosexuality was. She was well aware, however, that she was a deserted wife. Her unhappiness was clear to Lady Wilde, who wrote to Oscar on 3 November 1891: "Constance was here last evening. She is so nice always to me. I am very fond of her. She is so very lonely, and mourns for you".[25] A month later Speranza received her copy of Wilde's *A House of Pomegranates*, and wrote expressing not only her delight but that "Constance is looking well and is much pleased at the dedication to her".[26]

Dedication or not, while Oscar observed the formalities of marriage, his intellectual and emotional needs were now being served by the circle of young men who hovered around him. Wilde had written sententiously in *Dorian Gray* that "the one charm of marriage is that it makes a life of deception absolutely necessary for both parties", but in his own marriage the life of deception was practised by one partner only. Nevertheless, right up to the moment when the trials began, Oscar preserved the fiction that he was a conventionally married man. He justified his frequent absences from home by his need to have space to write, and as his literary career developed he had sufficient justification for this argument. He turned back to drama, and at last found his Muse.

George Alexander had taken over the St James's Theatre and asked Wilde for a modern play. Wilde temporised, but went to the Lake District with Robbie Ross and there wrote a script. By October, it was ready to read to Alexander, who was impressed and immediately offered Wilde a thousand pounds. Wilde asked for royalties, and thus earned seven thousand pounds in the first year. Alexander put the play into rehearsal early in 1892 under the tentative title *A Good Woman*. Under its final title of *Lady Windermere's Fan*, the play opened on 20 February 1892 and became the hit of the season.

On the opening night, Wilde was playing a double game. To outward appearances he was the successful married man, escorting his wife to see his latest play. Constance rose to the occasion, wearing a blue brocade dress modeled on the style of Charles I's era. It had a long, tabbed bodice, slashed sleeves, and was decorated with pearls and antique lace.[27] Lillie Langtry was in the audience, as were Richard La Galliene and his wife and Frank Harris. At the interval, Harris compared the play with the best of Congreve against the hostility of the critics. The audience agreed with Harris, and at the end Wilde responded to calls for the author from an audience in a state of euphoria. He appeared on stage smoking a cigarette and in high spirits. The cigarette annoyed the more conservative critics even more than the play, but critical comment had no effect whatsoever. The first night was a triumph, the whole season of the play a runaway success.

But Wilde's inner circle were taking part in a drama of a different kind. Wilde was surrounded by his entourage of young men, who included that night Robbie Ross, Bosie Douglas, Reggie Turner, who was the illegitimate son of Lord Burham, the young artist Graham Robertson, and a clerk at the Bodley Head Press called Edward Shelley. To Robertson, Wilde suggested buying a green carnation to wear as a buttonhole. "What does it mean?", asked Robertson. "Nothing whatever", Wilde replied, "but that is just what nobody will guess".[28] Wilde was again being disingenuous. The green carnation was the badge of a new cult, a long step beyond Pre-Raphaelite lilies. It signalled decadence, a secret sign for the young men who surrounded Wilde. It became well enough known for Robert Hichens to use it as the title of his book about Oscar and Bosie the next year. While Oscar denied publicly that he was the author of the book, on the green carnation he declaimed "I invented that magnificent flower".[29] After the curtain calls had finished, Constance went home while Oscar went on to dine with his entourage. Bosie Douglas went along to share Oscar's triumph. He loved the play, and always defended it as a delightful achievement. But he was still only one of the intimate circle.

If anyone was Wilde's lover at the time, it was Edward Shelley, whose low status as a clerk contrasted with the glittering youth surrounding Wilde. Yet if Wilde was courting Shelley, the relationship is far from proved. The defence in the Plea of Justification lodged by Queensberry's lawyers alleged gross indecency at a point between February and May 1892, but the charges relating to Shelley were withdrawn from the court. Whatever the truth of the relationship with Edward Shelley, it is clear that Oscar was more interested in him than in Lord Alfred Douglas. Bosie was merely another of the young men wearing the green carnation. He was stunningly good looking, Aesthetic, a student at Wilde's old Oxford college, and of similar sexual inclinations to Wilde. That was enough to admit him to the circle. But it did not lead immediately to the start of the affair.

Wilde's success greatly increased his attraction for Bosie Douglas, however, and very soon the Rubicon was crossed. It was certainly not the case that Wilde seduced an innocent Bosie, for Bosie was already well versed in decadence. The blackmail attempt which brought Wilde hot-foot to Oxford in the Spring of 1892 has never been clarified, but Bosie's subsequent reckless behaviour suggests it was a homosexual relationship, probably with a "renter", and quite likely, given his subsequent behaviour, to have involved letters carelessly left to fall into the wrong hands. It was the turning point in the relationship.[30] Once Wilde knew that Bosie was actively homosexual, a door was opened. In his *Autobiography*, Bosie recalls that what he calls "familiarities":

> began about nine months after I first met Oscar as a result of a long, patient and strenuous siege on his part. They were completely discontinued about six months before the final catastrophe, and were never resumed after he came out of prison. Wilde always claimed that his love for me was ideal and spiritual. I once, after he came out of prison . . . brought up against him that this was not strictly the case, and that there had been another side to it. He said: "Oh, it was so little that, and then only by accident, essentially it was always a reaching up towards the ideal, and in the end it became utterly ideal". Honestly, I believe he thought this to be true and meant what he said. In any case I am perfectly certain that his love

> for me, such as it really was before he went to prison, was the nearest he ever got to a pure and spiritual love.[31]

Bosie stated catagorically: "Of the sin which takes its name from one of the Cities of the Plain there never was the slightest question. I give this as my solemn word before God, as I hope to be saved. What there was, was quite bad enough."[32] What this was, Bosie spelt out to Frank Harris in a letter of 20 March 1925, before he fell out with Harris, in which he was brutally honest. He wrote that while it was hateful for him to speak of his physical relationship with Wilde, he had to be explicit. Some deep need to unburden led him to tell Harris that while sodomy – full physical intimacy – never took place, indecency of a public school type occured. More unusually, Wilde "sucked" him.[33]

The dating of nine months after a first meeting in July 1891 reinforces the view that the sexual and emotional relationship did not start before the Spring of 1892. Wilde appears to have been emotionally disengaged and looking for a relationship elsewhere in the Winter of 1891/2 – Edward Shelley had only a limited appeal, and the young poet John Gray was wooed. On a visit to Paris, André Gide fell under Wilde's spell – but, in the Spring of 1892, Bosie Douglas came to monopolise Wilde's attention. Wilde was entranced by the beautiful but irresponsible young man who had appealed to him for help. By early Summer 1892 he was inscribing a copy of his *Poems* "From Oscar, To the Gilt-mailed Boy at Oxford in the heart of June".[34]

From this point onwards, Oscar Wilde and Bosie Douglas were constantly in each other's company, and they flaunted their relationship. On 3 July, Oscar and Bosie went to Bad Homburg to take the waters, where Oscar met Bosie's grandparents and Alfred Montgomery took a deep dislike to him. On 7 July, Constance wrote sadly to her brother Otho: "Oscar is at Homburg under a régime, getting up at 7.30, going to bed at 10.30, smoking hardly any cigarettes . . . and of course drinking waters. *I only wish I was there to see it*". [*Original emphasis*][35] Although Constance did not understand what had happened to her failing marriage until much later, in taking Bosie to Bad Homburg and leaving her behind, Oscar had finally abandoned her.

And still, he was constantly surrounded by his circle of young men, many wearing the Green Carnation. But in 1892, and for the next three years, Wilde appeared to be no more than posing, flirting with homosexuality as he had long flirted with Roman Catholicism, without ever taking the plunge. For those of his circle such as Robert Ross, who was undoubtedly a practising homosexual throughout his life, and those on the fringe such as Max Beerbohm and Lionel Johnson, who had guessed at Wilde's inclinations, there was no secret. But outside the inner circle, it was commonly assumed that Wilde was merely posing.

Oscar's flirtation with young men such as John Gray, Edward Shelley, and now Bosie Douglas, may have caused comment. The author of *Dorian Gray* and *Salomé* attracted rumours, but it was commonly assumed that he was playing games. André Raffalovich, a friend of Wilde's in the late 1880s, reported that he was fascinated with the story of King James's favourite, Robert Carr who, on the eve of his trial for the murder of Sir Thomas Overbury, threatened to reveal that the King had slept with him. In consequence, two men were posted on either side of him during the trial with orders to stifle with pillows any attempt to mention James. Wilde studied Michaelangelo, Plato and Shakespeare for evidence of homosexuality, producing his essay "The Portrait of Mr W.H.", alleging that the Sonnets were addressed to a young male actor Shakespeare admired.[36] Before their friendship broke down, Wilde told André Raffalovich: "I do not think that the people who do these things derive as much pleasure as I do from talking about them".[37] And for most of Wilde's friends, talking about male love was as much as they suspected Wilde of doing.

Behind this smokescreen of dilettantism, Wilde cruised across the surface of London society, richly aware that his audience barely suspected that his decadence was more than a pose. Lionel Johnson, who did know, bitterly regretted having introduced Bosie to Wilde and had an acute sense of the disastrous course the two men were pursuing. He had long since abandoned the sense of knowing delight with which he had greeted *Dorian Gray*. In 1892, he wrote "The Destroyer of a Soul", a poem which, while not being openly addressed to Wilde, cannot but have been addressed to anyone else that he knew:

> I hate you with a necessary hate.
> First, I sought patience: passionate was she:
> My patience turned in very scorn of me,
> That I should dare forgive a sin so great,
> As this, through which I sit disconsolate:
> Mourning for that live soul, I used to see:
> Soul of a saint, whose friend I used to be:
> Till you came by! a cold, corrupting fate.

Why come you now? You, who I cannot cease
With pure and perfect hate to hate? Go, ring
The death-bell with a deep, triumphant toll!
Say you my friend sits by me still? Ah, peace!
Call you this thing my friend? This nameless thing?
This living body, hiding its dead soul?[38]

A Catholic convert who had dabbled in decadence, like so many Catholic literary men, Johnson was clearly repelled by Wilde's activities. His conversion had taken place in June 1891, almost at the moment at which he introduced Oscar and Bosie.[39] To a practising Catholic, Oscar Wilde could only represent a threat to Bosie Douglas's immortal soul.

Johnson was, however, in a tiny minority in even suspecting Wilde to be actively "decadent" rather than merely posing. To Society, Wilde continued to be an ambiguous figure whose talent for witty aphorisms and tragi-comic anecdotes made him an endlessly fascinating guest. Very few understood that Wilde had now formed a friendship with Bosie Douglas that had a greater significance than any other he had previously formed. Max Beerbohm, the writer and caricaturist, was one of the few who knew enough of both Oscar and Bosie to understand the secret game they were playing. He was the half-brother of Wilde's impresario, Beerbohm Tree, and a contemporary of Bosie at Oxford, his work having first seen the light of day in the *Spirit Lamp*. His closest friend was Reggie Turner, himself an intimate friend of Wilde's, who remained with Oscar, even to his deathbed. Beerbohm knew what the relationship of Oscar and Bosie meant, sketching them as a pair of grotesques, Fatman and Smallman.[40]

For those within the range of Wilde's wit and intellect, his presence could be overwhelming. His personality resonated in both London and Paris. Wilde's visit to Paris in late 1891 took the literary world by storm. Marcel Schwob, literary journalist, was his guide, though Pierre Louys formed an attachment that went deeper. Wilde's greatest impact was, however, on a close friend of Louys, André Gide. Gide was then twenty-one and just beginning the career that would take him to the Nobel Prize for literature. He was completely bedazzled by Wilde and, for three weeks, saw him almost daily. Gide could not keep away from Wilde and on the pages of his engagement diary for 11–12 December wrote in huge letters the single word WILDE! Gide then tore out the pages of his journals for the three weeks he spent in Wilde's company. What had he to hide? Wilde realised that Gide's troubled state of mind made him enormously receptive to his brilliant, paradoxical conversation and deliberately played upon it. He drove Gide to the edge of a mental breakdown.[41]

Gide himself was exceptional in every way, but the extraordinary power of Wilde's conversation could not be discounted by anyone who heard it. For no-one was this more true than Bosie Douglas. In his autobiography, Bosie frankly recalled:

> Whatever devotion I had for Oscar was certainly not founded on any physical admiration of mine for him. I loved him because he was brilliant and wonderful and fantastic and fascinating in his mind and in his conversation. His personal appearance, at any rate while I knew him, was always rather against him. When I first met him, I thought him comic looking. Afterwards I got used to his strange aspect, and my admiration for his brain and the dazzling brilliance and the spell-weaving enchantment of his conversation completely outweighed in my eyes the disadvantages of his appearance. When he got into his frightful trouble my love for him was deeply intensified by pity and compassion. There was nothing I would not have done for him.[42]

Robert Sherard had an exactly similar view of Wilde's golden tongue. Sherard defended him from the charge of arrogance, arguing:

> If he seemed to pontify, it was simply that he was such a delightful talker, and had a voice so melodious, that people simply stopped talking themselves, inviting him by their silence to continue . . . one simply had to listen, and was led from delight to delight, from surprise to surprise. I have never anywhere in the world met anybody even faintly resembling him in this gift. His conversation was indescribable. It charmed, touched, amused, inspired. One felt an enthusiasm for the man as one listened to him, the kind of enthusiasm that one experiences for Nature at the spectacle of some grand piece of scenery, some light on sea or land. One was lifted out of oneself.[43]

If Robert Sherard felt like this, a heterosexual friend who was far from being one of the inner circle, others were even more idolatrous. And if talk had been all there was, then Oscar's hold over intense young men would have had few serious consequences. However, the "shadow" side of Oscar's double life had taken him inexorably beyond the law into the twilit Victorian underworld of deviant sexual promiscuity.

THREE

Feasting with Panthers

Some time in May or June 1892, Oscar wrote to Robbie Ross from the Royal Hotel, Kensington, that "Bosie has insisted on stopping here for sandwiches. He is quite like a Narcissus – so white and gold. I will come either Wednesday or Thursday night in your rooms. Send me a line. Bosie is so tired; he lies like a hyacinth on the sofa, and I worship him. You dear boy, ever yours. . .".[1] This letter marks the new phase in Oscar's relationships, the ascendancy of Bosie Douglas, with the characteristically high-flown, flowery language that concealed to outsiders, the increasing physicality of the relationship. Robbie Ross was clearly meant to accept this and there is no real evidence that while Wilde was alive he displayed jealousy. In Wilde's circle, sexual fidelity was neither expected nor given. Ross knew that his place in Wilde's affections could only be threatened by resentment of Bosie Douglas and he behaved with admirable coolness. Others in Wilde's circle found themselves affected by the affair with Douglas with more serious consequences.

Bosie had pushed two others out of Wilde's affections, John Gray and Edward Shelley. John Gray was so close to Wilde that, aside from the coincidence of names, some thought him the original of Dorian Gray – he himself signed letters as "Dorian". Gray, Shelley and Douglas overlapped in the Spring of 1892, but Gray occupied first place. On 7 February at the Rhymers Club, with Wilde in the chair, Gray delivered a lecture on "The Modern Actor", arguing that art was manipulative and the artist a pariah. Wilde, from the chair, riposted that plays were best performed by puppets, with actors a second-best option whose personalities distorted the performance. The *Daily Telegraph* picked up this characteristically florid observation. Their reporter wrote a critical piece, to which Wilde was sufficiently concerned to reply by letter, claiming that his "acquaintance with Mr John Gray is, I regret to say, extremely recent",[2] which was untrue. The actors Charles Brookfield and Charles Hawtrey took the opportunity to satirise Wilde and his theory in a play, *The Poet and the Puppet.* The play ran in the West End as a lampoon of *Lady Windermere's Fan* from 19 May to the end of July 1892. Brookfield's extensive knowledge of gossip in the theatrical world about Wilde, his jealousy and hatred of Wilde were to make him one of his most dangerous enemies when the storm broke. In the Summer of 1892, however, Brookfield seemed merely an unimportant satirist of Wilde's ideas, Gray little more than another of the shallow young men around Wilde, propounding their shallow theories.

In June, Pierre Louys, the French writer who had become Wilde's closest friend among the French, arrived in England with a woman companion. Wilde immediately invited both to dine with him and Gray at the Café Royal.[3] Louys was extremely tolerant of Wilde's homosexuality, finding the *demi monde* fascinating. He admired Wilde's work immensely, and was so useful to Wilde in preparing the French version of *Salomé* for publication that Wilde dedicated the French edition to him. Though Louys was tolerant of the homosexual underworld, he was not naïve and came to realise that same sex love had darker aspects not immediately visible amid the superficial gushing recorded by Raffalovich.

Louys came to reconsider his initial impression of endless gaiety in the fall of 1892 as the relationship between Oscar and Bosie pushed John Gray out into the cold. Gray's last tribute to Wilde was an inscription in his translation of Bourget's *A Saint and Others,* to Wilde "My Beloved Master, Dear Friend, Homage".[4] It was a futile gesture and, soon after, Gray confessed to Louys that he felt outcast and was contemplating suicide. This tragedy was averted by André Raffalovich. He had long since fallen out with Wilde and it was poetic justice that Raffalovich then fell in love with Gray, made him the centrepiece of his lavish dinner parties, and installed him in Park Lane. In January 1893, Raffalovich replaced Wilde in paying John Lane for Gray's book of poems *Silverpoints.* By March, when the poems appeared, Gray told Louys that he had definitely broken with Wilde. Oscar had managed, by good fortune, to avoid a major disaster over his relationship with Gray.

Wilde indeed seems to have had no sense that any real danger could come from the careless way he conducted personal relationships. He was too immersed in living for the moment – "living for pleasure", as he described it in *De Profundis* – and caution was not part of his character. He took risks heedlessly, and over John Gray he was fortunate that events conspired to save him. His relationship with Edward Shelley was not so lucky. This had begun in the Autumn of 1891 when Wilde had met Shelley at the offices of Elkin Matthews and John Lane, Wilde's publishers. Shelley worked as one of Lane's clerks. Wilde had invited Shelley to dinner at the

Albemarle Hotel and, at the opening night of *Lady Windermere's Fan*, arranged for him to have the seat next to Louys. At the trials, Shelley would claim Wilde had later seduced him, and that he had been forced to quit his job because of ribald comments by other clerks. Luckily for Wilde, Shelley proved so poor a witness that the judge withdrew the charges relating to Shelley from the jury. Shelley claimed to be outraged by Wilde's approaches to him but, despite this, he had appealed to Wilde for money and assistance long after the Spring of 1892.

Shelley was altogether a spineless character, and it became clear in the court that Wilde treated him with benign contempt. Wilde admitted three gifts of money, one of which was for the train fare to Felbrigg, near Cromer in Norfolk, where he was staying with Bosie after returning from Bad Homburg. Shelley had not come; he was pestering Wilde for money as late as April 1894, and Wilde commented in a letter to Bosie that he had "had a frantic telegram from Edward Shelley, of all people! asking me to see him. When he came he was of course in trouble for money. As he betrayed me grossly I, of course, gave him money and was kind to him. I find that forgiving one's enemies is a most curious morbid pleasure; perhaps I should check it".[5] This was clearly not a significant relationship and, by the Autumn of 1892, it had faded before the rising sun of Bosie Douglas.

In the Summer of 1892 the affair entered its honeymoon period. Although Wilde later claimed bitterly in *De Profundis* that life with Bosie inhibited his writing, Bosie contested this with some justice. Wilde was working on his second light comedy, *A Woman of No Importance*, at Felbrigg during August and September, with Bosie sharing the cottage on vacation, Constance being elsewhere looking after the children. Sharing a cottage with Bosie did not prevent Wilde handing in the playscript to Beerbohm Tree in October of 1892. The quarrels which were to occur in 1893 were mercifully absent and, in the circles of the Douglas family, the friendship was so well established that it was accepted as significant by the early Autumn.

Wilde met the parents of his *amour*, Lady Queensberry by design, the Marquis by accident. Bosie's mother invited the Wildes to Bracknell. While there, she took Oscar for a long walk and discussed her fears for her favourite child. In *De Profundis*, Wilde later recalled sitting "in the yellowing woods in Bracknell with your mother. At that time I knew very little of your real nature . . . your mother began to speak to me of your character. She told me of your two chief faults, your vanity and your being, as she termed it, 'all wrong about money'. I have a distinct recollection of how I laughed. I had no idea that the first would bring me to prison and the second to bankruptcy."[6]

Queensberry, however, was much less approachable than Sybil. The Marquis never approved of the relationship, but initially was not offensive, although he told his son he must give up Wilde. Bosie, being of age, ignored his advice and told him so. Soon after, the couple were lunching at the Café Royal when Queensberry came in alone. Bosie went over and invited his father to join their table. The Marquis acquiesced with bad grace, but on sitting and listening to Wilde's charm in full flow, fell under the spell. Within ten minutes he was laughing at Wilde's jokes, Wilde playing cleverly on the Marquis's hostility to religion. After an hour, Bosie became bored and left the two older men to converse. The conversation went on until the late afternoon. Two days later, Bosie received a letter from his father in which Queensberry took back everything he had said about Wilde. He considered him charming and clever and did not wonder that Bosie was fond of him. Queensberry had heard from Lord and Lady Grey that Wilde was "perfectly all right in every way".[7]

Queensberry's good opinion did not last. It would not even have begun had Queensberry understood what his son and Wilde were doing. But neither were innocents and it is completely untrue that Wilde "perverted" Bosie. Until he was past thirty, Douglas never denied that he was homosexual. As he said in his *Autobiography*, "even before I met Wilde I had persuaded myself that 'sins of the flesh' were not wrong, and my opinion was of course vastly strengthened and confirmed by his brilliantly reasoned defence of them. I am trying to be fair to Wilde and not make him responsible for 'corrupting' me more than he did . . . I must say that it strikes me now that the difference between us was this: that I was at that time a frank and natural pagan, and that he was a man who believed in sin and yet deliberately committed it. . .".[8] Writing to Frank Harris thirty years afterwards, Douglas admitted that his instincts were for younger men, Wilde being the exception, and that he was homosexual in the 1890s. After Wilde's death he married and he became heterosexual. He regarded his earlier activities as prolongation of boyhood.[9]

From this it is clear that Douglas was active throughout the 1890s, mainly with lower-class boys and men. His story would be kept out of the courtroom, but events in the first part of 1893, emerging in court two years later, showed clearly that he had been knowingly active on his own account in the homosexual underworld of London.

When Oscar returned to town in the early Autumn, Bosie introduced him to Maurice Schwabe, nephew-in-law of the Liberal politician Frank Lockwood, and Alfred Taylor, the son of a rich cocoa manufacturer. The introduction set in train events that would lead Taylor and Wilde to the dock at the Old Bailey. A superficial but charming "queen", Taylor was not exactly a procurer but gave dinner parties at which "gentlemen" could meet out-of-work, working-class youths – remarkably easy to do, despite the formidable social code of Victorian prudery.

In the period before the Wilde trials made the existence of the homosexual underworld known to all who read the papers, neither the police nor any other authorities took serious notice of the "renters" or their clients. This was less because they were prepared to tolerate such immoral behaviour, as long as it didn't "frighten the horses" as the saying went, but because homosexual practice was really quite unthinkable and seldom came to the public notice. The Wilde trials would change this view, but at the time Douglas and Wilde cruised among the renters they moved in a world which was invisible to all except those who knew the entrées into this twilit subculture. Taylor had such knowledge, and introduced Wilde to Sidney Mavor, known as Jenny among his circle.[10] Wilde was instantly attracted, and invited Mavor and Taylor to dine at Kettner's the following evening, Bosie making up the party. Boris Brasol claims that Wilde ordered Thornhills in Bond Street to send Mavor a cigarette case on 3 October; an event which was later to come up at the trials.[11] Wilde certainly took Mavor to spend the night at the Albemarle. This was the "feasting with panthers" of which Wilde later boasted.

Mavor and Taylor were not themselves in any way threatening, but Oscar and Bosie were undoubtedly moving among very dangerous characters. Schwabe had picked up one Freddie Atkins at the Knightsbridge skating rink earlier that year. He realised that Atkins was no innocent, but failed to realise that he had a career as a blackmailer and was already known to the police. Schwabe introduced Atkins to Taylor in November 1892 and, through Taylor, Atkins came to know Wilde.[12] Wilde was immediately interested. Invitations ensued, and the prosecution at the Old Bailey would later allege gross indecency. Atkins, however, denied on oath that any impropriety took place with Wilde. Nevertheless, the landlady at his lodgings in Osnaburgh Street deposed that Wilde visited Atkins, and that afterward the maid complained at the state of the bed, claiming "the sheets were stained in a peculiar way".[13] Atkins' greatest threat lay in the fact that, at the magistrates' trial and again at the Old Bailey, he would claim that, while with Wilde in Paris, he had seen the playwright in bed with Schwabe, whose uncle-in-law, Frank Lockwood, had by then become Solicitor General.[14] Fortunately for all concerned, Atkins's career as a blackmailer enabled Wilde's barrister, Sir Edward Clarke, to destroy him as a witness, and Schwabe's involvement barely received a mention.

This was but a Pyrrhic victory. Oscar and Bosie were soliciting men with such recklessness that Queensberry was able to gather seriously damaging evidence against Wilde in 1895. He could equally easily have destroyed his own son, had he intended to. Sometime late in 1892, Bosie picked up a "renter" called Alfred Wood who, unknown to him, was another blackmailer with criminal connections. When Bosie tired of his charms, in January or February 1893 he passed him on to Wilde, introducing him by the appallingly indiscreet medium of a telegram.[15] Wilde met Wood by prearrangement in the Café Royal, plied him with food and drink, then took him back to Tite Street. Bosie, too, continued to see Alfred Wood, with fatal consequences.

While the affair was still passing through its honeymoon stage, Oscar took a short lease on the Devonshire house of Lady Mount-Temple at Babbacombe Cliff near Torquay. Constance had taken the boys there during the Summer of 1892 while Oscar was in Norfolk, and he renewed the lease over the following Winter.[16] This took Constance and the boys out of London in mid-Winter and allowed Oscar and Bosie to engage in what were, at the very least, passionate gestures. In January 1893, Bosie sent Oscar a sonnet entitled "In Sarum Close", the address in Salisbury near the cathedral where his mother had rented a house. It expressed jejune but intense feelings, with sentiments that were little more than juvenile doggerel, but which pleased Wilde immensely. He wrote back a letter that was to have serious consequences:

> My own boy, your sonnet is quite lovely, and it is a marvel that those red rose-leaf lips of yours should have been made no less for music of song than for madness of kisses. Your slim gilt soul walks between passion and poetry. I know Hyacinthus, whom Apollo loved so madly, was you in Greek days.
>
> Why are you alone in London, and when do you go to Salisbury? Do go there to cool your hands in the grey twilight of Gothic things, and come here whenever you like. It is a lovely place – it only lacks you – but go to Salisbury first. Always, with undying love,
>
> Yours Oscar.[17]

At the trials, it would be alleged that Bosie had charitably decided to give Alfred Wood some cast-off clothes, and that Wood "found" a bundle of letters among them, including this one. It is more likely that Wood simply searched Douglas's apartments for incriminating material and stole every letter from Wilde he could lay his hands on. Whatever the truth of the matter, he came into the possession of this letter from Wilde to Bosie Douglas, and immediately realised that it opened the possibility of blackmail. Wilde's letter, generally known as the "Hyacinthus" letter, now began to take on a life of its own.

Wood showed his finds to two professional blackmailers, Robert Cliburn and William Allen. Cliburn (or Clibborn), the older of the two, had already been convicted at Lewes Assizes in December 1890 under the name Robert Henry Harris, and both men were later to serve prison sentences for blackmail, seven years' penal servitude in the case of Cliburn.[18] Wood wanted to go to America, and his accomplices selected the Hyacinthus letter as the means of getting him there. A copy was made and sent to Beerbohm Tree, then producing *A Woman of No Importance*, on 21 April. Tree handed it to Wilde, remarking that its sentiments were open to misconstruction. Wilde airily replied that it was really a prose poem, and that if put into verse it could appear in an anthology such as the *Golden Treasury*.[19]

Despite his careless dismissal of the letter to Tree, Wilde was seriously alarmed, and privately agreed to purchase all the letters from Wood. He gave him thirty-five pounds to go to America. But when he examined the bundle, he discovered that the dangerous Hyacinthus letter was missing. Douglas and Wilde were acutely conscious of why this letter had disappeared, and persuaded Pierre Louys to produce a poetic version in French. This appeared in Bosie's Oxford magazine, the *Spirit Lamp* of 4 May 1893. At the Old Bailey in 1895, Queensberry's counsel, Edward Carson, would attack this attempt to turn the letter into aesthetic verse as "a very thinly veiled attempt to get rid of the character of that letter. A more thinly veiled attempt to cover its real nature has never been made in a Court of Justice".[20] Wilde and Douglas could, however, hope that with Wood in America and an airily literary version in print, they might never hear of the Hyathincus letter again.

No such good fortune ensued. Allen returned from the USA and turned up unannounced at Wilde's house. According to Wilde – we have only his side of the story – he treated the blackmailer with contempt. "I suppose you have come about my beautiful letter to Lord Alfred

Douglas. If you had not been so foolish as to send a copy of it to Mr Beerbohm Tree, I would gladly have paid you a very large sum of money for the letter, as I consider it to be a work of art". Allen replied that a man had offered him £60 for it. Wilde advised him to sell at that price, as "I myself have never received so large a sum for any prose work of that length". Wilde refused to pay for the letter, gave Allen half a sovereign for his cab fare, and remarked: "The letter is a prose poem, will shortly be published in sonnet form in a delightful magazine, and I will send you a copy of it". Allen then departed, crestfallen.

Five minutes later the bell rang and Wilde found Cliburn on his doorstep. To his surprise he presented him with the Hyacinthus letter with the comment, "Allen has asked me to give it back to you". Wilde was nonplussed and asked why. Cliburn replied: "He says that you were kind to him, and there is no use trying to 'rent' [*blackmail*] you as you only laugh at us". Wilde accepted the letter and the conversation became surreal. Wilde complained that the letter had become soiled, commenting, "I think it quite unpardonable that better care was not taken of this original manuscript of mine". Cliburn expressed regret, and was given half a sovereign for his pains. Wilde bantered: "I am afraid you are leading a wonderfully wicked life". Cliburn riposted "There is good and bad in all of us", and Wilde told him "You are a born philosopher". On this they parted, and Wilde closed the door on what he hoped was finally the end of the episode.[21]

Unfortunately for him, the blackmailers had made a copy of the letter which, eighteen months later, was to fall into the hands of his adversary, the Marquis of Queensberry. Wilde and Douglas could not know this. From their viewpoint, they had shot the rapids and come out unscathed. They may have realised that they were charting a very dangerous course in associating with characters like Wood, but neither could stop pursuing young men, though they were more cautious in the immediate future. The net effect of the Hyacinthus letter episode was to increase their confidence that they could handle any crisis, however dangerous, and they plunged on without regard for the consequences, only feeling an increased sense of comradeship through shared danger.

The only immediate fallout from the Hyacinthus episode was, indirectly, the collapse of Oscar Wilde's friendship with Pierre Louys. The Frenchman was tolerant of the homosexual *milieu*, being lost in admiration for Wilde. He started his letters to him "Cher Maître", and Wilde was flattered. Louys was granted entrée to Wilde's London society, becoming friendly with John Gray. He naïvely told André Gide about the exquisite manners of the homosexuals around Wilde, particularly their habit of lighting a cigarette, taking a puff, then offering it round the circle. In the Autumn of 1892, Louys began to have second thoughts, initially because John Gray confided in him that he was contemplating suicide following his rejection by Wilde. This could be dismissed as the fortunes of love, and Louys remained friendly with Wilde. Nevertheless, it clearly came as a great surprise to the Frenchman to find, on receiving a copy of the French version of *Salomé* on 22 February 1893, that Wilde had dedicated the edition "A mon ami Pierre Louys". He responded with a facetious telegram, which pained Wilde. By now Louys found the constant presence of the circle of young men around Wilde oppressive, writing to his brother on 22 April that, while Oscar had been charming, "I should have been glad if he had provided different company". Nevertheless, he was persuaded to turn the Hyacinthus letter into a poem in French, and it was published by Bosie with the legend "A letter in prose poetry by Mr Oscar Wilde to a friend, and translated into rhymed poetry by a poet of no importance".[22]

Louys was becoming increasingly unhappy with the games played by Wilde and his circle. He was even more deeply disturbed when he visited Wilde in his rooms at the Albemarle Hotel in late April.[23] Louys observed a bedroom shared by Oscar and Bosie, having one double bed with two pillows. He was then shaken by a visit from Constance, who brought Wilde his mail and pleaded with him to return home. Wilde made a joke of this, pretending that he had been away so long that he had forgotten the house number, and Constance smiled through her tears. Wilde made light of his behaviour, but could hardly have been unaware of Constance's distress. It was about this time, according to a story he told Madame Melba, that he tried to tell off one of his sons for being naughty and making his mother cry. His son then asked, poignantly: "What punishment would be reserved for naughty papas, who did not come home till the early morning, and made Mother cry far more?"[24]

Louys was disgusted by Wilde's treatment of his wife and children; he had not previously considered the family. Wilde tried to make light of Louys' outrage by commenting that he had been married three times, once to a woman and twice to men – presumably Douglas and Robbie Ross – but Louys refused to be mollified. When Wilde visited Paris in late May, Louys remonstrated with him on his treatment of his family. Wilde was unrepentant, and Louys told him he was breaking off relations.

Wilde looked sadly at him and said: “Goodbye, Pierre Louys. I had hoped for a friend. From now on I will have only lovers”.[25] After his downfall, Wilde would regret losing the friendship of both Gray and Louys.

But, in the Summer of 1893, with another theatrical success in *A Woman of No Importance*, criticism made no difference to either Wilde or Douglas. Wilde displayed an almost childish sense of his own self-importance. When the first run of the play came to an end in August, he turned up at the theatre pompously the worse for drink. Max Beerbohm wrote to Reggie Turner on 19 August that Wilde had arrived with Douglas, Robbie Ross and Aubrey Beardsley, posing as ancient Greeks on a Bacchanalian romp. Beerbohm was repelled by Wilde’s drunkenness. That Max Beerbohm could feel this about Wilde in the theatre of his half-brother, at the end of a successful run, and knowing Oscar and his circle as he did, tells us much about Wilde’s growing egoism.

Yet Wilde was on the crest of a wave; and, after the problem of the Hyacinthus letter had been swept under the carpet, behaved as if he were invulnerable. The relationship with Bosie was a well-kept secret, appearing no more significant to those outside the charmed circle than his “friendships” with Robbie Ross or the young illustrator of *Salomé*, Aubrey Beardsley. However, Bosie was about to become an increasingly visible and demanding presence in Wilde’s life. Until the Summer of 1893, Bosie had still been an undergraduate at Oxford. That year, however, his university career came finally to a halt. From that moment on, he would be able to devote all his emotional energies to his relationship with Oscar. And from that moment, Oscar Wilde found that the younger man had the stronger will and would make demands on him that he would ultimately be unable to fulfil.

* * *

As a student at Oxford, Bosie Douglas showed an insolent disregard for academic study. In fact, throughout his life, Bosie disliked any form of work, other than writing poetry and editing literary journals, at both of which he showed some talent. This was not likely to pay many bills, as his father pointed out to him; but Bosie was wholly indifferent to advice, particularly from that quarter. Lord Alfred Bruce Douglas had inherited a title and took the view that the world owed him a living. He expected to live a life of aristocratic indolence and literary endeavour, languidly engaging in cultural and sporting pursuits. This attitude would have made sense if he was the heir to a fortune, but as Bosie was the third son in an ancient system of primogeniture in which the eldest inherited the bulk of an estate, Bosie was never likely to inherit the money needed for a life of effortless leisure.

He never even conceded that this might pose problems. Despite entreaties from his parents, he frittered away his life at Oxford. He lived on an allowance from his father of £350, plus some money from his mother, apparently indifferent to what would happen if his father cut off his allowance and unwilling to follow his brothers in attempting to earn a living. Unlike his elder brother Drumlanrig, who attempted a career in politics as Rosebery's private secretary, he had no interest in life at Westminster and refused to train for a career. His brother Percy, equally feckless but less intelligent, was put into the Navy at the age of 12 and, being cashiered over an obscure scandal at 19, tried cattle ranching in Canada. He abandoned this to set out as a tea planter in Ceylon in 1894, and was then persuaded to seek his fortune in the Coolgardie gold rush in Western Australia. He had already married the daughter of an impoverished Cornish parson, infuriating his father beyond measure, but Percy was at least attempting to find his own fortune.[26]

Bosie's younger brother, Sholto, also made some attempts to earn his way. In the family tradition, Sholto was unstable and prone to disappearances. When he failed as a lieutenant in the Northamptonshire regiment he vanished so completely that Queensberry had to hire a private detective to find him – indirectly leading Queensberry to the method which would prove so crucial in his pursuit of Oscar Wilde. When he was found, the family decided to send Sholto abroad to get him out of mischief. Sybil purchased a fruit farm in Bakersfield, California, and in 1894 Sholto was sent to manage it. There, he married a local barmaid; when this unpromising beginning proved to have an unexpected pot of gold at the end of the rainbow – Sholto's wife unexpectedly came into money – the couple settled in Ontario to farm. Sholto had finally settled to a regular job.[27]

Bosie made no attempt to emulate his brothers by seeking a career, spurning the opportunities offered by his academic studies at Oxford. The inevitable result was that he was "ploughed" – sent down for a term and forced to resit after failing an exam – at Christmas 1892. His family were deeply worried. With his finals only six months away, he showed every sign of complete failure. In January 1893, Lady Queensberry consulted his closest friend, Lionel Johnson, who proposed that the family hire a crammer to get Bosie through his finals. He recommended a friend from Winchester and New College Oxford, Campbell Dodgson, later Keeper of Prints and Drawings at the British Museum. Dodgson was eminently well qualified and agreed to tutor Bosie for a month, Johnson advising him that Bosie "wants most help in logic, Aristotle, Bacon, History".[28] Dodgson accordingly responded to the emergency, only to find that his work as a tutor took a very strange turn indeed.

On 8 February, Dodgson wrote to Johnson describing what had happened: "As a tutor I am the merest fraud: only nobody seems to expect anything else".[29] Dodgson had gone to Winchester and Salisbury in pursuit of Bosie, eventually catching up with his pupil at his mother's house in Salisbury, but only after spending most of the day wandering in the cathedral cloisters waiting for Bosie to turn up. Bosie arrived too late to start work. He spent the evening editing the *Spirit Lamp* by telegram, only turning his attentions to Plato on the following morning. This lasted an hour and a half, after which he informed Dodgson they were going to Torquay to stay with Oscar Wilde. Oscar was at Babbacombe Cliff with Cyril, working on a new play, while Constance had taken Vyvyan to Florence. Dodgson spent the afternoon repacking the portmanteau he had just unpacked, Bosie looked for books, money, cigarettes and sent telegrams and, after a lunatic dash to the station – Dodgson finding himself in charge of a fox terrier and a "scarlet morocco dispatch-box, a gorgeous and beautiful gift from Oscar", they caught the train by the skin of their teeth.

An hour into the journey, Bosie remembered that he had not told Oscar he was coming, so a telegram had to be sent from Exeter en route. They arrived at about nine o'clock and dined luxuriously. Oscar painted an attractive picture of the party in a letter to Lady Mount-Temple, with a characteristically offhand reference to Constance to complete the scene: "Babbacombe Cliff has become a kind of college or school, for Cyril studies French in the nursery, while I write my new play in Wonderland (Lady Mount-Temple's boudoir, with pictures by Rossetti and Burne Jones) and in the drawing room Lord Alfred Douglas – one of Lady Queensberry's sons – studies Plato with his tutor for his degree in Oxford in June. He and his tutor are staying with me for a few days, so I am not lonely in the evenings. Constance seems very happy in Florence. No doubt you will hear from her. . .".[30]

Dodgson's account was less idyllic. He wrote to Lionel Johnson: "Our life is lazy and luxurious; our moral principles are lax. We argue for hours about different interpretations of Platonism. Oscar implores me, with outstretched arms and tears in his eyes, to let my soul alone and cultivate my body for six weeks. Bosie is beautiful and fascinating, but quite wicked. He is enchanted with Plato's sketch of democratic man, and no arguments of mine will induce him to believe in any absolute standards of ethics or of anything else. We do no logic, no history, but play with pigeons and children and drive by the sea. . ."[31]

It is not suprising that Dodgson regarded himself as a fraud. Babbacombe Cliff was the very parody of an educational establishment, and Wilde formalised this in a letter of thanks to Dodgson of 23 February, when he commented flippantly that he was "still conducting the establishment on the old lines and really think I have succeeded in combining the advantages of a public school with those of a private lunatic asylum, which as you know was my aim". To underline what he meant by this, Oscar included a "rule book", as follows:

BABBACOMBE SCHOOL

Headmaster – Mr Oscar Wilde
Second Master – Mr Campbell Dodgson
Boys – Lord Alfred Douglas
Rules:

Tea for masters and boys at 9.30am

Breakfast at 10.30

Work. 11.30–12.30

At 12.30 Sherry and biscuits for headmaster and boys (the second master objects to this)

12.40–1.30 Work.

1.30. Lunch

2.30– 4.30. Compulsory hide-and-seek for the headmaster.

5. Tea for headmaster and second master, brandy and soda (not to exceed seven) for boys.

6–7. Work.

7.30. Dinner, with compulsory champagne.

8.30–12. Ecarte, limited to five guinea points.

12–1.30. Compulsory reading in bed. Any boy found disobeying this rule will be immediately woken up.[32]

It is possible to detect a certain gentle charm in all this, and Rupert Croft Cook in his biography of Douglas has stated that Dodgson left a "most happy account" of his adventures as Bosie's tutor. Up to a point this is true. But Dodgson knew perfectly well that he was not being paid to act a part in an entertainment, and that he had not discharged his duties as a tutor. Indeed, had Wilde been less inclined to humour Bosie by playing fatuous games, he might have considered that he was storing up trouble for the future. However at this point the relationship was lighthearted and punctuated with schoolboy humour, which, for all its shallowness, made an indelible mark on Bosie. Thirty years later Bosie could still remember the jokes and told them to Croft Cook. The writer did not think much of their brilliance, but what mattered was the enjoyment that Wilde had in Bosie's company and the impact the stay had on the younger man. It was sweetness and light, an enjoyable experience that both men savoured and thought good.[33] No consideration of future problems spoilt the sunlit adventure; although, at the end, Wilde experienced another side of Bosie Douglas that should have alerted him to the dangers of encouraging Bosie to neglect his studies. Bosie lost his temper and Wilde saw for the first time the unpleasantness that a Douglas was capable of displaying. What provoked the row neither man ever revealed, but the seriousness of the quarrel is beyond dispute. From his prison cell, Wilde recalled it as the first breach in the relationship, setting a precedent that would recur with terrible effect:

> My fault was, not that I did not part from you, but that I parted from you far too often. As far as I can make out I ended my friendship with you every three months regularly, and each time that I did so you managed by entreaties, telegrams, letters, the interposition of your friends, the interposition of mine, and the like to induce me to allow you back. When at the end of March '93 you left my house at Torquay I had determined never to speak to you again, or to allow you under any circumstances to be with me, so revolting had been the scene you had made the night before your departure. You wrote and telegraphed from Bristol to beg me to forgive you and to meet you. Your tutor, who had stayed behind, told me that he thought that at times you were quite irresponsible for what you said and did, and that most, if not all, of the men at Magdalen were of the same opinion. I consented to meet you, and of course I forgave you. On the way up to town you begged me to take you to the Savoy. That was indeed a visit fatal to me.[34]

Wilde's bitterness was justified. The row with Bosie probably took place in February, not March 1893, Wilde never being very good on dates, but the memory of the actual quarrel is not in dispute. It set a pattern that would recur whenever Bosie lost his temper, white hot rage and vicious abuse following in an ominous pattern. Wilde could never break with Bosie or set limits to the relationship. Yet he was frightened by Bosie's rages and knew they spelt danger to him. Characteristically, Wilde forgave but did not forget. He took Bosie to the Savoy. This was possibly the setting in which Louys observed the bed with two pillows. Wilde later moved from the Savoy to the Albemarle, being unable to afford the cost of the most expensive hotel in London – but, while at the Savoy, he had written Bosie a most revealing letter:

Savoy Hotel
Victoria Embankment
London

(March 1893)

Dearest of Boys, Your letter was delightful, red and yellow wine to me; but I am sad and out of sorts. Bosie, you must not make scenes with me. They kill me, they wreck the loveliness of life, I cannot see you, so Greek and gracious, distorted with passion. I cannot listen to your curved lips saying hideous things to me. I would rather sooner (be blackmailed by every renter in London) than have you bitter, unjust, hating. I must see you soon. You are the divine thing I want, the thing of grace and beauty; but I don't know how to do it. Shall I come to Salisbury? My bill here is £49 for a week. I have also got a new sitting room over the Thames. Why are you not here, my dear, my wonderful boy? I fear I must leave; no money, no credit, and a heart of lead.[35]

With astonishing irresponsibility, Bosie left this letter lying about in a hotel and it was stolen, later to reappear to devastating effect, in the hands of Queensberry's counsel at the Old Bailey where Carson read it to the court. It is worth noting the vast sums Wilde was prepared to spend on hotel bills: £49 per week made the Savoy among the most expensive hotels in London. To put the sum into context, Rowntree's *Poverty: A Study of Town Life*, published in 1901, estimated that the breadline for a family of two adults and three children was £1–1*s*–8*d* per week, about £56 per year. Nearly a third of the British population lived on less. Wilde, whose income from the smash hit he was about to launch in the West End would be about one hundred pounds per week, was thus spending some forty times more than the poverty line on rooms at the Savoy, despite having no income of any consequence. He would complain in *De Profundis* that, between the Autumn of 1892 and his imprisonment in 1895, he spent with Bosie and on Bosie a total of £5,000.[36] This is a staggering sum – it can be multiplied a hundredfold to match today's prices – but it was hardly Bosie's fault that Oscar spent money irresponsibly. Oscar wished to live his life as a plutocrat, and did so regardless of whether he had money or not. He never even thought of the consequences.

Bosie, too, was irrepressible. He came defiantly that Spring to the end of his inglorious career at Oxford, basking not only in his relationship with Oscar, but also in the kudos that the *Spirit Lamp* had earned him in the homosexual community. Bosie had already published the poem "Two Loves", with its resonant "I am the Love that Dare not Speak its Name", giving the homosexual underworld a slogan which would echo down the decades. His editorship of the *Spirit Lamp* had established him in the Aesthetic movement as a figure of promise and had attracted the notice of John Adington Symonds, whose *A Study in Greek Ethics* ranked with anything Pater had written on Greek Love.

Symonds, who lived in Switzerland and Italy, had been elected a fellow of Magdalen and was a major historian. Aged 63 in 1893, sexually ambiguous (despite his scholarly interest in homosexuality he had been married with a daughter), he was fascinated by Bosie; and, on receiving an invitation to contribute to the *Spirit Lamp*, sent Bosie an article entitled "Beethoven's Concerto in E Dur", a slight piece on the composer's use of the pianoforte. A letter from him dated 30 March, which has survived, suggests a certain jealousy of Oscar Wilde, who had of course invited Bosie to London for the première of *A Woman of No Importance*. The key paragraph reads: "I daresay it is rather dreadful for you at Klein Schmalkaden. But you'll shake down. You can't be always pampered in the Savoy. It was very pleasant for Oscar pampering you, I doubt not. I wish you would come and see how I can make you comfortable, and feed your soul on honey of sweet-bitter thoughts – in Italy – in Switzerland – it is all the same".[37]

The phrasing is somewhat similar to Wilde's, but the relationship with Bosie was not to develop. Symonds died three weeks later. Bosie published his essay, together with an obituary, in the May edition of the *Spirit Lamp*. This edition also contained Louys' verse rendition of the Hyacinthus letter (Louys was named as translator), a short story by Robert Ross entitled "How We Lost The Book Of Jasher", a poem by Lionel Johnson, and a poem and two essays including a review of *Salomé*, by Douglas himself. Douglas relied heavily on his friends for contributions. It was in the last edition of all, published 6 June, that he carried Wilde's "The Disciple" and Beerbohm's "The Incomparable Beauty of Modern Dress". Bosie worked hard at the *Spirit Lamp*, but at the expense of his studies.

As Bosie moved unsteadily towards his finals in May, Oscar arrived to ensure that his friend's last weeks would be illuminated in a blaze of reflected glory. Bosie basked in the triumph of Oscar's progress through Oxford that Spring. He had to take what glory he could from this, for he had little of his own. In June, he produced one more edition of the *Spirit Lamp*, but did not turn up for his final examinations. Magdalen College expressed its disfavour, and Bosie rushed to remove his name from its books. Wilde encouraged Bosie, praising him for having, like Swinburne, decided to remain permanently undergraduate. Swinburne's example was hardly relevant, he had in any case a poetic talent greater than Bosie's. Coming from a man with a double First this seems flippant indeed. But, for the moment, Bosie's seemed an heroic gesture in the little circle surrounding Oscar Wilde. It would become clear in the months to come that Bosie's fate was now inexorably linked with Oscar's. In the Summer of 1893 this seemed to both men an infinitely delightful prospect.

For the Douglas family, however, their son's failure to gain a degree after four years of expensive study was anything but delightful.

FOUR

Queensberry Rules

Queensberry's reaction to his son's failure to gain a degree in the Summer of 1893 was to write to him what Wilde called "a very ugly, abusive and violent letter". Wilde continued, however, that the letter Bosie wrote in reply "was in every way worse, and of course far less excusable, and consequently you were extremely proud of it. I remember quite well your saying to me with your most conceited air that you could beat your father 'at his own trade'".[1] Bosie recalled matters differently, arguing in *Oscar Wilde and Myself* that he had missed the final exams because of illness and that Oxford had offered to confer on him an honorary degree if he returned in the vacation to take two papers. Bosie argued that he consulted his father on the matter, an unlikely course of action given the hostility between them, and that Queensberry opined that a degree was worthless. In consequence, Bosie refused to re-sit his exams.[2] Wilde's version of events carries conviction. Bosie – or his collaborator, Crosland – of whom more later – was gilding the lily where Bosie's failure at Oxford was concerned. Bosie was right to think his father despised academic success. But Bosie was being economical with the truth in suggesting that Queensberry was indifferent to his son's failure.

In the Summer of 1893, the hatred between father and son was merely simmering. Queensberry seems to have been appeased for the moment by suggestions that Bosie was intent on studying for the Bar. Nothing could be further from the truth. Bosie had no intention of pursuing a career in the law or anywhere else. Instead, he joined Oscar and his family as Oscar was working on his latest play *An Ideal Husband* and the two men frittered away the time in chitchat and frivolity. Bosie always recalled that Summer of 1893 as an idyllic period. Oscar Wilde was to see it as a calm punctuated by storms.

Oscar had taken a house on the Thames at Goring known as The Cottage, hoping inspiration would flow. In June, he does appear to have sketched a first act, but he was constantly interrupted by visitors, whom he could never resist. Even when Constance and the boys went back to London, he could not settle. In June he wrote to the artist Charles

Ricketts to discuss designs for the cover of his poem "The Sphinx", admitting: "I have done no work here. The river gods have lured me to devote myself to a Canadian canoe, which I paddle about. It is curved like a flower".[3] Bosie was never far from his thoughts. He had commissioned a drawing by William Rothenstein before Bosie left Oxford, and in May he had written to him that "You really must be painted, and have an ivory statue executed".[4] These were never carried out, but Bosie came to Goring on a visit with immense consequences.

The affair was superficially still in its honeymoon period, with Oscar almost pathetically anxious to please his beloved. Bosie came down from Oxford aristocratic, beautiful, and poetic. He wrote eloquent lyrics. He brought five servants with him, one of whom, Walter Grainger, was to be cited in the trials, most damagingly for Wilde. Wilde was induced to subsidise Bosie's lifestyle at the highest levels, not that Oscar needed much encouraging to spend money. According to Wilde in *De Profundis*, in the three months Bosie spent with Oscar at Goring, the two men managed to spend the astonishing sum of £1,340.[5] Wilde took the view that the future could only be an endlessly wonderful romp, and when Oscar and Bosie played on the banks of the Thames it seemed true. The flavour of that Summer is captured in an anecdote recorded by Frank Harris, which, despite Harris's tendency to pretend total recall, has the ring of authenticity. Harris remembers Wilde telling him:

> One afternoon it was sultry close, and Bosie proposed that I should turn the hosepipe on him. He went in and threw his things off and so did I. A few minutes later I was seated in a chair with a bathtowel round me and Bosie was lying on the grass about ten yards away, when the vicar came to call. "I am the vicar of the parish", he bowed pompously. "I'm delighted to see you," I said, getting up and draping myself carefully, "you have come just in time to enjoy a perfectly Greek scene. I regret that I am scarcely fit to receive you, and Bosie there" – and I pointed to Bosie lying on the grass. The vicar turned his head and saw Bosie's white limbs; the sight was too much for him; he got very red, gave a gasp and fled from the place. I simply sat down in my chair and shrieked with laughter.[6]

This juvenile baiting of the bourgeoisie was the keynote of an indolent Summer, but the note of lighthearted horseplay did not last. There was a serious breach, later recalled in *De Profundis* as the second major disruption of the year. The row took place in June, when some of Bosie's Oxford friends came to visit from a Saturday to a Monday – the presence of younger men always likely to cause tension in the relationship. What the quarrel was about is unknown, but Wilde recalled: "You made a scene so dreadful, so distressing that I told you we must part. I remember quite well, as we stood on the level croquet ground with the pretty lawn all around, pointing out to you that we were spoiling each other's lives, that you were absolutely ruining mine, and that an irrevocable parting, a complete separation was the one philosophic thing to do. You went sullenly after luncheon, leaving one of your most offensive letters behind with the butler to be handed to me after your departure. . .".[7]

But no parting between Oscar and Bosie was forever. Within three days, Bosie was telegraphing from London begging to be forgiven. And Wilde, who had taken The Cottage to please Bosie, had engaged his servants and was infatuated, took him back.

But he was sufficiently alarmed about the situation to give some thought to Bosie's immediate future. Wilde decided that allowing Bosie to remain idle and bored was a recipe for trouble, and so gave him the commission of translating *Salomé* from French to English for publication. It was a mistake: Wilde should have known that Bosie's schoolboy French was not up to the task, but once Bosie believed that his name would appear on the same title page as Oscar Wilde's, he could not see himself as a craftsman engaged on a task of work. The commission gave him an inflated view of his abilities, which even Wilde could not indulge in a work for publication. The storm broke at the end of August, when Wilde saw Bosie's translation, pointed out elementary errors, and reaped the inevitable fury. As Bosie broke into his most vicious tantrum yet, Wilde fled his wrath, taking the opportunity to leave the country to visit Dinard in Jersey.

He returned to the Albemarle Hotel,[8] only to find Bosie pursuing him in person and by abusive letter. Wilde claimed Bosie was furious at not being taken to Jersey, making unpleasant scenes at the Albemarle before Wilde left. He then sent equally abusive telegrams to Wilde via a country house where Wilde was staying. Bosie wrote that he was under "no intellectual obligation of any kind" to Wilde, and Wilde saw this as the excuse to end the affair. He recalled in *De Profundis* that: "I told you, I remember, that I thought it was your duty to be with your own people for a little, as you had passed the whole season away from them. But in reality I could not under any circumstances have let you be with me.

We had been together for nearly twelve weeks. I required rest and freedom from your terrible companionship. I saw in your letter . . . a very good opportunity for ending the fatal friendship that had sprung up between us, and ending it without bitterness."[9]

Wilde wrote to Bosie on 9 September with deliberate casualness that he hoped Bosie would get the proofs of *Salomé* soon but in fact he was trying Aubrey Beardsley as a translator. Poor Beardsley was even worse at French than Bosie, though essential for the incomparable brilliance of his illustrations. Furious four-way quarrels over responsibility for producing the English version of the play ensued, involving Oscar, John Lane, Bosie Douglas and Aubrey Beardsley, before Wilde adopted the compromise of a fulsome dedication to Bosie while keeping his name off the title page. Beardsley contributed only illustrations. By now there had been another reconciliation, apparently at the intercession of Robert Ross and the relationship resumed, though living together was not attempted.[10]

Wilde was now in no doubt about the grave threat that Bosie's ungovernable temper posed to him, and he had other worries about him. By November he was sufficiently concerned to contact Sybil Queensberry. On 8 November, he wrote a carefully worded appeal for help, suggesting that:

> Bosie seems to me to be in a very bad state of health. He is sleepless, nervous and rather hysterical. He seems to me quite altered. He is doing nothing in town. He translated my French play last August. Since then he has done nothing intellectual. . . he does absolutely nothing, and is quite astray in life, and may, unless you or Drumlanrig do something, come to grief of some kind. His life seems to me aimless, unhappy and absurd. All this is a great grief and disappointment to me, but he is very young, and terribly young in temperament. Why not try and make arrangements of some kind for him to go abroad for four or five months, to the Cromers in Egypt if this could be managed, where he would have new surroundings, proper friends, and a different atmosphere? I think that if he stays in London he will not come to any good, and may spoil his young life irretrievably, quite irretrievably. Of course it will cost money no doubt, but here is the life of one of your sons – a life that should be brilliant and distinguished and charming – going quite astray, being quite ruined. I like to think myself his greatest friend – he, at any rate, makes me think so – so I write to you quite

> frankly to ask you to send him abroad to better surroundings. It would save him, I am sure. At present his life seems to be tragic and pathetic in its foolish aimlessness.
>
> You will not, I know, let him know *anything about my letter.* I can rely on you, I feel sure. . .".[11] [*Original emphasis*]

This letter is less than frank. Bosie was certainly idle and highly strung, a combination that could produce the symptoms that Wilde revealed. However, there were other reasons why Bosie was sleepless, nervous and hysterical, and why a period in Egypt would be desirable. Bosie himself probably suggested the move as a solution to a serious crisis, for Wilde noted in *De Profundis* that the letter was written "with your knowledge and concurrence".[12] The suggestion of a visit to the Cromers could only have come from Bosie, for he was well aware that Ethel Errington, who had married Sir Evelyn Baring, was one of his mother's most intimate friends. Baring was Consul General and Diplomatic Agent in Egypt, in effect the Governor of the country. He had just been given a barony to become Lord Cromer and Cairo could provide not merely a escape, but potentially an entrance into the Diplomatic Corps. Such a career would solve the problem of Bosie's future, keep his father from interfering, and most desirable of all, get Bosie out of England on a semi-permanent basis. Lady Queensberry immediately saw the potential of a visit to the Cromers and this was rapidly arranged. However she could hardly have begun to understand the deeper reasons why Oscar Wilde wanted desperately to get Bosie out of the country.

Getting Bosie as far away from London was imperative, for he was up to his neck in a potentially disastrous scandal involving the inner circle of Wilde intimates. Beerbohm wrote to Reggie Turner at this time a muddled account of an affair centring on Robbie Ross, who:

> has returned to this country for a few days and of him there have been great and intimate scandals and almost, if not quite, warrants: slowly he is recovering but has to remain at Davos during his convalescence for fear of a social relapse. I may tell you that a schoolboy with wonderful eyes, Bosie, Bobbie, a furious father, George Lewis, a headmaster (who is now blackmailing Bobbie), St John Wontner (a police solicitor), Calais, Dover, Oscar Browning, Oscar, Dover, Calais and returned cigarette cases were some of the ingredients of this dreadful episode. . . .[13]

This muddle was clarified in 1919 by a letter from Oscar Browning to Frank Harris.[14] Browning's brother-in-law, the Revd Biscale Hale Wortham, kept a boys' school in Bruges. In 1893, Ross visited the Worthams and met a 16-year-old boy, Philip Danney, son of an army colonel. Ross invited the boy to stay with him in London during the Summer holiday. He mentioned this in a letter to Bosie, who rushed up from Goring and returned with Danney in tow. "On Saturday", according to Browning, "the boy slept with Douglas, on Sunday he slept with Oscar. On Monday he returned to London and slept with a woman at Douglas's expense". On Tuesday he returned to Bruges three days late, was quizzed by his headmaster, and the story came out.

The colonel was told. Police solicitors were consulted, and Ross and Douglas had to visit Bruges on 15 October to consult with Wortham. Fortunately, Colonel Danney was told that, while the offenders might get two years, his son would be ruined and, unlike Queensberry, decided to drop the matter. Ross stayed out of the country until early 1894 at Davos, while it became essential that Bosie leave the country at the earliest opportunity. This is the background to Wilde's letter of 8 November, though it is clear that Oscar had his own reasons for wanting Bosie safely abroad. In *De Profundis*, Wilde recalled bitterly the three months that Autumn when he met Bosie every day, living a life of conspicuous consumption, except for "the four days when you went abroad. I then, of course, had to go over to Calais to fetch you back. For one of my nature and temperament it was a position at once grotesque and tragic".[15] The passage from which this is taken is a sustained complaint by Wilde that Bosie prevented him from working in the Autumn of 1893 by selfishly demanding to be entertained, making the use of the words "grotesque and tragic" seem absurd. In the light of the Browning revelations, which both men would have understood to be the true meaning of the complaint, the words have profound significance. Yet Oscar could not seriously complain that Bosie was leading him towards disaster, for he knew what he was doing and was happy with a lifestyle lived at high pressure.

Others were less happy. Beardsley was so troubled by the *Salomé* quarrels that his tuberculosis intensified and he began spitting blood. For Beardsley, the endless conflicts were deeply distressing. He was seriously ill and all around him knew his health to be dangerously fragile. He was upset that neither Oscar nor Bosie Douglas took any account of his illness. His condition was terminal and he was to die, aged only 25, in March 1898. Quarrels such as those over *Salomé* threatened him with profoundly serious consequences and, in a letter to Ross, he berated Oscar and Bosie as "really very dreadful people". The controversies over *Salomé* reverberated, undermining Oscar Wilde's reputation as an entertaining jester. Those who knew about the Danney affair knew how dangerous the game was that Oscar and Bosie were playing. Will Rothenstein perceptively noted that Bosie "had been going in for the wildest folly in London, and, I imagine, will shortly have to take a tour round the world, or something of the kind".[16] Yet if Bosie was behaving with the wildest folly, Oscar was matching him almost stride for stride.

Wilde had taken chambers at 10–11 St James' Place in September 1893, rooms which he kept until the following March, to work undisturbed on a new play for John Hare. If he had used this as an excuse to be away from his family, it was less than the whole truth; for, enjoying life in the homosexual community was a major priority. This was becoming even more fraught than usual, for the authorities were taking a belated interest in this aspect of Wilde's circle. Charles Parker, one of the circle of young men who interested Wilde and was sharing lodgings with Alfred Taylor, was being watched by police. A plainclothes officer went to his lodgings in Little College Street and examined his rooms. Taylor promptly moved out, finding rooms at 3 Chapel Street, while Parker lodged at 50 Park Walk nearby. This situation may have induced Wilde to abandon the Albemarle Hotel as a place of assignation in favour of St James' Place. The proprietor, a Swiss called Aloys Vogel, later deposed that so many young men called on Wilde that his suspicions were aroused. Far from the chambers being a haven of peace and playwriting, Charles Parker, Sidney Mavor, Ernest Scarfe (friend of Taylor), Fred Atkins and a friend called Harry Barford, and Edward Shelley all visited Wilde, sometimes staying the night.[17]

Above all there was Bosie, who, after the first week, visited daily. Bosie had Wilde in thrall and the Autumn passed with increasing tension. By November 1893 the future with Bosie seemed so unattractive that Wilde desperately wished to break the relationship. Bosie sensed this, and it led to the fourth and most frightening of a year of terrible rows. The following day Wilde fled to France, having given his family "some absurd reason" for his sudden departure, and leaving a false address with his servant, fearing that Bosie would follow by the next train. Wilde sat in the carriage, speeding through France, "thinking what an impossible, terrible, utterly wrong state my life had got into, when I, a man of worldwide reputation, was actually forced to run away from England, in order to try to get rid of a friendship that was entirely destructive of everything fine in me either from the intellectual or the ethical point of view". Bosie soon discovered where Wilde was and sent telegrams full of remorse and entreaty, which Wilde ignored. Failing with these, he played his trump card, refusing to go to Egypt unless Wilde saw him.

Under this blackmail, Oscar Wilde consented to meet Bosie. In a meeting marked by great emotion, Wilde forgave the past – but carefully made no promises for the future. Returning to London the next day, he sat down in a turmoil, wondering "whether or not you really were what you seemed to be, so full of terrible defects, so utterly ruinous both to yourself and to others, so fatal a one to know even or to be with". After a week of thinking, Wilde was still unsure whether he was not mistaken in this estimate of Bosie's character, when he received a letter from Lady Queensberry confirming all that he felt himself. She wrote of Bosie's temper, which made her afraid to speak about her concerns, Bosie's irresponsibility in money matters, and the degeneration and change she felt had taken place. This was the letter in which Sybil – in Wilde's words – "admitted . . . with terror" that Bosie was "the one of my children who has inherited the fatal Douglas temperament". She wrote frankly that the friendship of Bosie and Oscar had intensified Bosie's faults, and she begged Oscar not to meet Bosie abroad.

Oscar was happy to concede. He assured Lady Queensberry that he had no intention of meeting Bosie abroad, and "begged her to try to keep you there, either as an honorary attaché, if that were possible, or to learn modern languages, if it were not; or for any reason she chose, at least during two or three years, and for your sake as well as for mine".[18] This appeared to be the end of the affair. In December 1893, Bosie Douglas left London for Cairo. That Christmas, Oscar celebrated with his family in the highest of spirits. But, while Oscar saw the dawning New Year of 1894 as a time to get his life back on an even keel, under the Middle Eastern sun, Lord Alfred Douglas was making it clear that his priority was to resume the affair at the earliest opportunity. The stage was set for an unequal struggle in which Bosie Douglas would pit his willpower against that of Oscar Wilde, and Wilde would find that "feasting with panthers" was only the least of the dangers he now faced.

FIVE

Rogue Elements

When Bosie Douglas arrived in Cairo in December 1893, he moved from his world of cosseted privilege on to an even higher plane. His life as the third son of a Marquis had accustomed him to luxury and indulgence. To be the guest of the Cromers, however, was to partake in the wealth and grandeur of the most powerful imperial ruling class in the world. Sir Evelyn Baring was considered the most brilliant and successful administrator in the British colonial machine. He was infinitely more than a mere civil servant – while nominally responsible to the Egyptian Khedive, the *Oxford History of England* notes that during his twenty-four years as British Consul-General of the Anglo-Egyptian Sudan, 1883–1907, he was virtual ruler of the country.[1] Baring was an exemplary empire builder. A cousin of Lord Northbrook, he had been Northbrook's secretary in India from 1872 to 1876 when Northbrook was Viceroy. He learnt imperial administration from Northbrook and was posted to Egypt to ensure British control of the Khedive's finances from 1878 to 1880, before returning to the Indian government as financial member of the Council in the era when Ripon was viceroy.

After the British conquest of Egypt in 1882, Gladstone appointed Baring as Consul-General, a post he occupied for almost a quarter of a century. He ran the colonial administration with skill, but had serious problems with the nominally independent government of the Khedive. He faced open rebellion in the Sudan to the south, where Dervish insurgents had claimed the life of General Gordon in 1885. The year 1893 had been particularly difficult. He had struggled to control the finances of the Egyptian government, which was heavily in debt to European bondholders. He quarrelled with Sir Herbert Kitchener, Sirdar of the Anglo-Egyptian army, who had developed detailed plans for the re-conquest of the Sudan, which Baring opposed as adding to his problems. Elevation to the peerage – he was granted the title Baron Cromer in 1892 – added prestige but did not ease his burden.

Entangled with Egyptian finance and Kitchener's preparations for the Sudan, he could not have particularly welcomed the task of providing a bolthole for Bosie Douglas. When his wife received the urgent entreaties of her oldest friend, however, the Cromers knew their duty. Bosie was immediately given *carte blanche* to stay in the imperial residence. It was clearly understood by all parties, with the possible exception of Bosie himself, that his future lay in becoming honorary attaché in some far-flung imperial outpost. Shortly after he arrived, he was observed by the young writer Robert Smythe Hichens, who was in a crowd at the Cairo races when he heard someone cry, "Here comes Cromer!" He saw an open carriage drawn by a pair of fine horses drive slowly by. In it were two people. One was the Great Man, Cromer, wearing a white top-hat. By his side sat a young man, almost a boy, fair, aristocratic, poetic-looking. Hichens did not know who he was and no-one told him. Later, he learned that he was the Marquis of Queensberry's third son. He was soon to meet Bosie Douglas face to face.[2]

For a young man who had only a few weeks previously been facing disgrace and imprisonment, Bosie's visit to the Cromers was a stunning transformation. Yet it was a transformation which Bosie did not reflect on. If he understood how narrowly he had escaped disaster, he did not show any visible sign of it. Instead, he appears to have believed that it was entirely appropriate that, when trouble loomed, he should be whisked away a thousand miles, at the expense of others, to be entertained by the most powerful man in Egypt and vested with the privileges of imperial power. The experience of 1893 reinforced Bosie's view that he was invulnerable. He had wasted his years at Oxford, failed to translate Wilde's *Salomé*, had no prospects and little money, and had by sheer irresponsibility arrived at the door of the police court. Yet when Nemesis beckoned, a magic carpet had arrived to transport him to a palace of Oriental opulence. For a young man of twenty-three, immature for his age, the lesson appeared to be that he enjoyed absolute protection by the title and connections he had inherited.

Bosie remained obsessed by his life in London and the relationship that dominated his life there, and his letters to his mother from Cairo indicate this. He wrote two long letters to Lady Queensberry from Cairo arguing with his mother over Oscar Wilde. The first was written shortly after his arrival in Egypt, unburdening himself of deeply felt feelings about Wilde. Lady Queensberry had talked with Bosie at length on the night before his departure, urging him to break with Wilde once and for all. It is likely that she had read Lionel Johnson's poem, "To The Destroyer of A Soul", for according to Bosie she had spoken of Wilde as having "ruined my soul". Sybil had not minced her words. She had told Bosie that she would almost like to murder Wilde, and begged her son to break with him. Bosie refused, his letter revealing adolescent petulance and a complete failure to apprehend the situation in which his family perceived him to be:

> Let me ask you, what do you propose to give me in exchange for this man, where am I to go for my quickening? Who is going to "feed my soul with honey of sweet-bitter thoughts"? Who is going to make me happy when I am sad depressed and ill at ease [*sic*]? Who is going to transport me out of this tedious world into a fairyland of fancy, conceit, paradox and beauty by the power of golden speech? . . .
>
> What do you propose to give me instead? That is what I ask. I am spoilt for society, I am a Bohemian and must remain one. Why can't you leave me alone, why can't you help me to do what I must do? Be nice to my friend, be just and kind, your present attitude towards him is so banal, so illogical, so shallow.
>
> There is one thing more that I must say something about, that is that you cannot do anything against the power of my affection for Oscar Wilde and his for me. I am passionately fond of him, and he of me. "There never was a better bargain driver". There is nothing I would not do for him, and if he dies before I do I shall not care to live longer. The thought of such a thing makes everything black before my eyes. Surely there is nothing but what is fine and beautiful in such a love as that of two people for one another, the love of the disciple and the philosopher. . .
>
> There is no good in saying any more except that while I perhaps have no right to say that Oscar Wilde is a good man, neither you nor anyone else has the right to say he is a bad man. A bad man I might admire intellectually, but I could never love, and what is more he could never love anyone faithfully, loyally, devotedly, unselfishly and purely as Oscar loves me. I cannot say more now, so goodbye. Please try and like my friend who is so dear to me
>
> With heaps of love, Ever your loving son,
>
> Bosie[3]

Of course, this frank admission of the relationship could hardly placate his mother. Bosie had foolishly mentioned the morality of goodness in his letter, approving Wilde's philosophy in *Dorian Gray*, that "there is no such thing as a moral or immoral book, a book is well written or badly written, that is all". Sybil took up the theme, comparing Wilde to Lord Henry Wootton in her reply. An exasperated Bosie wrote back, arguing that there was no comparison:

> You say "If Mr W. has acted, as I am convinced he has, the part of a Lord H. to you I could never feel differently towards him than I do, as the murderer of your soul". . . . If you come to look into your own analogy you will find that it breaks down on very important and very essential points. . . . Lord H.'s intention was to make Dorian Gray a sort of experiment in a philosophy which was to consist in a triumph of the body over the soul; to bring this about he encouraged him to sink his intellect to the position of a pander to his vices, he tells him to *do everything*; he is not to write a book, he is to do nothing but live, live, live for pleasure, while Lord H. looks on with a morbid and curious interest in the psychological study thus presented. . . . Now, if you are so extraordinarily wrong-headed, so deliberately blind, and so monstrously unjust, as to seriously draw an analogy between the attitude of O.W. to me, and Lord H. to Dorian Gray? I feel that anything I can say is utterly useless.
>
> Oscar has no desire to ruin my soul in order that he may have the pleasure of getting a morbid satisfaction from the contemplation of its ruin, he is merely a very brilliant and irresponsible and very impulsive creature who enjoys life thoroughly, and who wishes to be as happy as he can under the circumstances in which he finds himself placed. . . .
>
> As for what you say about what you call "eccentricities and peculiar views of morality", I am so far from deceiving myself by thinking that they are a special characteristic of my own, that I know them to be shared and to have been shared by nearly all the great minds for whom I have special respect both in ancient and modern times, and I should also like to tell you once and for all that I did *not* imbibe those ideas from Oscar Wilde and that he did *not* put them into my head and encourage them. I had formed them in my own mind and I was quite certain of their truth *two years* before I had ever seen him or even heard of him. When I first met him, it was the finding someone with a really great mind and genius who agreed with me, that made me like him, and since then, although you will probably not believe it, it is nevertheless a fact that I have had more influence on him than he has had on me. . . .

> Now do try and get out of your head this absurd idea about the ruin of my soul and all that. . . . I am so sick and tired of this sort of perpetual war that seems to go on whether I like it or not. Do let us for a change be a little more commonplace and a little less emotional. I am aware that in that respect I am as much to blame as anyone, I have in my blood the love of a scene and a tragedy, but I am convinced it is a mistake, and certainly in our family of all families somebody ought to make a determined stand against it. There is such a tendency to lift everything up on to the stilts of tragedy, we are such a theatrical family. Let us cease from this, and become a little bourgeois.[4] [*Original emphasis*]

While Bosie's style was jejune, his assessment of Wilde and his relationship with him was incisive. The view that he was not influenced in his views on morality by Wilde is clearly correct: he was exploring decadence well before he met Wilde. He was justified in saying that he had more influence on Wilde than Wilde had on him, though he could never have explained to his mother into what dark corners of Victorian society that influence had taken them both. Bosie's character sketch of Wilde was acute, for Wilde was indeed brilliant, irresponsible and very impulsive. At twenty-three, Bosie Douglas had a better understanding of Wilde perhaps than Wilde did of himself. His final comments were eerily prescient. His family did have in its blood the love of a scene and a tragedy. That he could not avoid this strain in his character would bring about his personal Calvary.

Bosie tried to close on a lighter note, mentioning that he had received letters from Francis (Drumlanrig) begging him to think of old times, Percy claiming his willingness to lay down his life for Bosie, and his father talking about his miserable and lonely life. Bosie in the end sent his mother a very mixed message, claiming that "there are times when my heart aches and my eyes fill with tears at the sense of the pitiableness of my position and the darkness of my future, and it is all really the result of a morbid imagination. I am perfectly happy really, and nobody enjoys life more thoroughly than I do".[5] The last note was false: while he was certainly enjoying his entertainment by the Cromers – and Egypt overall was a golden interlude – he could not fully enjoy it for, all the while, his obsession with Oscar Wilde haunted his waking hours.

* * *

For the next three months, Bosie could do nothing but enjoy Egypt. He moved out of the Cromer residence and took himself up the Nile. Perhaps not accidentally, Reggie Turner had turned up in Cairo, and entertained Bosie on a gilded barge owned by his half-brother, Frank Lawson. Turner was excellent company, and when he and Bosie were joined by E.F. Benson – "Freddie" – three sparkling wits came together for mutual entertainment. Benson was a son of the Archbishop of Canterbury and was nominally engaged in archaeology in Greece. However, as a novelist he had just scored a notable success with a novella based on the life of Margot Tennant, a young woman almost as successful at self-publicity as Wilde, who was to marry Asquith and eventually become Countess of Oxford and Asquith. The fame of *Dodo, a Detail of the Day*, had spread throughout the English community in Egypt. It excited the envy of Robert Hichens, in Egypt to recuperate after a bout of illness for, as a struggling journalist only a little older than Benson, he wanted to emulate Benson's success.

Hichens found his subject while in Egypt. He had travelled up the Nile to Luxor, arriving in the same hotel and at the same table as Reggie Turner, Freddie Benson and his sister, and Bosie Douglas. He fell into an intimacy with the other three men, being particularly drawn to Douglas when he learned of his friendship with Wilde, all of whose first nights Hichens had attended.

The holiday friendship with Douglas might have provided Hichens with nothing of substance, but Bosie promised to introduce him to Oscar Wilde when both were back in London. As this happened within months of the meeting in Egypt, Hichens secured the material, enabling him to fullfill his ambition to emulate Benson's success with *Dodo.* Hichen's novella *The Green Carnation* appeared in the Autumn of 1894. The stars of the book were Bosie Douglas and Oscar Wilde, loosely disguised as Lord Reginald Hastings and Mr Amarinth. The book was an immediate success and, while painting a sympathetic portrait of the relationship, made a large proportion of the book reading public aware of the relationship of Bosie Douglas and Oscar Wilde. Hichens sketched the circle around Wilde with barbed accuracy. When Mrs Windsor debated with her cousin Lady Locke about the young men who wore the Green Carnation, it was in terms that echoed Raffalovich: (Mrs Windsor) "Do you object to the Green Carnation?" (Lady Locke) "That depends. Is it a badge?" "How do you mean?" "I only saw about a dozen in the Opera House tonight, and all the men who wore them looked the same. They had the same walk, or rather waggle, the same coyly conscious expression, the same wavy motion of the head. When they spoke to each other, they called each other by Christian names. Is it a badge of some club or society, and is Mr Amarinth their high priest?"[6]

The two women discuss Bosie Douglas, and the conversation turns on the femininity of the circle around Mr Amarinth: (Lady Locke) "And has Lord Reginald Hastings got a woman's mind?" (Mrs Windsor) "My dear, he has a very beautiful mind. . . . He dares do anything. He is not afraid of Society, or of what the clergy and such unfashionable and limited people say. For instance, if he wished to commit what the copy-books call a sin, he would commit it, even if Society stood aghast at him. That is what I call having real moral courage".[7]

This sketch was painfully accurate, and when the book appeared late in 1894 public awareness of Wilde and Bosie was powerfully increased. Hichens suddenly realised the dangers of publicising Decadence in an anti-decadent society and withdrew the book from sale. It was too late. Queensberry had read the book and was consumed with fury.

None of this would have mattered if Sybil had succeeded in getting Bosie safely hidden in a foreign outpost, but all Lady Queensberry's plans to secure a diplomatic position for her errant son turned to dust. Sybil had enlisted the aid of her father and the Cromers to pull strings to secure for Bosie an honorary attachéship, the accepted route into the diplomatic service for youths with no training but a willingness to learn. Lord Currie, the ambassador at Constantinople, was induced to take Bosie on. Bosie was less than eager to secure the position. Instead of going straight to Constantinople he proceeded instead to Athens, where he spent a week visiting the sights and sitting in the Acropolis with Freddie Benson. He then went to Paris, admitting in his *Autobiography* that: "My longing to meet Oscar Wilde again was what made me go back to Paris".[8] It was not a diplomatic move.

Bosie claims that he told Cromer of his plans, and was unaware that Currie wanted him in Constantinople immediately. Whether this is true, or whether he simply thought that disobeying instructions was a matter of no consequence, it is impossible to tell. It is clear that he *thought* he would be going to Constantinople. On 30 March, he wrote to Kains Jackson, the writer and editor of the *Artist*, who had proposed to nominate him for the Authors Club. Bosie declined on the grounds that he would be going to Constantinople, so it was not worth pursuing the nomination.[9] Bosie probably did not intend to snub Currie, believing that a permanent diplomatic career was in prospect. This was an illusion, for the ambassador was so angry at what he believed to be a deliberate insult that he refused to have anything more to do with Douglas. Bosie for the rest of his life blamed, not himself for this turn of events, but Lord Currie's "middle-class fussiness". Looking back on the affair thirty-five years later he commented:

> I regard the whole incident as one of those numerous cases in which my most simple and harmless acts have been misconstrued and misrepresented. . . . If Lord Currie – who, to quote Wilde, did not "rise from the ranks of the aristocracy but was born into the purple of commerce" – had been a little more *grand seigneur* than he was he would not have made such a ridiculous fuss, and it would not have occurred to him (he was a newly created peer) that any assault on his dignity had been so much as dreamt of. However, there was the end of my diplomatic career, and I was in disgrace with my grandfather, Alfred Montgomery, and once more exposed to the mad-dog threats of my father.[10]

Bosie had annoyed Montgomery and infuriated his father, but he was not an innocent abroad. He wrote in his *Autobiography* that he was "delighted to escape the necessity of going to Constantinople, and to be able to get back to London".[11] He was unaware that this posed any problems for Wilde, dismissing as "deliberately untrue" Wilde's account of his reluctance to meet him again. Bosie's recollection was that as soon as he suggested meeting Wilde in Paris, Oscar telegraphed his delight at the prospect, and Bosie duly made his way to Paris via the Acropolis.

Oscar Wilde's view of the meeting is darker, more detailed, and more plausible. At Christmas 1893 he was in wonderfully high spirits, having resolved the issue of his relationship with Bosie to his own satisfaction. He claimed that, when Bosie wrote to him every post from Egypt, he tore up the letters. At the end of three months he was astounded to find that Lady Queensberry was urging him to write to Bosie, and sending him Freddie Benson's address in Athens. Wilde claimed he told Sybil he would have nothing to do with Bosie, who then found a chink in his armour by telegraphing Constance. Under pressure from his wife, Wilde felt he had to make some communication with Bosie. He wrote to Athens, telling Bosie, "time heals every wound but for many months to come I will neither write to you nor see you".[12] The message had the opposite effect to what Wilde intended: it fired Bosie's infatuation. Ignoring Wilde's rebuff he immediately began the journey to Paris, sending Wilde telegrams on route begging him to join him in the capital. Wilde declined. Bosie arrived in Paris late on a Saturday night to find a brief letter at the hotel telling Bosie that Wilde would not meet him. Wilde alleges that the situation that weekend became critical:

> Next morning I received at Tite Street a telegram of some ten or eleven pages in length from you. You stated in it that no matter what you had done to me you could not believe that I would absolutely decline to see you; you reminded me that for the sake of seeing me for even one hour you had travelled six days and six nights across Europe without stopping once on the way; you made what I admit was a most pathetic appeal, and ended with what seemed to me a threat of suicide, and not one thinly veiled. You had yourself often told me how many of your race there had been who had stained their hands with their own blood: your uncle certainly, your grandfather possibly; many others in the mad, bad line from which you come. Pity, my old affection for you, regard for your mother to whom your death under such circumstances would have been a blow almost too great for her to bear, the horror of the idea that so young a life, and one that amongst all its faults had still the promise of beauty in it, should come to so revolting an end, mere humanity itself – all these, if excuses be necessary, must serve as my excuse for consenting to accord you one last interview. . . .[13]

But it could not be "one last interview". Once Wilde had succumbed to Bosie's entreaties, he had crossed the Rubicon. Wilde recalled bitterly that, when they met, Bosie was overcome, "the tears . . . falling over your cheeks like rain" as they went to dinner at Voisin's and supper at Paillard's. Bosie displayed unfeigned joy, holding Wilde's hand whenever he could, displaying contrition, "so simple and sincere, *at the moment*", and behaving like a penitent child. Bosie had almost lost the thing he valued most, and his thankfulness at having regained it gushed like a torrent. Oscar Wilde was clever enough to know the dangers this posed. Yet though Wilde could recognise danger, he was too weak to avoid it. Bosie was triumphant. He had defeated his mother, his grandfather and Oscar himself by wrecking their plans to pack him off to a diplomatic career. Meeting Wilde in Paris, the relationship resumed its familiar pattern, but the balance of power had shifted. In the battle of wills, Bosie Douglas now had the upper hand. Oscar Wilde had gone reluctantly to meet him in Paris, yet resumed the relationship on Bosie's terms. Bosie may have been in floods of tears, but he had won.

Two days after returning to London, on 1 April 1894, the two men accidentally met Bosie's father and he drank wine with them, surly and suspicious. Queensberry's hostility to the relationship was about to enter a new and virulent phase which would meet with an equal and opposite reaction from his son. Oscar Wilde was caught in the middle, as the "theatrical Douglas family" were about to lift the affair on to the wobbling stilts of tragedy.

* * *

While Bosie was in Egypt, his father had written to him complaining that he was living a miserable and lonely life. The Marquis's self pity was justified, for at 49 he was a middle-aged man with few friends, a precarious social position, and little to occupy himself. His behaviour had cut himself off from the relationships which could sustain a man of his background. His quarrels with the Scottish peerage prevented him living out the last decades of his life as a pillar of his estate and community. His divorce alienated him from his family and respectable society in London. While the sporting fraternity had lower standards, his achievements were ancient history and in neither the racing nor boxing worlds had he reached sufficient heights to earn respect.

Only in the raffish sporting club known as the Pelican was Queensberry at home, tolerated rather than respected. The club in Gerrard Street was a meeting place for sporting aristocrats like the Dukes of Manchester and Hamilton, Lord Marcus Beresford, Lord Lonsdale – who had created boxing's Lonsdale belt – and the Marquis of Queensberry. The rough and ready democracy of the sporting world allowed less exalted persons to join: journalists, actors, business men and speculators prominent among them, and many dubious characters in the seedy world of the turf and the ring provided Queensberry with a degree of companionship. Queensberry was a star of the rowdy smoking room concerts. He would spend hours practising the latest music hall songs, hammering out the tune one-fingered on the piano. On one notable occasion he dressed up to look like music hall star Albert Chevalier while performing a spirited version of "Knocked 'em in the Old Kent Road". The concert ended after the police arrived because several champagne bottles had been thrown through the windows.

It was a poor substitute for sporting action. By mid-1893 Queensberry was facing physical decline with all the rancour of the Douglases at their worst. He could not resist attempting to be cock of the walk at a time when his legendary fighting prowess was becoming history. Frank Harris also frequented the club, and while Bosie was in Egypt in the winter of 1893/4 he met Queensberry for the first time, forming a deeply unfavourable impression. John Sholto Douglas:

> was perhaps five feet nine or ten in height, with a plain, heavy, rather sullen face and quick, hot eyes. He was a mass of self-conceit, all bristling with suspicion, and in regard to money prudent to meanness. He cared nothing for books, but liked outdoor sports and under a rather abrupt but not discourteous manner hid an irritable, violent temper. He was combatative and courageous as very nervous people sometimes are, when they happen to be strong willed – the sort of man who, just because he was afraid of a bull and had pictured the dreadful wound it could give, would therefore seize it by the horns.
>
> The insane temper of the man got him into rows at the Pelican more than once. I remember one evening he insulted a man who I liked immensely. Haseltine was a stockbroker, I think, a big, fair, handsome fellow who took Queensberry's wrath aside with a fair word, but Queensberry went on working himself into a passion, and at last made a rush at him. Haseltine watched him coming and hit out in the nick of time; he caught Queensberry full in the face and literally knocked him heels over head. Queenberry got up in a sad mess. He had a swollen nose and black eye and his shirt was all stained with blood spread about by hasty wiping. Any other man would have continued the fight or else have left the club on the spot: Queensberry took a seat at a table and sat there for hours silent. I could only explain it to myself by saying that his impulse to fly at once from the scene of his disgrace was very acute, and therefore he resisted it, made up his mind not to budge, and so he sat there the butt of the derisive glances and whispered talk of everyone who came into the club in the next two or three hours. He was just the sort of person a wise man would avoid and a clever one would use – a dangerous, sharp, ill-handled tool.[14]

Queensberry's extraordinary behaviour conformed to his manic aggressiveness throughout his life. However his behaviour during 1893 and 1894 was fuelled by a greater mass of resentments than normal, for his life was scarred by a series of disasters and humiliations far more serious than a beating in the Pelican club. His relationships with his family were spiralling to new depths, that with his eldest son and heir experiencing particularly serious difficulties.

When his first son Francis was born in 1867, the child automatically took the courtesy title of Viscount Drumlanrig. The rest of the family deferred to him throughout his childhood and adolescence as the next head of the family, but in a purely formal manner. Francis Douglas commanded the affections of his family, but little more. His mother looked on him as the least troublesome of her children, claiming that from the day of his birth he "never caused her to shed a single tear"[15] Wilde saw his character as one of "sweetness and goodness", yet though Francis was amiable, he was also limited socially and lacking virtually any personal depth at all. A relative described him as being "a highly nervous boy with considerable charm but no great intellect".[16] Despite an education at Harrow and Sandhurst he failed as a lieutenant in the Coldstream Guards. Like his brothers, he had little capacity for a career. Yet unlike them, he entered one which puzzled as much as it delighted those who knew him. He became the personal private secretary of Lord Rosebery.

Rosebery was Foreign Secretary in Gladstone's last ministry when he made the appointment – one of the most powerful, but enigmatic, figures in late nineteenth-century politics. Although well placed at the top of the Liberal Party, there were many Liberals who wondered why Rosebery stayed in their ranks. Archibald Philip Primrose, fifth Earl of Rosebery, was a landed aristocrat still supporting the Liberals at a time when the Lords had shifted overwhelmingly to the Conservatives. His personal values did not seem particularly Liberal. At Eton, he had confided to a friend that he had three ambitions – to marry an heiress, become Prime Minister, and own a Derby winner. He succeeded in all three. He was so unlike the mainstream of the largely nonconformist Party that many wondered privately whether he had joined them simply to become Gladstone's successor at the top? Leading politicians pondered his politics. The Liberal John Morley described him as "a dark horse in a loose box". Gladstone thought him "an incalculable man – one of the most incalculable I have ever known".[17] They were referring to Rosebery's unfathomable politics, well to the right of the Liberal Party mainstream.

Yet his character was just as curious in his private life as in public affairs. A contemporary biographer, E.T. Raymond, noted at the time "the man was a puzzle, and puzzles are always interesting".[18] But this was not so much a matter of a man playing a deep political game, as a man who was moody, imperious and too thin skinned to be predictable. A not unsympathetic biographer commented that "He had a tendency to be a law unto himself, resentful of outside interference, and easily angered by opposition or criticism. His temperament was notoriously uneven; he could be the most enchanting of companions, or he could be moody, severe and autocratic. When in this latter mood, so strong was his personality that he could shrivel conversation with a glance, and chance acquaintances meeting him in this frame of mind were often frightened of him".[19]

Why this imperious, gifted but unpredictable man abandoned politics in 1895 when at the height of his powers and at the pinnacle of his party has never been satisfactorily explained. His involvement with Drumlanrig may help explain the mystery. Lord Rosebery moved in the charmed circle inhabited by Alfred Montgomery, one of the wire-pullers of the Liberal Party. This was one of Queensberry's list of grievances against his father in law, for John Sholto Douglas affected to be a Conservative in politics, but more pertinently resented Montgomery's relationship with his eldest son. Drumlanrig was Montgomery's favourite grandson, Bosie later recalling that his grandfather was absolutely devoted to his oldest brother.[20] Montgomery invited his grandson to stay in his house in Hertford Street when his army career came to an end, and through this connection Drumlanrig met Rosebery. Rosebery decided he was the ideal man to become his private secretary.

It was a puzzling choice. Drumlanrig may have supported the Liberals, but not through real political convictions. Those who met him were usually impressed by his good manners, diffidence and amiability. But when they discussed politics with him they quickly found a mind hopeless lost in a maze of confusion and ignorance. Lady Paget met him at a country house party and was most impressed with him until raising the burning issue of the day, the support of the Gladstonian Liberal Party for Home Rule in Ireland. "He imparted to me", she later wrote incredulously, "that though he thought Home Rule might turn Ireland into Eden, he knew that the objections to it were so great that it could not become law, and that was the reason his party voted for it!"[21]

Political ignorance was clearly a problem for the private secretary of a major politician, but Drumlanrig was equally deficient in most of the other qualities of an aide-de-camp. In the world of political nepotism inhabited by Alfred Montgomery, none of this mattered. He had himself become the protégé of the Marquis of Wellesley (elder brother of the Duke of Wellington), who had made him his private secretary at the age of sixteen. Tongues wagged over a boy so young having so important a post when Wellesley was just about to become Viceroy of Ireland. Some imagined Montgomery was Wellesley's illegitimate son. Others whispered more quietly of a homosexual relationship. The rumours almost certainly reached the ears of the Marquis of Queensberry, increasing the suspicious hostility of Queensberry for his father in law. However, until Montgomery secured the post of private secretary to Rosebery for Drumlanrig, Queensberry was not much exercised by rumour. Even when Drumlanrig took up the post in a manner remarkably reminiscent of Montgomery's virtual adoption by Wellesley, Queensberry did not react. In May 1893, however, Rosebery decided to reward his new secretary with the post of Lord in Waiting to Queen Victoria and the temperature began to rise.

The problem was that the post required Drumlanrig to obtain an English peerage. Drumlanrig was reluctant, knowing how sensitive his father was to the lack of an English title. He had no desire to infuriate his father by entering the House of Lords, from which Queensberry had been so publicly excluded in 1880. According to Bosie, it took the combined efforts of Rosebery and Gladstone to persuade Drumlanrig, and only with the argument that he should firstly approach his father to see whether he had any objections. Drumlanrig did so with considerable misgivings. But Queensberry was delighted with the prospect of an English peerage in the family, and urged his son to accept. Drumlanrig was astonished, and insisted that his father put his agreement in writing, via a letter to Gladstone. Queensberry was happy to do so, and Bosie recalled that "he wrote to Gladstone thanking him and expressing great satisfaction at the honour done by Her Majesty to his son".[22]

This was a magnanimous gesture: but, as so often with Queensberry, geniality proved a passing phase. By 5 June, a month after he had given his approval, resentment over the slight done to him by the Lords welled up and he was in combatative mode. He bombarded Gladstone with letters, and on 20 June one of these was read out at a cabinet meeting. Rosebery strongly advised Gladstone to ignore Queensberry, and the Prime Minister did so. This only inflamed the Marquis still further and he turned his anger on to the Foreign Secretary, whom Queensberry now identified as the source of his humiliation.

Queensberry began to fire off abusive letters in all directions. Not only did Gladstone receive further correspondence along with Rosebery, but Queen Victoria herself received some of the Marquis's bilious letters. The source of Queensberry's ire was no longer just the question of the English peerage. He informed the Queen ominously that he considered Lord Rosebery to be a "bad influence" on his son. What he meant by this he left deliberately obscure, but there is little doubt that he was hinting at a homosexual relationship between the two men – Rosebery was unmarried at the time, his wife having died in 1890. Queensberry was now paranoid, believing that he was the victim of a plot co-ordinated by his former wife and involving the highest personages in the state. On 6 July he wrote a letter to Alfred Montgomery making accusations against Sybil for inciting plots against him, exonerating Montgomery for what he regarded as the plot over Drumlanrig's peerage, with the extraordinary statement that "your daughter's conduct is outrageous, and I am now fully convinced that the Rosebery-Gladstone-Royal insult that came to me through my other son, that she worked that – I thought it was you. I saw Drumlanrig here on the river, which much upset me. It shall be known some day by all that Rosebery not only insulted me by lying to the Queen, which makes her as bad as him and Gladstone, but also has made a lifelong quarrel between my son and I."[23] What Queensberry could mean by this nonsense is unfathomable, but in the summer of 1893, Queensberry's paranoia and homophobia led to a simple reaction. Learning that Rosebery had been ordered by his doctor to Bad Homburg to cure an unspecified illness (Rosebery was prone to unspecified illnesses) the Marquis set out hotfoot across Europe to confront the Foreign Secretary.

When he arrived in Germany, Queensberry prowled about outside Rosebery's hotel threatening to thrash him with a whip. Rosebery attempted to make light of this, writing to Queen Victoria that: "It is a material and unpleasant addition to the labours of Your Majesty's service to be pursued by a pugilist of unsound mind".[24] But Queensberry on the rampage was no laughing matter. The Prince of Wales, who was in Homburg at the time, intervened and the Chief of Police was called in to get rid of the Marquis. He reported to Rosebery that "The Marquis of Queensberry, in consequence of the entertainment I had with him, found it advisable to part this morning with the 7 o'clock train for Paris".[25] Queensberry went home with his tail between his legs. The next time he returned to his prejudices on homosexuality, he would be equally manic, but infinitely more cunning.

This reversal did nothing to soothe Queensberry's chronic conflicts with his family. He fell almost without a pause into a dispute with his second son, Percy. Lord Douglas of Hawick, as he was formally titled, was a happy-go-lucky young man with irrepressible optimism and none of the melancholic, destructive tendencies which plagued his male line. "My brother Percy", Bosie later wrote, "was the kindest hearted and sweetest tempered man I ever met".[26] This may have been true, but Percy was also feckless and irresponsible. He was a man who made promises which he had every intention of fulfilling but no practical means of carrying out. Oscar Wilde was to learn bitterly that Percy Douglas was generous to a fault in promising money which he did not have.

Percy had reached twenty-four in the summer of 1893, and had already spent half his years trying to master a career, without success. After failing to make a naval career and spending a brief period cattle ranching in Montana, he returned home no nearer settling into a paying occupation and Queensberry decided he should try an army career. Percy accepted his father's decision. But before he could apply for Sandhurst his abysmally poor education had to be improved and he was packed off to a crammer in Cornwall. No sooner had he arrived in Cornwall than Percy fell in love with the daughter of a local Vicar. Anna Maria Walters was pretty, charming and modest. Her father, Revd Thomas Walters, was a respectable member of an ancient family. Although Queensberry was inevitably likely to object to a marriage into a clerical family, had Percy courted his beloved with discretion and above all pursued his army career with success, he could probably have won his father over. But discretion was not in the Douglas character, and Percy conformed to the family type. He promptly decided to marry Minnie Walters.

Queensberry had rational grounds for objecting to the marriage. Percy depended entirely on an allowance from his father, and a family would add to the burdens Queensberry was financing. He objected to his son marrying before he could support a family, but Percy did not take the hint. He married on 11 September 1893, in a ceremony which attracted a fair amount of publicity and further incensed his father. The ceremony in his view was another Montgomery plot designed to undermine his authority. His sons seemed to take a fiendish delight in flaunting his paternal authority. Behind the scenes, Alfred Montgomery and his daughter seemed to the Marquis to be supporting and controlling the process. Immediately after the marriage, Queensberry destroyed what was essentially a rational case based on well founded objections to what his son had done by pouring his feelings into a series of manic letters sent to the newlyweds. He completely lost his head, attacking Percy as "white livered", though Percy was certainly no coward. Still worse, Queensberry wrote to Minnie attacking her as an adventuress who had trapped his son into marriage through a desire for his title and fortune – although he had otherwise objected to the marriage on the grounds that Percy had no money, no fortune, and few prospects. Later, Queensberry wrote to Revd Walters accusing his "stuck-up, pauper, impertinent daughter" of "forcing herself into my family and marrying my son, a mere boy and younger than herself, in defiance of my consent".[27]

Percy never forgave these attacks. He could – just – overlook his father's attacking him as an insolent boy, but he could never forgive the attacks on his wife. He ignored his father's threats to cut off his allowance and abandoned his army career. A few months after marriage, he set out for Ceylon to make his fortune as a tea planter. In Ceylon he met the Honorable David Carnegie, youngest son of Lord Southesk, and was quickly convinced that the Coolgardie gold rush in Western Australia offered a better chance of fortune. The two men promptly embarked for the Antipodes chasing a literal pot of gold at the end of a highly speculative rainbow. While Percy was out of the country, Queensberry's life staggered from one disaster to another.

When he wrote to Bosie complaining that he was lonely, his complaints had a peculiar ring to them, for John Sholto Douglas was newly married for the second time. Yet his marriage relieved none of his problems, for it was the greatest disaster and most curious decision of all. He went for a holiday in Eastbourne in November and his friends and family were astonished to learn from the press that, on the 7th of that month, he had been married to a Miss Ethel Weeden. The news leaked out via the Eastbourne Gazette, which reported four days later that the union had been concluded by licence and was private. Indeed, so private had it been that none of the bride's family knew about it, nor any of Queensberry's friends or relations. Apart from the Registrar and his deputy the only witnesses at a decidedly furtive affair were a Mr J. Hillman and Queensberry's valet, Tom Gill.

This was a gift to gossip mongers. The certificate put both partners as being of "full age". But whether Ethel Weeden was yet twenty-one was doubted. How had the couple met? Her parents, Mr and Mrs de Courcy Atkins, were pillars of the local Liberal Party, her mother having married again after her first husband died. Mrs Atkins attended the fashionable

St Saviour's church, and her two daughters went to the church's weekly "Penny Readings". These were the circles into which the raffish, Tory-inclined and atheistical Marquis of Queensberry was unlikely to be invited. It was a most unlikely match, and it was not surprising that it collapsed almost immediately. Whether Queensberry left his new bride the day after the ceremony, as Bosie was later to allege, or the family stepped in to take Ethel away before real damage was done, cannot be established. Oscar Wilde, observing proceedings with relish, managed to obtain inside information and in early November 1894 wrote to Bosie that "I heard all the details of the divorce of the Scarlet Marquis the other day: quite astonishing. Arthur Pollen told me all about it; he came to tea one afternoon".[28] Arthur Pollen had acted for Queensberry. Wilde was shrewd enough not to write privileged information in a letter and there is no knowing what he had heard.

All that is known for certain is that immediately after the marriage, Ethel and the Marquis were parted and the bride started proceedings for annulment. The annulment would not come through until October of 1894. But the collapse of his second marriage reverberated around the little circle in which the Queensberry family moved, as Queensberry was well aware. His humiliation was intensified by the stories circulating about his two elder sons. Moreover, he had become aware that his third son was as problematic as his first two had proved to be. While Queensberry was engaged in dealing with the collapse of his marriage and his disputes with his eldest sons, he had little time to deal with Bosie, and seems to have accepted that Bosie was going to Egypt to settle down and join the diplomatic corps. The failure of this project in the spring of 1894 alarmed him, for he was never indifferent about his son's futures. He was even more alarmed when he discovered that not only was Bosie back in London, but that he was in the company of Oscar Wilde. On returning to England at the end of March the two men had fallen back into their old habits of dining at the best restaurants. An encounter at the Café Royal was probably inevitable. When it took place on 1 April, all Queensberry's prejudices were inflamed.

No quarrel took place immediately, but Queensberry did not fall under the spell of Wilde's charm as he had at their previous meeting. Instead he drank wine and kept his counsel, observing carefully the relationship between the two men. Returning to Carter's Hotel in Albemarle Street, he wrote a letter that effectively started a civil war with his son. Queensberry wrote:

Alfred

It is extremely painful for me to have to write to you in the strain that I must; but please understand that I decline to receive any answers from you in writing in return. After your recent hysterical impertinent ones I refuse to be annoyed with such, and I decline to read any more letters. If you have anything to say, do come here and say it in person. Firstly, am I to understand that, having left Oxford as you did, with discredit to yourself, the reason of which were fully explained to me by your tutor, you now intend to loaf and loll about and do nothing? All the time you were wasting at Oxford I was put off with an assurance that you were eventually to go into the Civil Service or to the Foreign Office, and then I was put off with an assurance that you were going to the Bar. It appears to me that you intend to do nothing. I utterly decline, however, to just supply you with sufficient funds to enable you to loaf about. You are preparing a wretched future for yourself, and it would be most cruel and wrong for me to encourage you in this. Secondly, I come to the more painful part of this letter – your intimacy with this man Wilde. It must either cease or I will disown you and stop all money supplies. I am not going to analyse this intimacy, and I make no charge; but to my mind to pose as a thing is as bad as to be it. With my own eyes I saw you both in the most loathsome and disgusting relationship as expressed by your manner and expression. Never in my experience have I seen such a sight as that in your horrible features. No wonder people are talking as they are. Also I now hear on good authority, but this may be false, that his wife is petitioning to divorce him for sodomy and other crimes. Is this true or do you not know of it? If I thought the actual thing was true, and it became public property, I should be quite justified in shooting him at sight. These Christian English cowards and men, as they call themselves, want waking up.

Your disgusted-so-called father,

Queensberry[29]

This was an extremely dangerous letter, for while Queensberry clearly entertained suspicions of Wilde he was cunning enough only to refer to posing. At this stage Queensberry was relying on little more than clubland rumour, and innaccurate rumour at that. Constance was not suing for divorce: the danger was that Queensberry thought she was. Such a letter required the most circumspect response if it was not to trigger a vendetta. But Bosie was incapable of circumspection. Reading only criticism, he noted only that his father wanted no more letters from him, and he replied on 2 April by telegram. The message was simple, abusive and designed to wound. It read simply "What a funny little man you are". Wilde was shown the letter and the reply and saw immediately that this was a declaration of war, and that he would be caught in the middle. He objected, but his objections were too late. The telegram was the opening shot in a bitter conflict between Bosie Douglas and his father. Wilde would inevitably become a catspaw in the vendetta, and his fate would turn on the exchange of blows between two manic figures, father and son sharing the same blighted characteristics, over which he would have no control.

News of the letter and the telegram reverberated around the Queensberry circle and became public knowledge. By September, Robert Hichens would be weaving it into his portrait of Wilde, Douglas and Queensberry in *The Green Carnation.*[30] Hichens regarded the quarrel as a lighthearted disagreement. Those more intimately involved, who knew what the "Fatal Douglas Temperament" was and saw both John Sholto and Alfred Bruce Douglas bearing it in a virulent form, could only view this escalation of the quarrel with deep foreboding.

* * *

News of the quarrel between Bosie and his father soon reached Sybil. She was deeply alarmed by the conflict. After all her exertions to get Bosie out of the country, away from Wilde and into a stable career, she had accomplished nothing and faced an increasingly savage quarrel between Bosie and his father over Wilde. Her instinct was to send Bosie abroad again, and as he had always wanted to go to Florence she gave him money on condition he left immediately. Bosie arrived at the Palazzo Ferroni in mid-April, where Sybil could not have known that his host, Lord Henry Somerset, was the elder brother of that former Privy Councillor who had been forced to flee England in 1889 over the Cleveland Street brothel affair. Henry, too, was homosexual, had indeed contributed a poem to the *Spirit Lamp*, and gone abroad after the failure of his marriage.[31] Bosie's eclectic choice of host confirms that he saw himself then as an accepted member of the international homosexual fraternity.

If Sybil hoped to put an emotional distance between Wilde and her son, she failed, for now Wilde could not live without Bosie. Shortly after the magazine of the Decadents, the *Yellow Book*, appeared for the first time in April, Wilde wrote: "I miss you so much. The gay, gilt and gracious lad has gone away. How I envy you under Giotto's Tower, or sitting in the loggia looking at that green and gold god of Cellini's. You must write poems like apple blossom. The *Yellow Book* has appeared. It is dull and loathsome, a great failure, I am so glad".[32] He wrote again a couple of days later, modifying his spiteful opinion of the *Yellow Book* to praise Max Beerbohm's essay on cosmetics. Letters were not enough; within weeks he was with Bosie in Florence.

Oscar and Bosie took an apartment for a month, but only stayed a fortnight – perhaps because they were observed by André Gide, who wrote to his mother on 28 May that he had seen Wilde.[33] He noted that Wilde preferred not to be identified. Wilde rapidly returned to London, only to find that the Queensberry situation was becoming ominous. The Marquis had been seeking information in London restaurants. Far worse, on 30 June he turned up at Tite Street to confront Wilde in person. Queensberry and Wilde gave differing accounts of their encounter, Queensberry claiming Wilde showed him "the white feather", Wilde that he outfaced the Marquis and ordered him out of the house. Whatever went on between them, there is little doubt that the Marquis, who had taken along a witness whom Wilde believed to be a bruiser intended to intimidate, was hoping to provoke him into an indiscretion. Wilde kept his nerve, and Queensberry was temporarily checked.

That Bosie's father was prepared to visit his home shocked Oscar. He found it more unnerving even than the fact that Queensberry "goes from restaurant to restaurant looking for me, in order to insult me before the whole world, and in such a manner that if I retaliated I would be ruined, and if I did not retaliate I would be ruined also"[34] Wilde perceived with great acuity, the trap which Queensberry was setting for him. He did not lack for advice. If Frank Harris is to be believed, he warned Wilde of the dangers he faced at precisely this time. "'It's the old, old story', I said, 'You are putting your hand between the bark and the tree, and you will suffer for it'. But he would not or could not see it. 'What is one to do with such a madman?' he asked pitiably. 'Avoid him,' I replied, 'as you would a madman, who wanted to fight with you, or conciliate him; there is nothing else to do'."[35]

Instead, after Queensberry's visit, Wilde decided to seek a legal remedy. This alarmed the Queensberry family and a person later named in the trial only as "a member of the Queensberry family . . . who was also a member of Parliament" came to see Wilde to smooth over any difficulties and persuade Wilde to drop Bosie. Wilde named this person in *De Profundis* as "plausible George Wyndham", the cousin of Sybil's who was a leading Tory politician. He was not able to prevent Wilde going to the solicitor, but may have undermined Wilde's resolution to push legal action to a conclusion.[36] Wilde initially contacted George Lewis, the outstanding lawyer in cases of sexual scandal of the time. Lewis, however, wrote to Wilde on 7 July declining as he was acting for Queensberry.[37] Robert Ross recommended his own solicitor, Charles Humphreys, who duly wrote to Queensberry on 11 July, concerning: "certain letters written by your lordship, in which letters you have most foully libelled him, and also your son, Lord Alfred Douglas. In these letters your lordship has mentioned exalted personages, and Mr Oscar Wilde . . . has instructed us to give you the opportunity of retracting your assertions . . . . If this be done at once it may prevent litigation, but unless done forthwith no other course will be left open to us but to advise our client as to the proper course to adopt to vindicate his character."

Queensberry replied on 13 July: "I certainly shall not tender to Mr Oscar Wilde any apology for letters I have written to my son. I have made no direct accusation against Mr Oscar Wilde, but desired to stop the association as far as my son is concerned."[38] This was a clever response putting Wilde into the position of having to expose the allegations against him if he were to take legal action. In the Summer of 1894 Wilde was too cautious to take such a dangerously fraught step. Queensberry had made no accusations, for despite his suspicions he was cunning enough not to make any accusations which he could not prove in court. And as he had revealed in his letter to Alfred Montgomery of 6 July, this he could not do. He told Montgomery:

> Your daughter must be mad by the way she is behaving. She evidently wants to make out that I want to make out a case against my son. It is nothing of the kind. I have made out a case against Oscar Wilde and I have to his face accused him of it. If I was quite certain of the thing I would shoot him on sight, but I can only accuse him of posing. It now lies in the hands of the two whether they will further defy me. . . . I don't believe Wilde will now dare defy me. He plainly showed the white feather the other day when I tackled him – damned cur and coward of the Rosebery type. As for this so-called son of mine, he is

> no son of mine, and I will have nothing to do with him. He may starve as far as I am concerned.[39]

Only lack of evidence prevented Queensberry launching an all-out assault on Oscar Wilde.

Had Queensberry exerted himself, the evidence that his detectives discovered before his trial in 1895 might well have come to hand much earlier. On 12 August, police raided a house in Fitzroy Street, Bloomsbury, taking a number of men into custody, including two in female costume, alleging they had committed homosexual acts. Among their number was Alfred Taylor, who was to stand trial with Wilde in 1895. Wilde wrote to Charles Spurrier Mason from Worthing that "It is a dreadful piece of bad luck, and I wish to goodness I could do something for him, but . . . as I have no play going on this season I have no money at all. . . . Let me know what Alfred intends doing after next Monday is over, and how you yourself are going on in your married life".[40] This was a dangerous letter. At Wilde's first trial it would be alleged that Mason had gone through a form of marriage with Taylor, explaining the reference to marriage here and establishing that Wilde knew about it. Had Queensberry made the connections in the Summer of 1894, Wilde's position would have become untenable far earlier than Spring 1895.

Nevertheless, in the Summer of 1894 he was more troubled than he would admit. While he floated apparently serenely above his troubles, those troubles were pressing in on him. He lived well, inviting Reggie Turner to dine with him and Bosie at Kettner's in June,[41] and apologising to Ada Leverson, "The Sphinx", in July for not dining with her at Willis's, the most famous and fashionable restaurant of the decade, because of a prior engagement.[42] Yet he was desperately hard-up and wrote to Bosie in mid-July to say that he had turned down an invitation from Reggie Turner and others to go to Paris owing to lack of money. More significantly, Wilde wrote:

> Besides, I want to see you. *I can't live without you.* You are so dear, so wonderful. I think of you all day long, and miss your grace, your boyish beauty, the bright sword play of your wit, the delicate fancy of your genius, so suprising always in its sudden swallow-flights towards north or south, towards sun or moon – and above all you yourself. The only thing that consoles me is what the Sibyl of Mortimer Street (whom mortals term Mrs Robinson) said to me. If I could disbelieve her I would, but I can't, and I know that early in January you and

> I will go away together for a long voyage, and that your lovely life goes always hand in hand with mine. My dear wonderful boy, I hope you are brilliant and happy.[43] [*Original emphasis*]

Wilde, with his fey spirituality, was always much impressed by clairvoyants, and Mrs Robinson's prophecy was fulfilled in January 1895 when Wilde and Douglas travelled to Algiers. However, Wilde was reporting selectively. Mrs Robinson had also predicted, with chilling prescience: "I see a very brilliant life for you up to a certain point. Then I see a wall. Beyond the wall I see nothing".[44]

Neither the worldly advice of Frank Harris nor the prophecies of Mrs Robinson made much difference to Wilde, but he was forced to confront his financial problems by turning to the pen. In July he asked George Alexander for £150 to go away to write a new play. The money must have arrived, for, shortly after, Wilde wrote to Bosie that he was going to Worthing where he had taken a small house with his family for the Summer, and though this had no writing room he planned a new comedy. He invited Bosie to visit, complaining ominously that: "Your father is on the rampage again – been to the Café Royal to enquire for us, with threats etc. I think now it would have been better for me to have had him bound over to keep the peace, but what a scandal! Still, it is intolerable to be dogged by a maniac".[45]

Like Rosebery, Wilde found Queensberry's mania intolerable. Bosie, however, quite enjoyed the growing conflict with his father. On 19 August he wrote to Percy in Australia referring to his father as "that brute" and retailing the quarrels with Queensberry at length. In Percy he had an ally who hated the Marquis as much as he did. Drumlanrig was more circumspect and indeed had much to be worried about. His nephew, later the 11th Marquis, wrote that his uncle declined to be seen in public with Bosie and Wilde, and left London in order to avoid the possibility of being seen in public with either.[46] Bosie now took the drama to lengths that the pacific Wilde recalled with understandable bitterness from his prison cell three years later.[47] He deliberately escalated the conflict. He wrote his father a crudely naked threat:

> As you return my letters unopened, I am obliged to write on a postcard. I write to inform you that I treat your absurd threats with absolute indifference. Ever since your exhibition at OW's house, I have made a point of appearing with him at many public

> restaurants such as The Berkeley, Willis's rooms, the Café Royal, etc., and I shall continue to go to any of these places whenever I choose and with whom I choose. I am of age and my own master. You have disowned me at least a dozen times, and have very meanly deprived me of money. . . . If O.W. was to prosecute you in the Central Criminal Court for libel, you would get seven years penal servitude. . . . If you try to assault me, I shall defend myself with a loaded revolver, which I always carry; and if I shoot you or if he shoots you, we shall be completely justified as we shall be acting in self-defence against a violent and dangerous rough, and I think if you were dead many people would not miss you – A.D.[48]

This violent, ignorant missive was intended to intimidate Queensberry. Bosie was indeed carrying a pistol, and he was characteristically irresponsible in handling it. He fired it, apparently by accident, in the Berkeley, frightening Wilde tremendously. The news stopped Queensberry in his tracks, and there was a temporary cessation of his harrassment. Negotiations followed, and Queensberry wrote to Wilde's solicitor on 18 July that: "Since seeing you this morning I have heard that the revolver has been given up. I shall therefore not insist on taking the step I threatened to do to-morrow of giving information to the police authorities. However if this is to go on, and I am to be openly defied by Mr Oscar Wilde and my son by further scandals in public places, I shall have no other resort but do [*sic*] as I have threatened and give information to Scotland Yard as to what has happened."[49]

Any respite was welcome, but relations between Bosie and his father were now pregnant with menace. If Queensberry swallowed his rage he only did so to plot his next moves with greater care.

Bosie continued to do nothing with his life and, when he received Oscar's invitation to Worthing, he accepted. Bosie enjoyed visiting Wilde at Worthing despite the cramped conditions. Underneath the outward decorum and the humour of the school playground which he and Oscar habitually displayed when together, sharp emotions were held in tension when others were present. These would burst out into another violent quarrel when the two were alone but, at Worthing, they were never alone. Whatever strain there was did not prevent Wilde producing the most sparkling of his comedies, *The Importance of Being Earnest*, thus throwing doubt on the claim Wilde made in *De Profundis* that whenever he and Bosie were together, he was distracted from writing anything of note.

And, on the surface, all was well. After Bosie left Worthing, Wilde wrote him a ponderously cheerful letter praising his latest poem as full of "light lyrical grace" and gossiping about "Percy" – probably not Bosie's brother but an unidentified boy – Alphonso, who was "still in favour", and Stephen. Alphonso was Alphonso Conway, a newspaper boy whom Wilde had met on the beach. Wilde took him to Brighton and bought him a new suit. These were however peripheral relationships. Nothing really mattered to Wilde but Bosie, and he wrote that Bosie was "more to me than any one of them has any idea; you are the atmosphere of beauty through which I see life; you are the incarnation of all lovely things. When we are out of tune, all colour goes from things for me, but we are never really out of tune. I think of you day and night".[50] The language is poetic, but the note reflects a reality that was obscured by later arguments and in particular by Wilde's attack on Douglas in *De Profundis*. In his prison letter, Wilde gave a portrait of Bosie and their relationship so negative that it is hard to understand why the two men were attracted to each other. The relationship must have been founded on mutual enjoyment of each other's company, but was overshadowed by the more dramatic quarrels and reconciliations. It could not have survived had the two men not found one another's company immensely pleasurable.

Nevertheless, the emotional overstatement of Wilde's famous prison letter is undoubtedly there, and Oscar's view that he and Bosie were never really out of tune was rapidly put to the test. In mid-September, he invited Bosie to go to France for three days, suggesting Dieppe. Bosie demurred, and the two settled for Brighton in October. But, as they were preparing to make this visit, they found themselves confronted with an unpleasantly public description of their relationship. On 15 September, the anonymously authored novella, *The Green Carnation,* appeared. It was an instant success, and placed the two originals of the book's central characters, Mr Esmé Amarinth and Lord Reginald Hastings, in a spotlight the originals did not welcome. Wilde and Lord Alfred Douglas recognised themselves instantly, and knew that the author was Hichens. He had met Wilde three times after returning from Egypt, and wrote the book easily, reading some of the chapters to Max Beerbohm and Reggie Turner. Beerbohm should have realised that the book would be dangerous to Wilde; but, if he did, he did not warn Hichens, who was blissfully unaware of the likely outcome.

Nor did Wilde initially grasp the threat, although the thesis of the book was that Bosie's character was being swallowed up by Wilde's – this was the belief which drove Queensberry – and, still more dangerously, the book had Bosie chasing a boy. Both Bosie and Wilde read it, though neither of the two initially thought the book dangerous. Bosie called on Hichens. He professed himself delighted with the book and took Hichens to dinner. In the restaurant Bosie was recognised – Hichens was unknown – and when journalists present quizzed Bosie about the authorship of the book, Hichens' identity was revealed. If Bosie regarded *The Green Carnation* as delightful, Wilde was increasingly alarmed. As rumours that Wilde wrote the book circulated, he wrote to the *Pall Mall Gazette* on 1 October in very sharp terms to deny authorship: "Kindly allow me to contradict, in the most emphatic manner, the suggestion, made in your issue of Thursday last, and since then copied into many other newspapers, that I am the author of *The Green Carnation.* I invented that magnificent flower. But with the middle-class and mediocre book that usurps its strangely beautiful name I have, I need hardly say, nothing whatever to do. The flower is a work of art. The book is not".[51]

There was more than artistic vanity involved here: Wilde had begun to appreciate the effect the book would have on Queensberry. Hichens had included the "What a funny little man" incident in the text. The Scarlet Marquis, as Wilde called him, would be particularly infuriated by this public display of his private correspondence in a most humiliating manner. Hichens had portrayed the incident in the most unflattering terms, describing Reggie/Bosie's progress through the West End: "Presently he passed an elderly gentleman with a red face and small side whiskers. The elderly gentleman stared him in the face, and sniffed ostentatiously. 'What a pity my poor father is so plain,' Reggie said to himself with a quiet smile. Only that morning he had received a long and vehement diatribe from his parent, showering abuse upon him, and exhorting him to lead a more reputable life. He had replied by wire – 'What a funny little man you are. Reggie'. The funny little man had evidently received his message."[52]

Such a public portrayal of the quarrel between father and son could only inflame Queensberry still further. If Bosie Douglas was unable to see this, Oscar was intelligent enough, but he and Bosie still behaved as though they were invulnerable. The visit to Dieppe lapsed and the two men went off to Brighton. As always when the two were together, left to their own company they fell into a violent quarrel.

Three years later, Wilde was to paint Bosie's conduct over the four days from 10–13 October with apparently total recall. No sooner had they arrived in Brighton than Bosie fell ill with influenza. Wilde waited on him, claiming not only that he provided luxuries of fruit, flowers, presents and books, but that he remained with Bosie, either in the next room or sitting with him, entertained him and procured grapes from London as Bosie did not like the hotel variety. After four or five days, having to finish the play, Oscar took cheap lodgings. The next morning, he himself went down with 'flu. Bosie travelled to London on business, promising to return that afternoon. Instead, he did not return until late the next day, by which time Wilde was in a fever, inconvenienced by being in a bedroom two floors up from the sitting room, and without a manservant. He assumed Bosie would be in attendance: Bosie was not there.[53]

What followed was a nightmare: Oscar claims he did not see Bosie for two days, during which he could not even get the milk that the doctor had prescribed. When Bosie did turn up, Oscar asked him to get a book to read. No book arrived. Bosie pleaded that he had ordered the book but it had not been delivered. Wilde later discovered this was untrue. Oscar asked Bosie to come back after dinner and sit with him. Bosie agreed, ungraciously but by eleven o'clock Bosie had not returned and Wilde left a note in his room reminding of him of his promise. By three a.m. Bosie had still not returned and Wilde dragged himself down to the sitting room to find water. Instead, he found Bosie.

A terrible row ensued. Wilde paints a picture of a Bosie falling on him "with every hideous word an intemperate mood, an undisciplined and untutored nature could suggest. . . . You accused me of selfishness in expecting you to be with me when I was ill: of standing between you and your amusements: of trying to deprive you of your pleasures. . .". Wilde dragged himself back to bed, disgusted. The following morning Bosie visited him, only to repeat the assertions of the night before. Wilde told him to leave his bedroom, but when he lifted his head from the pillow found Bosie still there. Bosie suddenly moved towards him, laughing maniacally, and Wilde was so terrified that he fled down two flights of stairs and rang for the owner of the lodging. Bosie returned, scooped up the money lying around the rooms, and left with his luggage. Wilde recalled from his prison cell: "I recognised that the ultimate moment had come, and recognised it as being really a great relief. . . . Ill as I was, I felt at ease. The fact that the separation was irrevocable gave me peace".

Two days later, Wilde got a letter from Bosie. In this he repeated his accusations of the quarrel, mocking Wilde with his having dined at the Grand Hotel and put the cost of the meal down to Wilde's account. More ominously, according to Wilde, he:

> congratulated me on my prudence in leaving my sickbed, on my sudden flight downstairs. "*It was an ugly moment for you,*" you said, "*uglier than you imagine*". Ah! I felt it but too well. What it really meant I do not know: Whether you had with you the pistol you had bought to try to frighten your father with . . . whether your hand was moving towards a common dinner knife that by chance was lying on the table between us: whether, forgetting in your rage your low stature and inferior strength, you had thought of some special insult, or attack even, as I lay ill there: I would not tell . . . all I know is that a feeling of utter horror had come over me. Only once before in my life had I experienced such a horror at any human being. It was when in my library at Tite Street, waving his small hands in the air in epileptic fury, your father, with his bully, or his friend between us, had stood uttering every foul word his foul mind could think of, and screaming the loathesome threats he afterward with such cunning carried out. . . .[54] [*Original emphasis*]

Bosie concluded his letter with the comment: "When you are not on your pedestal you are not interesting. The next time you are ill I will go away at once." Wilde commented savagely that he "felt almost polluted, as if by associating with one of such nature I had soiled and shamed my life irretrievably. I had, it is true, done so, but I was not to learn how fully till just six months later on in life". He resolved to return to London on Friday 19 October in order to see Sir George Lewis personally and request him to write to Queensberry to say Wilde had resolved "never under any circumstances to allow you to enter my house, to sit at my board, to talk to me, with me, or anywhere and at any time to be my companion at all".[55] On the Thursday night after receiving the letter, Wilde believed that the following day he would by speaking to Lewis at last begin to move on to a new stage in his life, without Bosie Douglas.

But on 19 October, Wilde did not return to London. That morning he opened his newspaper and was dumbfounded. The previous day Francis Douglas, Viscount Drumlanrig, Bosie's eldest brother and heir to the family estate, had been found dead in a country ditch. He had been killed by a single cartridge, discharged by his own shotgun. The charge had entered the mouth, fracturing the lower jaw, and passed through the roof of the mouth into the brain. He had died instantly.[56]

* * *

Drumlanrig's death devastated the Douglas family and immediately destroyed Wilde's resolution to break with Bosie. The tragedy struck with greater force because it came completely without warning. Drumlanrig had been the least problematic of the Queensberry children, despite the storms surrounding his work with Rosebery. His amiability was acknowledged, and he seemed to have avoided the worst excesses of the Douglas temperament. He had survived the rows of 1893 and continued to work unobtrusively for Rosebery When entering the Lords as Baron Kelhead he had kept his head down politically in a particularly turbulent period in the history of the Liberal Party. He made his maiden speech in the Lords on 25 June 1894, on the minor issue of the Prevention of Cruelty to Children Bill. Drumlanrig left the chief points of the Bill to be dealt with by the Lord Chancellor, and confined himself to generalities about supporting the activities of the Child Protection Society with the forces of the state. It was a competent but plodding speech about a minor issue.[57] Drumlanrig never spoke in the Lords again.

Nor did he appear to play any role behind the scenes in the events surrounding the resignation of Gladstone and the elevation of Rosebery to the premiership in the spring of 1894. As the Grand Old Man came to the end of his long career there was intense conflict within the cabinet over who should replace him. Whatever intrigues went on, however, Drumlanrig played no visible role in drumming up support for his employer. In fact Drumlanrig played no visible role at all, whether before Rosebery became premier on 2 March or afterward. When Gladstone resigned that day, Victoria did not ask his advice and used her prerogative to select Rosebery. Despite being a reasonably popular figure with the public – Rosebery had been Chair of the London County Council, and while Foreign Secretary had negotiated a settlement to solve a major coal strike – he was neverthless isolated in the House of Lords and needed all the support he could obtain. Drumlanrig appears to have offered none.

To all outward appearances this amiable but none too political young man was largely absorbed in his own affairs that summer, for he entered into a relationship. The details of the courtship are not recorded, but in the middle of October he proposed to Alix Ellis, daughter of Major General Arthur Ellis, an equerry to the Prince of Wales. In order to introduce Drumlanrig to the Ellis family, he was invited to a family gathering at Quantock Lodge in Somerset.

On 18 October the women went on an afternoon drive while the men went out shooting. Drumlanrig went off with his prospective brother in law, Gerald Ellis, and three other young men. They trudged across two miles of country shooting at pheasants with little success. Drumlanrig winged a bird but it flew off and he left the party to search for it muttering 'I think my bird is in the hedge'.[58] After he was gone for some minutes a single shot was heard from the field into which he had disappeared. "Where can his lordship be?" asked one of the keepers. "I hope he has not shot himself" one of the Party commented, but the keeper replied "Oh no, we won't think that". But Gerald Ellis gave his gun to a keeper and hurried back through a gap in the hedge. He found Drumlanrig lying on his back parallel with the hedge, and quite dead. The gun was lying across his stomach. The muzzle was towards the hedge and his arms were stretched out on either side. In a macabre echo of his grandfather's death, he was killed by a single shot from a double barrelled gun.

An inquest was held at Quantock Lodge two days later. The coroner concluded that the gun had gone off accidentally while Drumlanrig was climbing over the hedge, though how the gun could be fired accidentally in such a way as to fracture the lower right jaw and blast a cartridge through the mouth into the brain was not explained – the gun had to be pointing upward from below head height, a curious position in which to hold a gun while climbing a hedge. Nevertheless, public opinion did not want to comment on the possibility of suicide, though some mentioned the parallels with his grandfather's death and the suicide of his uncle. Most public comment, however, talked of a promising career tragically ended and an engagement pathetically cut short. Privately, tongues wagged – while Queensberry had no doubt that what had happened was connected with his long-held suspicions about the relationship of his son and Rosebery. The father's grief was genuine and intense: but the death of his son could not lead to reconciliation with his family. On 1 November he wrote to Montgomery a semi-literate letter of extraordinary savagery:

> Sir,
> Now that the first flush of this catastrophe and grief is passed, I write to tell you that it is a *judgement* on the whole *lot of you*. Montgomerys, The Snob Queers like Rosebery & certainly Christian hypocrite Gladstone the whole lot *of you*! Set my son up against me indeed and make bad blood *between* us, may it devil on your own heads that he is gone to his rest and the quarrel between us not made up between him and myself. It's a gruesome message: If you and his mother did

> not set up this business with that cur and Jew friend (?) *Liar* Rosebery as I always thought –
>
> At any rate she [*Lady Queensberry*] acquiesced in it, which is just *as bad.* What fools you all look, trying to ride me out of the course and trim *the sails* and the poor boy comes to this untimely end. I smell a Tragedy behind all this and have already *got Wind* of a more *startling one.* If it was what I am led *to believe,* I of all people could and would have helped him, had he come to me with a confidence, but that was all stopped by you people – we had not met or spoken frankly for more than a year and a half. I am on the right track to find out what happened. *Cherchez la femme,* when these things happen. I have already heard something that quite accounts *for it all.*
>
> Queensberry[59] [*Original emphasis*]

This was the turning point in the crisis within the Douglas family. Drumlanrig's death changed everything – or rather it changed Queensberry, for he was now focussed on the issue which seemed to have come to blight his life, taking the life of one son and threatening the life of another: homosexuality. Queensberry is often dismissed as mad, but from any point of view his views were entirely rational. He saw the death of Drumlanrig as being rooted in a homosexual affair, something which has never been proven but which is certainly not impossible. He saw another son engaged in a similar affair, and assumed that he was similarly at risk. These are not irrational beliefs. That Queensberry being who he was then took on a crusade with obsessional fervour is hardly the action of a normal man. But he believed he was defending Bosie against a terrible fate. When the issue came to court, jurymen, journalists and politicians, who were certainly not insane, overwhelmingly endorsed his view.

Queensberry was now bent on a crusade to save Bosie whatever the cost. And the cost of saving Bosie was to destroy Oscar Wilde, even if this meant a ferocious fight with Bosie himself. Queensberry believed he could destroy Wilde while leaving Bosie unscathed. Bosie would believe that he and his mother were the true objects of his father's crusade, a view which his defenders still maintain, but it is abundantly clear that his object was to save Bosie and destroy Wilde. Bosie did not accept this at the time, but in later middle age it dawned on him that his hatred for his father had obscured his understanding of his father's motives.

The effect of Drumlanrig's death on Wilde was instantaneous. His resolution of the previous night to abandon the relationship flew out of the window. In *De Profundis* Wilde wrote: "What you had been to me in my sickness, I could not be to you in your bereavement. I telegraphed at once to you my deepest sympathy, and in the letter that followed invited you to come to my house as soon as you were able. I felt that to abandon you at that particular moment, and formally through a solicitor, would have been too terrible for you".[60] Bosie returned to Wilde "very sweetly and very simply, in your suit of woe"[61] seeking consolation and help, "as a child might seek it". Wilde was too good hearted to do other than admit Bosie once again to his affections. The terrible quarrel of Brighton was forgotten. The dance resumed again, and to the same music. Wilde may have been unaware that he was now being pursued by a father maddened with grief and implacably determined to sever his relationship with his son. It was however from this point that the collision of Wilde and Queensberry became inevitable. Wilde was determined to maintain his relationship with Bosie, Queensberry was equally determined to break the relationship. Nothing in the behaviour of Wilde or Douglas suggests that they were aware of the dangers. In the autumn of 1894 Wilde seems to have treated Queensberry as an irritant rather than a serious threat. Queensberry's second divorce, which was held in camera, intrigued him and, after charming Ethel Weedon's lawyer into indiscretion, delightedly wrote to Bosie on 5 or 6 November with his news as if retailing no more than a tattle of minor gossip. If news of Queensberry's furious temper following the death of Drumlanrig had reached Wilde's ears, there was no sign.

Nor is there any sign that Wilde felt he should modify his snubbing of bourgeois prejudices following the publication of *The Green Carnation*. Wilde's public was becoming hostile and he felt uncomfortable when at the theatre. In early November he wrote to Bosie complaining: "I went to Haddon Chambers's play. . . . The bows and salutations of the lower orders who thronged the stalls were so cold that I felt it my duty to sit in the Royal Box with the Ribblesdales, the Harry Whites, and the Home Secretary: this exasperated the wretches. How strange to live in a land where the worship of beauty and the passion of love are considered infamous. I hate England; it is only bearable because you are here".[62] [*The persons sitting with him were the Queen's Private Solicitor, the Master of Buckhounds, and Asquith, who would soon be prosecuting him. TF*] England, it was clear, also hated Oscar Wilde, but Wilde saw no danger. Frank Harris recalled that "He was now utterly contemptuous of criticism and would listen to no counsel. He was gross, too, the rich food and wine seemed to ooze out of him and his manner was defiant, hard. He was like some great pagan determined to live his own life to the very fullest, careless of what others might say or think or do".[63]

Wilde and Douglas appeared to think that what others said or thought about them was of no consequence. However, at the end of 1894 the two men took a careless step which would fatally wound them. An Oxford friend of Bosie's, Jack Bloxham, proposed a homosexual undergraduate magazine similar to the *Spirit Lamp*, called the *Chameleon*. Bosie contributed two poems, one of which contained the immortal phrase "The Love That Dare Not Speak Its Name". "The Two Loves" was as close to an open espousal of homosexuality as Douglas ever dared. By itself it might have passed unnoticed, but Bosie could not but involve Wilde. Bosie asked Wilde for a contribution, and Oscar was willing to please. He sent a collection of "Phrases and Philosophies for the Use of the Young" which were intended for the Saturday Review, but easily diverted to help the cause. Unfortunately for Wilde, Bloxham penned a blasphemous and obscene story of a priest who, having fallen hopelessly in love with a beautiful boy, poisons the sacrament and kills both himself and the boy. When the *Chameleon* appeared in December, the story of "The Priest and the Acolyte" attracted severe criticism. Jerome K. Jerome drew attention to it in the magazine *To-Day* on 29 December and recommended police action.[64] The police took none, but the magazine never appeared again. And although only a hundred copies were printed, one fell into Queensberry's hands, becoming a weapon that he would use against Wilde in court.

Bloxham did not have the courage to publish the story with an author's name. Wilde was popularly thought to be the author, though Ada Leverson believed John Gray to have written the story. Wilde wrote that "'The Priest and the Acolyte' is not by Dorian, though you are right to discern from internal evidence that the author has a profile [*ie, is beautiful. TF*]. . . . The story is to my ears too direct; there is no nuance: it profanes a little by revelation . . . still it has interesting qualities, and is at moments poisonous, which is something."[65] This flippancy showed a dangerous blindness: Wilde was now less than six months away from trial and imprisonment, and Wilde's association with the *Chameleon* would be used against him by the prosecution. Douglas's poem was also dragged through the mud. Yet neither of them seemed to have any awareness of the possibly dangers in writing for a journal of this kind, living their lives without any heed of the shadows gathering round them.

Wilde was possibly too busy to consider the implications of what he was doing. Over Christmas 1894 his play *An Ideal Husband* went into rehearsal, and Wilde insisted the cast rehearse on Christmas Day, alienating some members. The play opened on 3 January 1895 scoring an instant success. The Prince of Wales attended the opening night, as did Balfour, Chamberlain and many government ministers. Wilde's great success was not yet the peak of his achievement. George Alexander was then in rehearsal with *The Importance of Being Earnest*, and Wilde wanted to stay to interfere in the first production of his masterpiece. Bosie wanted a holiday, however, and as he could never deny Bosie anything, Wilde weakly acquiesced. To Ada Leverson he wrote ambiguously, "I begged him to let me stay, but so beautiful is his nature that he declined at once".[66] On 17 January they went to Algeria, a common haunt of wealthy homosexuals behaving as sex tourists, Wilde and Douglas conforming to type. Wilde wrote to Ross that "the beggars here have profiles, so the problem of poverty is solved".[67] Wilde sometimes affected to be a socialist. That Wilde regarded male prostitution as an answer to poverty illustrates that his proclaimed socialism was intolerably superficial.

His attention was certainly not with Constance and the children. Around this time Wilde effectively deserted his family, quitting the Albemarle Hotel without leaving a forwarding address. Wilde could not have known that his wife was in serious straits. She had fallen downstairs at Tite Street, injuring her arm and back – the latter with very serious consequences. On the 28th she wrote to Robbie Ross asking him to get in touch with Wilde as she did not know how to reach him. She was overdrawn at the bank and hoped Oscar would be able to send her some money. Ross, always a good friend to Constance and her children, immediately telegraphed Wilde's address and offered to send five pounds. Constance did not complain at her treatment, but pathetically asked Ross to tell her when her husband had returned to England.[68]

Despite allegations that Ross was jealous of Bosie Douglas's command of Oscar Wilde, there is little doubt that Ross and Douglas were close at this time and Douglas shared his secrets with Ross, as did Wilde. The two tourists immersed themselves in the attractions of Moroccan life, Wilde writing to Ross that "Bosie and I have taken to haschish: it is quite exquisite; three puffs of smoke and then peace and love. Bosie wakes up at night and cries like a child for the best haschish".[69] Bosie fell in love with an Arab boy, and went off to Biskra with him, finding that he had to sign innumerable forms, according to André Gide, who met Wilde and Bosie in Morocco. Douglas was enamoured with the boy, and wrote to Robbie Ross from Biskra an explicit account of their relationship. This letter was dangerous, and was used by Ross against Douglas when relations fractured after Wilde's death.[70] Douglas even claimed Ross threatened to blackmail him with the letter. At the time, however, Ross was the intimate confidant of both men.

Wilde took Gide off to Algiers, where he arranged for him to pair off with an Arab musician, bursting into what Gide later described as "satanic laughter" when he realised Gide did not know how to make the arrangements. Wilde confided to Gide that he was being pursued by Queensberry. Gide warned him of the risk. Wilde could only shrug his shoulders. Wilde returned to London for the opening of his new play, while Bosie remained in Algeria. Bosie was infatuated with his boy, and only a greater passion could take him back home. That passion was hatred for his father, which always overruled all other interests. Bosie returned home when he received a telegram from Percy announcing that their father had turned up at the opening night of *The Importance of Being Earnest* to create a scene. He immediately rushed back to London via Paris, understanding that his father was resolved on a fight to the finish, and determined to fling himself into the fray with equal fury. Oscar Wilde was caught in the crossfire between Bosie and his father, and wholly ill-equipped to cope with a war fought without quarter.

SIX

The Storm Breaks

By February 1895, Oscar Wilde's public and private lives were converging towards the critical moment. Wilde was the dramatist of the hour, with two sparkling comedies playing to packed houses in the West End. The success of *An Ideal Husband* in the first weeks of the New Year was quickly outclassed by that even more perfect confection, *The Importance of Being Earnest,* hailed then and now as an unquestioned masterpiece. Even as his audiences cooled rapidly towards his intolerable public displays of arrogance, and the Decadence he supported, Wilde was ironically becoming critically regarded as the finest writer of light comedy in the British theatre since Congreve and Sheridan. In the murky world of Wilde's private life, however, events were moving towards a *denouement.*

It is frequently supposed by his admirers in the modern "gay" movement and outside it, that Oscar Wilde was imprisoned as a result of a homophobic act of state repression. Nothing could be further from the truth. The state was not interested in Wilde's private life, which was overtly that of a happily married man, and it had even less interest in the aristocrat, Bosie Douglas. Despite the massive Moral Purity campaign launched by the National Vigilance Association after the passage of the 1885 Criminal Law Amendment Act, neither the NVA nor the police authorities had any real interest in actively prosecuting homosexuals. Of course, were the activities of the *demi-monde* to become widely known to the public, pressure would no doubt have mounted to do something. However, there was at the time no real evidence that a homosexual sub-culture existed or posed a threat to "respectable" opinion.

When Wilde joined Asquith, then Home Secretary in a Liberal Government, in his box at the theatre the previous November, he had done so in the absolute belief that he was impregnable. Despite the strong prejudices and suspicions about decadence entertained by most Victorians, no serious attempt had ever been made to investigate that sub-culture, or to pry into the reality behind the public antics of a few artistic young men wearing green carnations. It was for the most part an amusing expression of *fin de siècle* high spirits, which a powerful nation, confident in its place in the world, could easily afford to tolerate. Wilde, too, could be confident that his repeated flouting of the law would go undiscovered and unpunished. Without Queensberry's very public vendetta, and the inexorable momentum of his unfolding personal tragedy, this confidence might well have been justified.

Nevertheless, what Oscar Wilde and Bosie Douglas did in bed together and with others was both illegal and ran deeply counter to the strongest prejudices of Victorian society. They must have known how dangerous their behaviour was becoming. Other homosexuals knew, they conducted their affairs circumspectly in private, and with a due regard for public opinion. Wilde and Douglas were carelessly open in consorting with renters, while Douglas's perverse habit of leaving incriminating letters lying around was to provide Queensberry with some of his most damaging evidence. The truth may be less that the couple did not consider their own vulnerability, but that, in some perverse way, they felt they had to test it to the limit. For Wilde, certainly, and probably for Bosie as well, the dangers in what they were doing must have lent added spice to the encounters.

So, what was the state of the law at that time? The famous Labouchère amendment to the 1885 Criminal Law Amendment Act did not replace the earlier, much harsher law, but added to the statute book a new, lesser offence that did not require proof of buggery. Thus, by requiring a lower level of evidence, it made prosecution easier. The testimony of one man that another had attempted indecency was all that was required; and, since the man making the allegation did not allege sodomy, he was virtually immune from prosecution. This was a blackmailers' charter, for male prostitutes could now threaten their clients that they would testify against them if they were not bought off. Both Wilde and Douglas knew this, they had both been threatened with blackmail before. For Wilde, this potential threat made consorting with renters and blackmailers more deliciously alluring – he described it in *De Profundis* as ". . . feasting with panthers". The danger was half the excitement. ". . . Clibborn and Atkins were wonderful in their infamous war against life. To entertain them was an astounding adventure".[1] It is impossible that Wilde did not know about the Amendment, in fact he regarded Henry Labouchère, the radical Liberal MP behind it, highly. In 1882, in a letter to Mrs George Lewis, Wilde named his three heroes as the actor Henry Irving, the painter Whistler, and the politician Labouchère. There is no reason to suppose he was writing with tongue in cheek.[2]

The increase in legal penalties failed to deter Wilde and his companions; indeed the evidence suggests a growth in homosexual activity and male prostitution. Female prostitutes complained that they were suffering a loss of business from the increased activity of the renters. This apparent growth in male prostitution may have happened in part because the authorities were reluctant to prosecute under the 1885 Act for fear of giving increased publicity to an activity the police found difficult to prevent. There was only one instance of the Labouchère Amendment being used. This was in 1889, when a male brothel was discovered in Cleveland Street, near London's Tottenham Court Road. Upper-class men had been picking up telegraph boys from the General Post Office, and one was identified as the Prince of Wales's equerry, Lord Arthur Somerset. The Conservative government of Lord Salisbury delayed action, and Somerset escaped to exile on the continent, while other leading figures fled to America. Only relatively minor figures were finally prosecuted. Whether the government was warned off other prosecutions by this scandal is not clear, but there were no more until 1895, when Oscar Wilde left them with no choice but to prosecute him. There was certainly no concerted effort to use the provisions of the 1885 Act, either before the Cleveland Street scandal or after. Two prosecutions in a decade is scarcely evidence of a crusade.

Wilde could not have been unaware of the Cleveland Street affair, which received massive press coverage. When the *Scots Observer* criticised *Dorian Gray* it did so with a reference to "disgraced noblemen and perverted telegraph boys", unmistakably a reference to Cleveland Street. Moreover, Henry Somerset, elder brother of Arthur, had entertained Bosie in Florence in the Spring of 1894. Both Somerset brothers had to go into exile because of homosexual activities. Wilde could not have been unaware of this either. He was certainly aware of rising public prejudice against him, as shown by his reception by theatregoers in November 1894, despite his enormous success as a playwright, hostility which led him to taking refuge in a box with Asquith. Yet even at this late date he seems to have perceived no danger. There was simply no indication that the authorities regarded homosexuality as an issue. Indeed, Wilde could still call on their protection. When Queensberry opened his vendetta by disrupting the opening night of *Earnest*, the police did not take his side. While suspicion about Wilde's sexuality must have grown over the years, Wilde was nevertheless lulled into the dangerous belief that he could invoke the Courts to protect him against Queensberry. It was a wholly reasonable belief, given the failure of the state to take action against homosexuality.

Indeed, the authorities seemed wholly indifferent to whatever Wilde might do in private, unless Queensberry could produce irrefutable evidence to obtain a prosecution. But he had none. He had the Hyacinthus letter stolen by Alfred Wood, a copy of the *Chameleon*, and he listened avidly to the rumours going around the London clubs about Wilde's conduct. But his frequent threats to go to Scotland Yard were mere bluster. He dared not go to the police and so had to choose his ground carefully. In his letter to Bosie of 1 April 1894, he had been careful only to accuse Wilde of posing, and he was cunning enough to stick to this position. There was no law against posing; nor against accusing someone of it.

Queensberry's strategy in February 1895 was therefore to provoke a public disturbance so great that Wilde would be forced to go to law, at which point Oscar would have to reveal what Queensberry had said about him. Queensberry hoped that then the whole Pandora's Box of suspicious activities would spring open and destroy Wilde. His aim was to do this without embroiling Bosie and the family in a public scandal. It is an error to suppose that Queensberry's principal aim was to break the rebellious Bosie, and that Wilde merely got in the way. Queensberry had no intention at all of harming the boy. He aimed to "save" him, as he saw it, in a profoundly moral sense. To do this, he had to force Wilde into an action that would destroy his glittering reputation: the most important thing in the writer's life. It is remarkable that the super-intelligent Wilde, with his "double First", blundered so easily into what Queensberry later derisively called the "booby trap". The first opportunity Queensberry had of creating a scene was the opening night of *The Importance of Being Earnest*, which was bound to be a glittering occasion.

To make sure his protests would cause a sensation, the Marquis took along a bunch of rotten vegetables to throw on to the stage. But his plan backfired. Algy Bourke, one of Bosie's cousins, revealed the plot, leading the business manager at the St James' theatre to cancel the booking and notify the police. When Queensberry arrived at the première on the night of 14 February, twenty unsympathetic constables barred the entrances. The Scarlet Marquis was furious at being thwarted once again, and Wilde bragged in a letter to Bosie in Algeria that "I had all Scotland Yard – twenty police – to guard the theatre. He prowled about for three hours, then left chattering like a monstrous ape. Percy is on our side.

I feel now that, without your name being mentioned, all will go well".[3] Bosie arrived home shortly afterwards and, in an excess of theatricality, bought Oscar a swordstick for Wilde to defend himself against his father.

With the police now apparently protecting him against the raging Queensberry, Wilde may have been encouraged to consider the disastrous step of going to law. He contacted his solicitors unsuccessfully, with a view to having Queensberry bound over. On 28 February, Messrs Humphreys, Son and Kershaw wrote: "We have met with every obstruction from Mr George Alexander the Manager and his staff at the Theatre who declined to give us any statements or to render any assistance to you in your desire to prosecute Lord Queensberry".[4] Despite the towering reputation of Wilde filling their theatre, Alexander and his staff had no stomach to get involved in the feud, which could only damage their theatre's reputation. It was the first in a series of setbacks. Humphreys, completely out of his depth amid the complexities of Wilde's affairs, commented hopefully that "such a persistent persecutor as Lord Queensberry will probably give you another opportunity sooner or later of seeking the protection of the law".[5] This was precisely what Wilde was afraid of.

In fact, Queensberry had already done so. On 18 February, he went round to the Albemarle Club to confront Wilde. Wilde was not in, and Queensberry decided to let him know that he had visited. He left his card, but to make sure Wilde understood that the visit was hostile, scribbled on it in his terrible handwriting the famous message, which he later claimed read "To Oscar Wilde, posing somdomite" [*sic*], though some read the message as: "To Oscar Wilde, ponce and somdomite", which would have been worse. While Queensberry was unable to spell the word, even at this stage he was cunning enough not to make a direct accusation of sodomy. He handed the card to the hall porter, who put it in an envelope and entered the date and time of receipt on the outside. The envelope was then left awaiting Wilde's return.

Wilde was at this time entertaining Bosie Douglas at the Avondale Hotel in Piccadilly, and running up a large bill in consequence. He later accused Bosie of bringing a companion to stay: thus Wilde had a bill to contend with of £140 for a ten-day stay. The bill was large enough to have serious consequences.

Wilde visited the Albemarle on Thursday 28 February and read the card. With a sinking feeling, he realised that Queensberry would pursue him until he was cornered. His immediate instinct was to run away. In

De Profundis he bitterly blamed Bosie for his not being able to take this action, for on account of his reckless spending he was barred from leaving the Avondale. "The hotel people absolutely refused to allow me to go. . . . The proprietor said he could not allow my luggage to be removed from the hotel till I had paid the account in full. That is what kept me in London. Had it not been for the hotel bill I would have gone to Paris on Thursday morning".[6]

It seems absurd that Wilde could not escape Queensberry and that the affair was to turn on a hotel bill, of all things. Wilde was a successful playwright with two hit plays running in the West End. Yet his financial extravagance was stupendous and his lack of funds entirely plausible. Just before the discovery of the card, he had written to George Alexander thanking him for a cheque for £300 and asking for the balance, commenting that he was "already served with writs for £400, rumours of my prosperity having reached the commercial classes, and my hotel is loathesome to me. I want to leave it".[7] But he could not do so. Had he tried to leave, the hotel management would immediately have sought an injunction to prevent him leaving the country. With Oscar turned back at Dover, Queensberry would have had every encouragement to re-double his attacks. Wilde could see no immediate alternative to confronting his persecutor. On reading the card he wrote immediately to Bosie and Robbie Ross, pleading for help. To Robbie, he wrote: "Since I saw you something terrible has happened. Bosie's father has left a card at my club with hideous words on it. I don't see anything now but a criminal prosecution. My whole life seems ruined by this man. The tower of ivory is assailed by the foul thing. On the sand is my life spilt. I don't know what to do. If you could come here at 11.30 please do so tonight. I mar your life by trespassing ever on your love and kindness. I have asked Bosie to come tomorrow."[8]

It is clear from this that Wilde had now decided on a criminal prosecution, and the letter suggests he had come to this decision without consulting anyone else. If this is the case, Wilde could not later plausibly suggest, as he does in *De Profundis*, that he was forced into the prosecution by Bosie, although he certainly egged him on. When Robbie Ross turned up that night, Bosie was already there. He saw the opportunity to bring down his father, and was primed for battle. Ross was more circumspect. Like George Lewis, who later said that Wilde should have torn up the card, Ross saw dangers ahead. But Bosie was insistent, and the three agreed that Wilde should see Humphreys the following day. Thus, on

Friday 1 March, Wilde went round with Ross and Bosie to the solicitor's office to seek advice on charging Queensberry with criminal libel.

In prison, Wilde would recall, with loathing, "the memory of interminable visits paid by me to the solicitor Humphreys in your company when . . . you and I would sit with serious faces telling serious lies to a bald man, till I really groaned and yawned with ennui"[9] Humphreys asked him questions about the truth of Queensberry's allegations, Wilde denied them; and, by telling these lies, crossed his Rubicon. Confident that Queensberry had no hard evidence to back up his suspicion, he took a calculated gamble that the truth would not come out in court.

But the pleasure-seeking Oscar had less stomach than Bosie for the fight. His only real attempt to escape from the trap Queensberry had set was to plead that he could not afford the lawyers' fees, which was true. Bosie jumped in at once, claiming the Queensberry family would be happy to pay the costs to rid themselves of the embarassment of his father. Sybil's rich relations were dangled; they would be happy to pay any amount to bring Queensberry down. However, in a letter Wilde wrote immediately afterward to Ernest Leverson, Ada's husband, asking for £500 "on account", it was Percy, Bosie's brother, who was expected to pay half the costs, and Lady Queensberry the rest.

Bosie had no right to claim that his family would produce the money. Sybil had money, but not easily accessible, and it is far from certain that she had or would have given consent to use her money to defend Wilde. Where Percy was concerned, he had little money to offer. He might be the Douglas heir, but he was penniless and had no career. Bosie managed himself to scrape together £360,[10] but Wilde never saw a penny from the relatives. He offered to repay Leverson within 7–10 days, a desperate promise, for the Douglases proved a broken reed. However, he was in too weak a position to challenge Bosie. He solemnly denied the truth of the allegations and Humphreys closed the interview then and there, sensing an easy victory ahead. If Wilde was telling the truth, then from a purely legal point of view the case was clear-cut. And all those present agreed that this was so, though only Humphreys was unaware of the key point on which the case would turn: Wilde was lying.

The party proceeded to the police court and swore out a warrant for Queensberry's arrest. The following day a detective from "C" Division formally arrested the Marquis at his hotel. Queensberry was triumphant. "I have been trying to find Mr Oscar Wilde for nine or ten days", he told the inspector. "This thing has been going on for about two years".[11] Wilde and Bosie Douglas were also pleased with their work, thinking their prospects were immensely favourable. On 13 March, characteristically disregarding the effect of their actions on public opinion, they went for a week's holiday to Monte Carlo. When they returned, Humphreys, having heard that *Dorian Gray* would be put into the case, asked Wilde to find an expert witness to testify that it was not immoral. Wilde went to see Frank Harris, who agreed to stand by him, but was appalled to find Wilde had discovered that Queensberry had copies of his letters, for which he had paid blackmailers. Harris, an experienced journalist, advised Wilde that whatever the rights and wrongs of the case – it seems extraordinary, but the worldly wise Harris still imagined his friend was only "posing" as a homosexual – no jury would convict Queensberry for trying to protect his son. Wilde was sufficiently frightened to agree to meet Harris in the Café Royal the next day.

It was a momentous meeting. Wilde came to the meeting alone. For moral support, Harris had brought with him George Bernard Shaw. He had consulted contacts in the office of the Department of Public Prosecutions, with ominous results. They were convinced Wilde was guilty of indecent behaviour and that a prosecution would follow. Harris told Wilde: "Let us begin by putting the law courts out of the question. . . . Don't forget that if you lose and Queensberry goes free, everyone will hold that you have been guilty of nameless vice. Put the law courts out of your head. Whatever else you do, you must not bring an action for criminal libel against Queensberry. You are sure to lose it; you haven't a dog's chance . . . don't commit suicide".[12] Harris advised Wilde to drop the case, leave with Constance for Paris, and write to *The Times* to say he had fled because of the impossibility of getting a fair trial. He appealed to Shaw, who agreed with his advice. Faced with this solid advice from two experienced and intelligent friends, Wilde's resolve began to weaken.

At precisely the moment when Oscar was considering Harris's argument, however, Bosie joined the party. Harris repeated what he had told Wilde. Bosie immediately stood up and, without attempting to counter Harris's pessimistic views with reason, "cried, with his little white, venomous, distorted face, 'such advice shows you are no friend of Oscar's!'" and walked out. To Harris's astonishment, Wilde mechanically repeated Bosie's words: "It is not friendly of you Frank; it really is not friendly" and followed his lover out of the door. Harris turned to Shaw and asked if he had said anything in the heat of the argument which might have offended Oscar or Douglas? Shaw commented that he had not; he had nothing to reproach himself with. Both Bosie and Shaw later confirmed the accuracy of Harris's description of the scene and for once there is no tincture of suspicion that Harris was making up an improbable event.[13]

None of the four men involved ever forgot this meeting. Thirty years later, Bosie confirmed to Harris that he was afraid Wilde would throw up the case from cowardice and his one aim was to get Wilde out of the restaurant immediately. Bosie believed that he could win the case by demonstrating that his father was a monster. He did not grasp that in a libel case evidence of character was irrelevant: the only relevant facts were whether the statement was true, and uttered in the public interest. On both counts, Queensberry was unbeatable. Harris was correct in predicting that Queensberry would win. By marching Oscar Wilde out of the Café Royal, Bosie thought he was marching Oscar to a decisive victory, but he was taking him to disastrous defeat.

In early March, Oscar and Bosie were convinced they would win. This view was reinforced by a ranting letter Queensberry wrote to Percy's wife Minnie, nine days after being arrested and two days after being committed for trial:

> I have now in my possession a copy of a most odious work, suppressed on account of its utter filth, which will be produced at my trial to substantiate what I have said about this Oscar Wilde, who wrote it. In this same publication are two so-called poems, if filthy gibberish strung together can be called poetry, by Alfred and signed by his name, and headed "In Praise of Shame", and "Two Loves", the last ending up with the words – "I am the Love that Dare not Breathe [*sic*] its Name", meaning Sodomy. The story by Wilde is of a priest and a boy and of their unnatural and hideous love as they call it, Percy and his brother must have been mad to go into Court with this fellow. . . . If Percy saw this publication it might convince him of the utter folly of his, and of his brother backing this man up, when I am doing all in my power to keep Alfred out of it. He goes and throws himself on our swords that mean to hack the other fellow to pieces, and which we can do without touching Alfred. As I said, you must all be mad.
>
> Queensberry.[14]

The mistaken view that Wilde had written "The Priest and the Acolyte" bolstered his belief that Queensberry had little evidence to go on. Wilde could easily prove in court that he was not the author, a contention Queensberry had to withdraw when the issue came up in cross-examination. But even if Wilde had been right in assuming Queensberry had no evidence, the evident intention of Queensberry to claim he was defending his son, which Bosie found impossible to accept, placed him in an enormously strong position before a jury of Victorian men. Frank Harris understood this vital point, Oscar Wilde and Bosie Douglas never did.

Percy was bound to have told Oscar and Bosie about this letter, and it must have been a factor in the otherwise inexplicable move the two then made. They left for a holiday in Monte Carlo. To do this at a time when both sides were marshalling for a decisive legal action seems deeply irresponsible. The only rational explanation is that each took the view that, if the *Chameleon* was the strongest card Queensberry could play, the verdict was a foregone conclusion. But Queensberry was far more cunning than either imagined. He was delighted to be facing Wilde across a public courtroom. He now put an extensive detective network on the case, working behind the scenes with deadly efficiency, digging up the evidence that would damn Oscar Wilde forever.

* * *

Legal proceedings opened on 2 March with the magistrates' hearings. Wilde was outwardly confident, although Frank Harris had warned: "An English court of law gives . . . no assurance of a fair trial. I am certain that in matters of art and morality an English court is about the worst tribunal in the civilized world . . . all British prejudices will be against you. Here is a father, the fools will say, trying to protect his young son. If he has made a mistake, it is only through excess of laudable zeal. You would have to prove yourself a religious maniac in order to have any chance against him in England".[15] Queensberry knew this only too well. When asked by the magistrate whether he had anything to say, he replied: "I have simply, your worship, to say this. I wrote that card simply with the intention of bringing matters to a head, having been unable to meet Mr Wilde otherwise, and to save my son, and I abide by what I wrote".[16] Nevertheless, Wilde's legal advisors were confident, and even Queensberry's lawyers had doubts about the case.

George Lewis dropped out of Queensberry's team after the magistrate's committal proceedings on 2 March, and was replaced by a new solicitor, Charles Russell. Russell immediately hired a young barrister then making a formidable reputation. Edward Carson had rejected Russell's first approach, not because of his acquaintance with Wilde but because he thought Queensberry would lose. Carson's biographer, Marjoribanks, asserts that at this stage that there was nothing to go on but hearsay and the construction of certain books.[17] Carson's initial pessimism was understandable, but he was soon convinced Queensberry could win. Russell had set in motion an extensive detective network to turn up evidence against Wilde. This rapidly produced enough ammunition for the coming battle to convince Carson that success was possible. Carson took up the brief on the morning of 9 March, the date of the resumed hearing at the magistrates' court. He learned that the Savoy Hotel had put Russell's team in touch with Charles Parker, and that Parker had agreed to become a Crown witness and affirm that indecency with Wilde had in fact taken place.[18] Nevertheless, Carson was still inclined to believe his new client should plead guilty. The word of one man against that of another would not be enough.

Russell's team of detectives, however, was working with extraordinary efficiency – helped by Charles Brookfield, whose theatrical work gave him personal knowledge of Wilde's activities and who now intended to settle old scores. Brookfield induced the commissionaire at the Haymarket to provide the names and addresses of Wood and the other blackmailers who had used the Hyathincus letter. More importantly, he told the detective Littlechild to visit a prostitute who attributed the fall off in her business to the activities of Wilde and the rent boys. She told him to visit the home of Charles Taylor, in Chelsea. He did so, and discovered a kind of postbox with details of rent boys linked with Wilde.[19] On the basis of this evidence he found William Allen and Robert Clibborn in Broadstairs, followed by Wood, Walter Grainger, Alfonso Harold Conway and others. Queensberry's team were soon on the trail of Edward Shelley, Herbert Tankard (a page at the Savoy) and, most damagingly, Maurice Schwabe, nephew of the wife of the Solicitor General, Sir Frank Lockwood.[20]

Meanwhile, Frank Harris was sounding out the Public Prosecutor's office on the Wilde issue and discovered that "his guilt was said to be known and classified".[21] Yet the Prosecutor was not officially involved in the first trial, so could have no legal reason for investigating. Politicians and legal officials were following events closely even before the trial opened but had no right to intervene. However, their attention was focussed on the trial by personal connection. Certainly the fact that Schwabe was involved would soon be known to Lockwood, and through him Asquith, the Home Secretary, who knew Wilde. The Liberal political élite, then in government, had every reason to be deeply alarmed by events. Their alarm would increase after the Grand Jury stage.

Wilde's legal team responded to the involvement of Carson by employing a heavyweight of their own – Sir Edward Clarke, a formidable barrister who had made his name cross examining the Prince of Wales in the notorious Baccarat case. Humphreys brought Wilde to Clarke's chambers, where Clarke stated: "I can only accept this brief, Mr Wilde, if you can assure me on your honour as an English gentleman that there is not and never has been any foundation for the charges that are made against you".[22] Wilde forebore to tell him he was an Irishman, and solemnly stated that the charges were "absolutely false and groundless". Was this further proof of Wilde's arrogant belief in his own impregnability, or by now, mere braggadocio? Even as he lied, Queensberry's detectives were uncovering sufficient evidence to destroy him completely as a witness.

Rumours about Wilde were a major reason why Queensberry had decided to pursue his vendetta, and he had used the Rosebery connection to buttress his case. But the powers-that-be would not have been willing to allow the connection to the Prime Minister to become a matter for public speculation. An administrative error, however, now ensured the link became an open secret.

Criminal law required a Grand Jury to be empanelled to consider whether the evidence presented in the magistrates' court justified proceeding to a full High Court hearing. According to Marjoribanks in his *Life of Carson,* a French citizen who had lived in England for many years was empanelled by accident. Seeing the Wilde case was in the lists, he did not point out the error and thus heard all the evidence. Crucially, the letters of Queensberry were read out. These had not been read out in the magistrates' court, and would be treated with some delicacy by the High Court. However, in the privacy of the Grand Jury they were read out in full. Rosebery's name was mentioned. The Grand Jury proceedings were not reported in the British press, but the juror ensured the information reached France, from where it rapidly returned. Rosebery's name began to be linked to Wilde's in the bars and clubs of London. The Liberal Government, headed by the very same Lord Rosebery, could not fail to treat the rumours with mounting concern.

Disturbing though the rumours were, they were still insubstantial and of no importance unless Queensberry could show hard evidence against Wilde. By the end of March, he was in a position to do so. He had returned his plea of justification on 30 March and, when Wilde returned from France, his solicitor showed him the main evidence that the defence now planned to put before the court. It was a shattering blow, for it listed names, dates and places on which Wilde was alleged to have committed gross indecency, with ten men being specifically named. This was far worse than anything Harris had foreseen. A wise man at that stage would have thrown in the towel and fled abroad. Even though Oscar's friends still had no idea that the evidence was so damaging, they urged him to do just that. Two days before the trial was due to open at the Old Bailey, George Alexander urged him to go abroad. Wilde mockingly replied, "Everyone wants me to go abroad. I have just been abroad, and now I have come home again. One can't keep going abroad, unless one is a missionary, or, what comes to the same thing, a commercial traveller." It was a hollow jest.[23]

Yet Wilde appeared totally confident of victory. He took comfort from his seer, "the Sibyl Robinson", wiring "The Sphinx", Ada Leverson on 25 March that she prophesied "complete triumph".[24] Bosie stood behind Wilde, convinced that he would be allowed to testify as to his father's loathsomeness, and that Clarke had agreed to allow him to do so. Yet in law the issue of Queensberry's character was irrelevant, and Clarke claimed later that it had never arisen. When questioned on this point in 1929 he wrote that: "The question of Lord Queensberry's character was quite irrelevant to the case, and was never mentioned in my instructions or in consultation, and if an attempt had been made to give such evidence the judge would of course have peremptorily stopped it."[25] Clarke was correct. Queensberry's character was completely irrelevant. The issue was merely whether the evidence supported his allegations.

On the evening that the trial opened, 3 April, Wilde wired Ada Leverson to excuse him from dining, as: "We have a lot of very important business to do. Everything is very satisfactory".[26] And, indeed, the first day had gone well. Queensberry had pleaded not guilty, claiming the libel was true and was published in the public interest. Clarke presented Queensberry's letters with discretion, skirting around awkward questions involving notable personages. Clarke focussed on the Hyacinthus letter, which Wilde defended in cross-examination. Wilde claimed that he had told the editor of the *Chameleon* he thought "The Priest and the Acolyte" was indecent. He made it clear he had not written the story. Carson then cross-examined on his relationship with Bosie, the *Chameleon*, Wilde's Aesthetic philosophy, and *Dorian Gray*. While Carson focussed on literature, Wilde was on strong ground and his witticisms and moral stance on literature were favourably received by the court. He denied morality had any relevance to literature, commenting: "you might cross-examine me as to whether King Lear or a sonnet by Shakespeare was proper".[27] When Carson moved on to Wilde's relationship with Edward Shelley, however, there was a flash of temper – Wilde fussily objected to Carson calling Shelley an "office boy" – and a curious incident when Wilde was allowed to write down the name of a third person who had been present at dinner with him and Shelley in October 1892. The name Wilde wrote down was that of Maurice Schwabe – nephew-in-law to the Solicitor General, Frank Lockwood. While the jury did not know the name, it is inconceivable that the incident did not get back to Lockwood. Wilde parried questions about his relations with blackmailers and young men with ease, jesting when Carson called Alphonse Conway "a newspaper seller". "It is the first time I have heard of his connection with literature", mocked Wilde.[28] The court liked such sallies and press comment that evening favoured Oscar.

The following day, the tide turned. Carson doggedly pursued Wilde's interest in lower-class young men. Wilde responding that he liked youth of any class: "I recognize no social distinctions at all of any kind; and to me youth, the mere fact of youth, is so wonderful that I would sooner talk to a young man for half an hour than be even – well, cross-examined in court".[29] The court relished this, and Oscar became over-confident. Asked to identify a cigarette case as one he had given to Sidney Mavor, Wilde flippantly replied, "no, really, I could not. I have given so many that I could not recognize it."[30] Wilde was bored and, appearing able to counter Carson easily, lapsed into carelessness. Carson asked him about Bosie's servant, Walter Grainger, who had waited on Wilde in Bosie's rooms at Oxford. Carson asked: "Did you ever kiss him?" Wilde replied flippantly "Oh dear no. He was a particularly plain boy. He was, unfortunately, extremely ugly". It was the mistake Carson had been waiting for. Carson turned the tables on Wilde immediately:

"Was that the reason why you did not kiss him?" – "Oh, Mr Carson, you are impertinently insolent."

"Did you say that in support of your statement that you never kissed him?" – "No. It is a childish question."

"Did you ever put that forward as a reason why you never kissed the boy?" – "Not at all."

"Why, sir, did you mention that this boy was extremely ugly?" – "For this reason. If I were asked why I do not kiss doormats, I should say that I do not like to kiss doormats. I do not know why I mentioned that he was ugly, except that I was stung by the insolent question you put to me and the way you have insulted me throughout this hearing. Am I to be cross-examined because I do not like it?"

"Why did you mention his ugliness, I ask you?" – "Perhaps you insulted me by an insulting question."

"Was that a reason why you should say the boy was ugly?" (Here, the witness began several answers almost inarticulately. His efforts to collect his thoughts were not aided by Mr Carson's staccato repetition: "Why? why? why did you add that?") At last the witness answered: "You sting and insult me and try to unnerve me; and at times one says things flippantly when one ought to speak more seriously. I admit it."

"Then you said it flippantly?" – "Oh yes, it was a flippant answer".[31]

Up to this point Wilde had cruised through the court proceedings with a confident front, bluffing the jury into thinking he had nothing to worry about. But from this point onwards he was on the defensive, and with his confident façade disintegrating it became clear that his denials were those of a man now unsure of his ground. When the defence cross-examination of Wilde finished, Clarke discussed the letters from Wilde to Bosie, being hampered by Queensberry's deep emotion, for the first time shown from the dock. "Every now and then he turned to the man in the witness box [*Wilde*] and ground his teeth and shook his head at the witness in the most violent manner. Then, when the most pathetic parts of the letters came, defendant [*sic*] had the greatest difficulty, apparently, in restraining the tears which welled up in his eyes and forced him to bite his lips to keep them back".[32] Bosie had wished to present his father as a monster. But, as Harris had predicted, Queensberry came over as a man naturally defending his son against a threat of vice. When the prosecution closed its case in mid-afternoon and Carson opened for the defence, this was precisely his first point: "Lord Queensberry withdraws nothing . . . he has said or written. He has done all these things with premeditation and a determination, at all risks and hazards, to try to save his son. Lord Queensberry's conduct has been quite consistent throughout, and if the allegations made against Mr Wilde are correct, then, counsel submits, his Lordship was justified in taking any steps that would put an end to the disastrous acquaintance his son had formed."[33]

Carson attacked Alfred Taylor: "a most notorious character (as the police would tell the court). . . . Whether Taylor was a procurer in this sense, the fact remained that on Tuesday last (2 April) he was in company with Mr Wilde at the latter's house in Tite Street, and that he had not been produced by the prosecution. . . . Mr Oscar Wilde had undertaken to send Lord Queensberry to gaol, but it was remarkable that the only witness who could have supported Mr Wilde's asseverance of innocence had not been called".[34] Carson again spoke of *Dorian Gray* and the *Chameleon*, and came dangerously close to linking Bosie with the culture he was attacking by commenting: "There was in this same *Chameleon* a poem which showed some justification for the frightful anticipations which Lord Queensberry entertained for his son. Was it not a terrible thing that a young man on the threshold of life, who had for several years been dominated by Oscar Wilde, and had been "adored and loved" by Oscar Wilde, as the two letters proved, should thus show the tendency of his mind on this frightful subject? What would be the horror of any man whose son wrote such a poem?"[35]

Carson was close to asserting that Wilde had corrupted Bosie. It was a dangerous argument – for it opened Bosie to be accused of the same crimes as Wilde – and Carson rapidly moved on. "He [*counsel*] was not there to say anything had ever happened between Lord Alfred Douglas and Mr Oscar Wilde. God forbid! But everything showed that the young man was in a dangerous position in that he acquiesced in the domination of Mr Wilde – a man of great abilities and attainments. Lord Queensberry was determined to bring the matter to an issue; and what other way was open to him than that which he had chosen?"[36] Carson now focussed on the Hyacinthus letter, scorning the suggestion that it was a "prose poem" which had, uniquely, been turned into a sonnet because of its beauty. Wilde, he alleged, wanted to divert attention from this rather than any of the other four letters stolen precisely because it had fallen into the hands of blackmailers and he could not get it back. Carson argued that Wilde had helped send Wood to America to get rid of his damaging evidence. "No doubt, Mr Wilde hoped never to hear of him again. But, as a matter of fact, Wood would be examined by the jury".[37]

This was a body blow. Wilde was staggered to learn that Wood had been brought back from America. As Carson closed for the day, Clarke and his legal team had to face the fact that the next day renters and blackmailers would be brought into the witness box to testify against Wilde. That evening there were no brave assertions that everything was very satisfactory. Clarke considered the situation overnight and came to the conclusion all was lost. The following morning Wilde did not appear in court to hear Carson enumerating his relations with young men. He had been advised by Clarke to stay away while the barrister attempted damage limitation. One of Wilde's legal team, Matthews, came to him and told him: "If you wish it, Clarke and I will keep the case going and give you time to get to Calais". Wilde astonishingly replied that he would stay, though Robbie Ross urged him to accept the offer. Clarke meanwhile was conceding defeat as gracefully as he could.[38]

The barrister stopped Carson in full flight as he began his opening remarks. He addressed the judge coolly, accepting that: "Having regard to what has been referred to by my learned friend in respect to the matters connected with the literature and the letters, I feel we could not resist a verdict of not guilty in this case – not guilty having reference to the word 'posing'. I would ask to withdraw from the prosecution. I am prepared to submit to a verdict of not guilty. I trust this may make an end of the case."[39] The judge instructed the jury to find that Queensberry was justified in claiming that Wilde posed as a sodomite, and that his publication of the allegation was for the public benefit. The jury immediately found for a not guilty verdict. Queensberry, beaming with delight, was discharged. The crowd inside and outside the Old Bailey cheered him as he exited the court. Female prostitutes, it is said, danced on the pavements, gleeful that their competition might now be reduced.

Wilde now left the building. Accompanied by Percy and Bosie, he drove to the Holborn Viaduct Hotel, shadowed by Queensberry's detectives. They had lunch, and Oscar Wilde wrote to the *Evening News* that: "It would have been impossible for me to have proved my case without putting Lord Alfred Douglas in the witness box against his father. Lord Alfred Douglas was extremely anxious to go into the box, but I would not let him do so. Rather than put him in so painful a position I determined to retire from the case, and to bear upon my own shoulders whatever ignominy and shame might result from my prosecuting Lord Queensberry".[40]

This was a most unwise letter, emphasising as it did the link between Oscar and Bosie in such an unmistakable manner. However legally dubious it was, it suggested that Wilde had been convinced by Bosie Douglas that he could blacken his father's character and win the case. Wilde was now vulnerable and in shock. He cast desperately around for a way out, visiting George Lewis for advice. Lewis could only reply: "What is the good of coming to me now? I am powerless to do anything. If you had had the sense to bring Lord Queensberry's card to me in the first place, I would have torn it up and told you not to make a fool of yourself".[41] It was too late for such advice. Wilde's friends were now urgently advising flight. He sent Robbie Ross to cash a cheque for £200, which suggests that perhaps he was intent on going. But instead he went to the Cadogan Hotel and sat indecisively waiting for events. Robbie Ross and Reggie Turner urged him to take the train to Paris. Ross had seen Constance, who in her distress hoped that Oscar would go abroad. Wilde prevaricated, perhaps hoping that he would avoid prosecution.

As the tension mounted, Bosie left for the Commons to consult his cousin, George Wyndham, to see whether the government was considering prosecution. It was. The hunter had become the hunted. Having failed to clear himself of the allegation of "posing" as a sodomite, the issue had now become one of whether he had actually practised what he had preached. Charles Russell had made prosecution inevitable by sending the Queensberry papers to the Public Prosecutor the moment the trial ended. The politicians could not avoid acting. The papers were full of sensations, quoting Queensberry on his release as sending a rhetorical message to Wilde that "If the country allows you to leave, all the better for you. But if you take my son with you, I will follow you wherever you go and shoot you!"[42]

The government knew it could not allow Queensberry any latitude. With the Rosebery connection exposed, and the Solicitor General's nephew-in-law named as a member of Wilde's circle, the stakes were too high. Wilde had to be brought to book that afternoon. Immediately on receipt of the evidence, a representative of the Public Prosecutor sent it via Scotland Yard to the Bow Street magistrate, who received it around 3.30 p.m. Meanwhile, a group of senior politicians, including the Home Secretary Asquith, the Attorney General, Sir Robert Reid QC, and the Solicitor General, Sir Frank Lockwood, met to discuss the case. So senior a group could not have met without prior arrangement, and there can be little doubt that the fact that two of them were involved in Wilde's circle concentrated their minds. According to Mason, Asquith issued orders that wherever Wilde might be found he should be stopped.[43] It was, however, the Bow Street magistrate who actually issued the warrant.

Soon after five o'clock a reporter from the *Star*, Thomas Marlowe, came to the hotel and told Wilde he had seen a message on the press tapes that a warrant had been issued for his arrest. The blood drained from his face, but still he did not move.[44] He remained with Robbie Ross and Reggie Turner, drinking glasses of Hock and seltzer until, shortly after six o'clock, two detectives arrived, announcing that they held a warrant for Wilde's arrest on a charge of committing indecent acts. Oscar asked if he could write a letter and this request was granted. It was his last act as a free man, and he used it to write to Bosie. The letter contained the sad little message that: "I will be at Bow Street Magistrates Police Station to-night – no bail possible I am told. Will you ask Percy, and George Alexander, and Waller at the Haymarket, to attend to give bail. Will you also wire Humphreys to appear at Bow Street for me. Wire to 41 Norfolk Square, W. Also, come to see me. Ever Yours, Oscar".[45]

Wilde was then escorted out, his little knot of friends trailing behind, leaving the room empty. When Bosie arrived from the Commons he found only the glasses from which they had been drinking and the letter Wilde had left him. As he read it, he finally understood that, in the last twenty-four hours, his lover had reaped the whirlwind Frank Harris had predicted. Having refused to flee to safety, Wilde would now suffer the torture of public prosecution.

125–145
notes 248–249

SEVEN

The Trials of Oscar Wilde

Standing alone in the emptiness of the lounge of the Cadogan Hotel, Bosie Douglas now came face to face with the consequences of suing his father. He and Oscar had gambled on sending Queensberry to prison, had lost, and now faced disaster. Wilde was to be deserted by most of his friends as the crisis developed, but it is not the case that Bosie Douglas deserted him. He must have realised that he was now vulnerable to the backlash that was developing against Wilde's circle, yet he was wholly focussed on the fate that was now overwhelming his lover. While others rushed to save their skins, there is little doubt that Bosie showed absolute loyalty to Oscar, disregarding his own safety. The myth that Bosie was a Judas who betrayed Oscar in his hour of need – and was to betray him again in Naples – has no foundation in evidence. Bosie stayed in touch with Wilde until he was given no choice but to flee the country, and only ceased attempts at communicating briefly when it became clear that Wilde's prison regime would not allow it. To the confused mind and shattered ego of Oscar Wilde, however, it probably did not seem like that. Someone must have been to blame; and the bitter accusations of betrayal that followed have resounded down the years, regardless of the fact that they were not really justified.

Bosie's first action was to take a cab to Bow Street, where he found that Oscar had been locked up in a cell for the night. He was forbidden either to see him or to stand bail. The inspector on duty told him that even if bail were to be granted by a magistrate, he alone would not be allowed to stand surety. Bosie then followed Oscar's instructions, visiting the theatrical managers Alexander and Wallace at their theatres, the Haymarket and St James's, where Oscar's plays were running, asking them to stand bail. Both refused. It was becoming unwise to be associated with Wilde; panic-stricken, they took his name off the playbills. Shortly afterwards, the plays themselves folded.

Public animus against Oscar Wilde was now intense. The *Daily Telegraph* expressed a characteristic view in its editorial of Saturday 6 April. Looking back on the previous day's sensations, it described Queensberry as "this sorely provoked and cruelly injured father", and went on to report: "As for the prosecutor, whose notoriety has now become infamy, he made no appearance yesterday upon the scene, and he has since been arrested at the instance of the Treasury on a charge of a very grave character. This being so, as regards any further influence which he can exercise upon social, literary or artistic matters, and the contempt and disgust felt for such a character being fully met by the hideous downfall of the man and of his theories, we may dismiss the prisoner without further remark". The editorial continued to lambast Wilde for several more column inches, describing him as "the evil figure which disappears from London society".[1] Others expressed similar views with less eloquence. Among the telegrams of congratulation Queensberry received from around London's clubland was one bearing the pointed message "Every man in the City is with you. Kill the ******!"[2]

In this hysterical atmosphere, it is hardly surprising that Wilde's friends deserted him. Robert Ross had been named in reports of the arrest, and had to resign from several clubs. His mother insisted he go abroad and, to overcome his resistance, offered £500 for Wilde's defence. She also agreed to help Lady Wilde financially, now that Oscar's royalties would dry up.[3] Ross had no choice but to take himself off to Calais, before settling at Rouen. Reggie Turner and Maurice Schwabe also decamped. Robert Sherard, Ada and Ernest Leverson, and Frank Harris remained loyal, but most of Wilde's circle dropped away.

For Bosie, however, there was never any question of following their example. For a young man of only 24, the weeks following his father's acquittal were a test of fire from which he never flinched. He continued to seek to have Wilde bailed. The day after the arrest, Saturday 6th, he asked Constance Wilde's cousin, Adrian Hope, to help. Hope refused after "a most painful interview".[4] Bosie remained in the bosom of his family, but hardly with their sympathy. Presumably, they were pulling strings to keep him from joining Oscar in the dock. This was difficult, for while no-one was anxious to look too closely at the evidence against him, his loyalty to Wilde, expressed in daily visits to him in prison, appeared to invite such a fate.

Bosie was determined to stand by Wilde publicly. His family tried to defend him, but Bosie wished for no such defence. He sought desperately instead to find ways to defend his friend. Bosie visited Wilde every day, first at Bow Street then in Holloway, which was at the time a remand prison. They sat facing each other in a kind of box separated by a long corridor about a yard wide patrolled by a warder. Oscar was slightly deaf and had great difficulty hearing because of the babble from other boxes adjacent. As the two looked at each other, the tears rolled down Oscar's face. Oscar wrote to More Adey and Robert Ross on 9 April, wistfully commenting: "Bosie is so wonderful. I think of nothing else. I saw him yesterday"[5] and to Robert Sherard on 16 April, "I am ill – apathetic. Slowly life creeps out of me. Nothing but Alfred Douglas's daily visits quicken me into life, and even him I see only under humiliating and tragic conditions."[6]

The magistrates' court proceedings began on 6 April, continued on 11 April and concluded on the 19th with Wilde being committed for trial, the magistrate refusing bail on grounds which Bosie recklessly criticised in a letter to the *Daily Star*, condemning press and judicial prejudice against Wilde.

His courageous protests were futile. Wilde's legal team did not regard such public interventions as being helpful, and they renewed pressure to get Bosie out of the country. Sir Edward Clarke had volunteered to defend Wilde without fee, recognising that Wilde had no money. Indeed, Queensberry had demonstrated the savagery of his nature by demanding Wilde be driven into bankruptcy to pay his costs from the libel action. Queensberry knew Wilde was in debt and had no source of income now his plays had closed. It was pure malevolence that led Queensberry to unleash the bailiffs. Tite Street on 24 April saw a disgraceful knockdown sale of Wilde's effects with the maximum inefficiency and least return to the creditors. The manuscript of Wilde's *A Florentine Tragedy* was stolen in the mayhem. Queensberry was presumably pleased by this outcome, which had serious consequence for Wilde's wife and children. But Queensberry was now victorious, and demanding the spoils of war, whatever the cost to non-combatants.

In the courtroom, Wilde would face an unequal struggle. Charles Taylor was to be tried alongside Wilde. The fact that the two cases would be tried together tipped the odds against acquittal still further against Wilde. And, as the police court proceedings developed, witness testimony lengthened the odds still further. A largely unnoticed but crucial moment came when Atkins, describing a trip to Paris with Wilde, stated that he had seen Wilde in bed with a man, and named Schwabe, only to be cut short by the prosecuting counsel, Charles Gill. Schwabe's name had not been spoken in the first trial, Wilde being allowed to write it down. Lockwood could hardly fail to know now that his relative had been exposed. The stakes were rising for all concerned.

As the police court proceedings ground on, Wilde struggled to muster his defence with what resources he had. Robert Sherard raised his hopes that circles of artists in France would raise money for him, but even Sarah Bernhardt preferred to keep her distance, making promises to send money and fixing appointments to see Sherard, which she never kept.[7] Oscar's brother Willie was making life even more difficult by writing what Wilde called "monstrous letters" and indulging in public controversy which hurt Wilde deeply. By 23 April, with the trial pending, Wilde was deeply depressed and wrote to Ada Leverson after meeting his counsel – who advised a speedy trial – and Bosie, who wanted the trial put off: "I don't know what to do. My life seems to have gone from me. I feel caught in a terrible net. I don't know where to turn. I care less when I think that he is thinking of me. I think of nothing else."[8] In *De Profundis*, Wilde would blame Bosie Douglas bitterly for his fall. At the time, though, it is clear that only Bosie's love sustained him through his ordeal.

Wilde's legal team were right to advise an immediate trial; the longer the proceedings dragged on, the more Wilde's reputatation suffered. Bosie, however, believed to the end of his life that Oscar's lawyers were not committed to a wholehearted defence, which could have been won by a spirited exposure of Queensberry as a monster. Realistically, he had to let them take the course they advised, and give way to the pressure to go abroad. On 23 April, he saw Oscar in prison for the last time. Douglas later recalled that, on the day of their parting, Wilde kissed the end of his finger through an iron grating in the prison, and begged him not to alter his attitudes and conduct towards a fallen man.[9] It would be two and a half years across an immense gulf of suffering before they saw each other again.

On 24 April, Bosie took the train to Calais, where he was joined by Robbie Ross. Together, they agonised over the reports of the trial in the English newspapers which arrived each morning. Wilde, alone in London, faced his trial with a mixture of fatalism and fortitude, but at least had a role to play. Bosie could merely watch helplessly, with only searing memories to sustain him. From this point on, the relationship would be sustained by a shared agony made the more unbearable by the knowledge that their hated enemy had totally outfoxed them.

* * *

Queensberry now became a gloating spectre at the feast as Oscar Wilde, his morals and lifestyle were paraded in the dock. With the state now in charge of the prosecution, the Scarlet Marquis could sit back in court and observe, a malevolent presence that to the defendant seemed pure torture. Oscar appeared at Bow Street magistrates' court, charged with gross indecency under Section 11 of the Criminal Law Amendment Act of 1885. Although Queensberry had hinted at sodomy, a felony carrying a possible twenty-year sentence, Labouchère's Amendment did not require proof of penetration to secure a conviction. The crime of gross indecency was classed as a misdemeanour. This was an offence with a lower burden of proof and shorter sentence than a felony. Conviction required only the sworn testimony of one of the participants, which made it an easier charge to prosecute than sodomy, although the consequences were severe enough. The fact that the authorities chose to prosecute Wilde under this lesser Act suggests they were not certain they would get a conviction if a higher level of proof were required, or that they feared the public effects of a really severe sentence, or both.[10] In addition, it was perhaps thought possible that Wilde might name names, to the embarrassment of the Establishment.

Whatever machinations were going on behind the scenes, when Wilde was arrested on 5 April the warrant alleged the committal of "acts of gross indecency with various male persons on 20 March 1893 and divers other dates". It was further alleged that Wilde was associated with Alfred Taylor, who procured young men for Wilde. Taylor was arrested and brought into the court while the first hearing was taking place. Charles Parker and his brother William gave evidence against Wilde. Alfred Wood alleged impropriety with Wilde, but in the one ray of hope for Wilde's defence team, when Sidney Mavor gave evidence he denied any impropriety, to the surprise of the prosecution. This was owing to Bosie's intervention at an earlier stage in the hearing before going abroad. Bosie Douglas later claimed he had met Mavor in the corridor outside the Bow Street court and urged him to keep silent, appealing to class prejudice as Mavor was "a gentleman and a public school boy", unlike the majority of Oscar's boys.[11] Bosie also sent £50 to Taylor's defence lawyer to assist in his defence. He did not know Taylor, but was grateful he had not turned Queen's evidence. He was not inactive on Wilde's behalf.

While renters could damage Wilde, their evidence was legally dubious. The most serious allegations were by two workers at the Savoy Hotel, Antonio Migge, who testified that in March 1893 he saw a young man in Wilde's bed, and Jane Cotter. Their evidence was sufficient to have Wilde remanded and the magistrate, Sir John Bridges, refused bail.

Three magistrates' court hearings were required before the case could be committed to the Old Bailey, Wilde being called back on 11 and 19 April. When Parker came back to court on 11 April he was dressed in new clothes, allegedly bought by Queensberry.[12] The Marquis played no part in the trials of Oscar Wilde, but his presence hung over proceedings and outside the court the civil war in the Queensberry family continued. In what would nowadays be considered as grossly prejudicial behaviour, Queensberry conducted a vigorous intervention in the letters columns of the newspapers. While he himself did not appear for the prosecution, the prosecution case rested heavily on the evidence turned up by his detectives, a fact which was to be exploited by Wilde's defence. The evidence of the men who had known Wilde was tainted and thus questionable. At the second magistrates' hearing, Charles Parker admitted being involved in extortion after committing impropriety with a gentleman.[13] The prosecution could not control such dubious witnesses. Atkins let slip that he had seen Maurice Schwabe in bed with Wilde in Paris, and though he was immediately silenced by Gill, the prosecutor could not stop Atkins revealing that Wilde had not only put his arms around a waiter, but also embraced Lord Alfred Douglas.[14] Bosie's presence however remained on the margins of the trial, as both prosecution and defence sought to exclude him.

The prosecution's reliance on dubious evidence from men flirting with illegality weakened their case, particularly where Atkins was concerned. Atkins denied he had been involved in extortion with the blackmailer Burton, but this was a claim Clarke would completely destroy. Various servants gave evidence of the lives of Taylor, Atkins and others which served only to underline how furtive and unreliable these men were. Taylor was damaged in the third hearing by unshakeable testimony from Charlie Parker that he had gone through a mock ceremony of marriage with one Charles Spurrier Mason, Taylor playing the part of the bride, dressed in women's clothing. Wilde had known about this, as his letter to Mason in 1894 indicates. The evidence was sufficient for the magistrate to commit both Wilde and Taylor for trial at the Old Bailey. The charges were that they had conspired together to procure the commission by Wilde of acts of gross indecency with persons named, and that Taylor had attempted to commit an "abominable crime" on Charlie Parker. The joining of the two men's names on a charge of conspiracy materially damaged Wilde's chances of acquittal. On 23 April, the Grand Jury found true bills and trial was brought on.

The first trial of Oscar Wilde began on 26 April on twenty-five counts, all of misdemeanour. The one charge of felony, against Taylor, had been dropped. The indictment alleged gross indecency with men including the Parker brothers, Frederick Atkins, Sidney Mavor, Alfred Wood and Edward Shelley. There were five charges of conspiracy arising out of alleged procurement. The prosecution case was far from overwhelming as it depended on the testimony of renters, some of whom had been involved in blackmail. Clarke's defence strategy depended on exposing the weaknesses in the prosecutions' witnesses, and Wilde's lawyers set out to damage their credibility.

The first two days of the trial became a war of attrition between a prosecution cross-examination seeking to establish misconduct, and defence cross-examination seeking to damage credibility. Parker alleged indecent behaviour by Wilde at the Savoy Hotel, at Taylor's lodgings in Chapel Street, Wilde's rooms in St James' place, and even at Tite Street. Clarke responded by exposing Parker's role in the blackmailing of Wood and Allen, and suggested he had stolen clothes from an employer. Alfred Wood's examination took a similar form. He alleged indecencies with Wilde at Tite Street, while Clarke cross-examined him on the blackmail of a gentleman and how he came by the Hyacinthus and other letters. Atkins talked of his visit to Paris, and again implicated Maurice Schwabe as having been in bed with Wilde. Atkins claimed no impropriety took place with Wilde, but this did not save him from merciless cross-examination in which Clarke proved him to have been an experienced and cynical blackmailer and to have perjured himself in the course of his testimony. Edward Shelley was similarly undermined as a credible witness.[15]

However, the evidence of servants was not so tainted and as such was infinitely more dangerous to Wilde. A Mrs Mary Applegate testified that the bed at Atkins' lodgings was in a state after Wilde had visited. "The sheets were stained in a peculiar way", she said.[16] The testimony of the two servants at the Savoy was equally credible and very damaging to Wilde. On the third day, the masseur, Antonio Migge deposed that on entering Wilde's bedroom at the Savoy to administer massage he saw a boy sleeping in Wilde's bed. The masseur's evidence was confirmed by Jane Cotter, the chambermaid, although she also let slip that Lord Alfred Douglas occupied the adjoining room (it was Bosie's "boy" they had seen). Wilde's bedsheets were "stained in a peculiar way", in the time-honoured phrase, and she had drawn the attention of the housekeeper to them. This worthy, Mrs Annie Perkins, testified that she remembered the incident and "gave instructions accordingly".[17]

The testimony against Wilde was bad enough; worse, Bosie's name kept cropping up. On the first day at the Old Bailey, Parker admitted he had been introduced to Taylor by Lord Alfred Douglas.[18] Later in the day, Alfred Wood, recounting the story of the Hyacinthus letter yet again, revealed that, while living with Taylor, he had received a telegram from Bosie Douglas asking him to introduce himself to Wilde at the Café Royal.[19] Even before Jane Cotter mentioned Bosie's name, it was clear his was the shadow beyond the gate. To Bosie, reading the reports of the case in Calais and receiving letters from Wilde daily, what mattered was not that the case was going badly, but that the only untainted evidence was that of the servants at the Savoy. This increased his agony, for Bosie was troubled by private knowledge.

On the third day of the case, Bosie telegraphed Sir Edward Clarke offering "certain information" which, though prejudicial to himself, would help Wilde. He also offered himself again in the witness box, possibly to trot out the stories of the monstrous father whom he had wanted to portray in the libel trial. This would have been even less relevant to the charges Wilde now faced at the Old Bailey, so it is unlikely that this is in fact what Bosie intended to offer. In *De Profundis,* Wilde claimed that "the sins of another were being laid to my account", and that he could have "saved myself at his expense, not from shame, indeed, but from imprisonment".[20]

What Wilde meant by this has never been explained, but there can be little doubt that the other person at the Savoy was Bosie Douglas. It might have been a noble gesture, but it would have been suicidal for Bosie to have returned to testify that it was he, not Oscar, who had had a boy in bed at the Savoy. Even if Bosie could thus disprove the servants' evidence, it would not have changed the outcome. Clarke was mortified by the prospect of the emotionally unstable Douglas in the witness box. Recognising the absurdity of the position, Wilde, too, reinforced his prohibition. So, Douglas stayed in France, and the emotional bond between him and Oscar Wilde reached new levels of intensity as his personal anguish and sense of helplessness intensified.[21]

Doggedly, Clarke fought a steadfast rearguard action against the state's witnesses, with some success. On the fourth day, the prosecution withdrew the conspiracy charges. Clarke had argued for this, partly to get the two cases heard separately, and partly to allow Wilde to go into the witness box. The latter move could now be made. Clarke now put the literary evidence into the frame and this turned into a discussion of the *Chameleon* and, in particular, the poems of Alfred Douglas. Gill cross-examined on the poem "Two Loves", and this sparked Wilde into life. When Gill put the question, "What is the 'Love that Dare not Speak its Name'?", Wilde burst into eloquence, describing:

> a great affection of an elder for a younger man, as there was between David and Jonathan, such as Plato made the very basis of his philosophy, and such as you find in the sonnets of Michael Angelo and Shakespeare. It is that deep spiritual affection that is as pure as it is perfect. It dictates and pervades great works of art like those of Shakespeare and Michael Angelo, and those two letters of mine, such as they are. It is in this century misunderstood, so much misunderstood that it may be described as the "Love that Dare not Speak its Name", and on account of it I am placed where I am now. It is beautiful, it is fine, it is the noblest form of affection. There is nothing unnatural about it. It is intellectual, and it repeatedly exists between an elder and a younger man, when the elder has intellect, and the younger man has all the joy, hope and glamour of life before him. That it should be so, the world does not understand. The world mocks at it and sometimes puts one in the pillory for it.[22]

This was magnificent, and produced a spontaneous burst of applause from the public gallery, mixed with some hissing. It made an unforgettable impression on those who heard it, and summed up the essence of what Oscar Wilde thought his relationship with Bosie Douglas to be. Max Beerbohm in the gallery heard it and wrote to Reggie Turner that Oscar had been superb. Wilde gained confidence, and his denials of the evidence of the witnesses, notably those at the Savoy, were delivered with emphasis. He denied he suspected anything abnormal in Taylor's life, and dismissed a letter from Mavor asking to break off the relationship as "impertinent". He denied, too, having anything to do with Bosie's poems.

This at last gave Clarke something to build on, and his final address to the jury developed the theme of unreliable witnesses with effect. "As to the affection which Mr Wilde has expressed in the letters which have been put in, he has himself described it as a pure and true affection, absolutely unconnected with, alien to, irreconcilable with the filthy practices which this band of blackmailers you have heard has been narrating".[23] The point about blackmailers was telling. Clarke contrasted Wilde's openness with the witnesses set against him, though with Shelley he dwelt on his hysterical personality. The testimony of the servants at the Savoy was ridiculed as unreliable, and when Clarke sat down after an emotional appeal to the jury to put the circumstances of the trial out of their minds there was a murmer of appreciation. Wilde wrote a note of thanks. Gill now stood up, cleverly countering the charge of tainted evidence by pointing out that the men in the case were accusing themselves of "shameful and infamous acts, and this they would hardly do if it were not the truth".[24] The judge interrupted his speech to strike out the charges referring to Sidney Mavor, which had been denied. Nevertheless, the charge sheet against Wilde and Taylor remained formidable.

While the trial was grinding on, Wilde wrote to Bosie every day. On the evening of 29 April, Oscar wrote to Bosie from Holloway prison a moving statement of his love:

> My dearest boy,
> This is to assure you of my immortal, my eternal love for you. To-morrow all will be over. If prison and dishonour be my destiny, think that my love for you and this idea, this still more divine belief, that you love me in return will sustain me in my unhappiness and will make me capable, I hope, of bearing my grief most patiently. Since the hope, nay rather the certainty, of meeting you again in some world is the goal and the encouragement of my present life, ah! I must continue to live in this world because of that. . . .
>
> I am so happy that you have gone away! I know what that must have cost you. It would have been agony for me to think that you were in England when your name was mentioned in court. I hope you have copies of my books. All mine have been sold. I stretch out my hands towards you. Oh! may I live to touch your hair and your hands. I think that your love will watch over my life. If I should die, I want you to live a gentle peaceful existence somewhere, with flowers, pictures, books, and lots of work. Try to let me hear from you soon. I am writing you this letter in the midst of great suffering; this long day in court has exhausted me. Dearest boy, sweetest of all young men, most loved and most lovable. Oh! wait for me! I am now, as ever since the day we met, yours devoutly and with an immortal love,
> Oscar[25]

These sentiments had the profoundest effect on Bosie. In his *Autobiography* he would suggest that before the trials his passion for Wilde was cooling, but that the trials rekindled the fire. It is certainly clear that the bond between the two men was intensified by the enforced parting and suffering of the trials. The idea that Bosie betrayed Wilde by leaving him to his fate is pernicious, particularly as there is abundant evidence that he obeyed the injunction given here to wait for Wilde. This fixed resolution and his desire to defend Wilde against his enemies would guide his course for the next two and a half years.

The trial continued towards an inconclusive draw. The judge summed up the charges in four questions:

1. Do you think that Wilde committed indecent acts with Edward Shelley and Alfred Wood and with a person or persons unknown at the Savoy Hotel or with Charles Parker?
2. Did Taylor procure or attempt to procure the commission of these acts or any of them?
3. Did Wilde and Taylor or either of them attempt to get Atkins to commit indecencies?
4. Did Taylor commit indecent acts with Charles Parker or William Parker?

The jury retired on 1 May from 1.30 to 5.15, when they reported that they had agreed to a negative on question three, but could not agree on the remainder. They were discharged and a re-trial ordered. The judge refused bail, but, on 3 May, Willie Matthews, acting for Wilde, convinced Judge Pollock in chambers that in a trial for a misdemeanour bail had to be granted. The judge fixed a sum of £5,000. Wilde was required to provide half, with two others providing sureties. One was Percy Douglas, finally fulfilling his promises of financial support. The other was the Revd Stewart Headlam, a Church of England vicar and early Fabian socialist, barely known to Wilde but an admirer of Wilde's demeanour and a critic of the public mania against him. A mob threatened to stone his house because of this action. While Wilde waited for a decision, he wrote to Ada Leverson on 3 May, commenting in passing that he had had no letter from "Fleur-de-Lys" – one of two pet names he used for Bosie – and that "I wait with strange hunger for it". Later the use of this alias would infuriate Wilde immeasurably. Two letters arrived the following day, and he was visited by Frank Harris.[26] In this way the time passed until Travers Humphreys carried out the formalities for bail at Bow Street on 7 May and Wilde was then released.

Queensberry's reaction to this showed him at his most monstrous. Wilde and Percy Douglas drove to the Midland Hotel, St Pancras, where Oscar took rooms. He was about to sit down to dinner when the manager asked him to leave, as a mob had gathered outside. The mob is generally thought to have been paid by Queensberry. Wilde sought refuge in hotels across North London, but everywhere the mob followed, threatening the manager of one hotel to "sack the house and raze the street if you stay here a moment longer".[27] Terrified and exhausted, Wilde shook off his pursuers and made for his mother's house, arriving at midnight. His brother let him in and later testified that he collapsed across the threshold "like a wounded stag".[28] Alas, the pursuit by Queensberry's thugs was not the worst of the ordeal Oscar Wilde was facing. He would now be prosecuted by politicians determined to secure a conviction. The government took the prosecution out of the hands of Charles Gill, and put it in the hands of the Solicitor General, Sir Frank Lockwood. Lockwood had both political and personal reasons for pursuing Wilde to the bitter end.

* * *

The decision to prosecute Wilde and Taylor a second time was not uncontroversial, particularly as the prospect of the Solicitor General involving himself in a relatively minor case, however notorious, seemed an excessive use of government power. Lockwood was approached by persons wishing to see the prosecution abandoned, notably Edward Carson, who visited Lockwood to ask "Cannot you let up on the fellow now? He has suffered a great deal". Lockwood replied: "I would, but we cannot, we dare not. It would at once be said both in England and abroad, that owing to the names mentioned in Queensberry's letters, we were forced to abandon it."[29] Queensberry's malign shadow again hovered over the proceedings.

The names mentioned in Queensberry's letters were at first sight marginal – at least those read out in court. Only one letter read out actually mentioned names of distinguished personages: this was the letter of 6 July 1894 to his father-in-law, Montgomery, ranting about Wilde being a "damned cur and coward of the Rosebery type" and that Sybil had been responsible for him being denied an English peerage while Drumlanrig received one, to wit: "I am now fully convinced that the Rosebery–Gladstone–Royal insult that came to me through my other son, that she worked that. . .".[30]

None of this was potentially incriminating in terms of the charges against Wilde, and it was smoothly covered over by Carson with the comment:

> It had been suggested that the names of those distinguished persons were in some way or other mixed up in Lord Queensberry's letters with the charges against Mr Wilde. The references were of a purely political character, arising out of the fact that the late Lord Drumlanrig was made a member of the House of Lords, of which his father was not a member. Rightly or wrongly, Lord Queensberry felt aggrieved that an honour should have been conferred on his son which was not given to him. That was how the names of eminent politicians and statesmen came to be mentioned.[31]

This was plausible, and disposed of the Rosebery issue as far as the press was concerned. Anyone who knew the correspondence which had not been read out in court, particularly Queensberry's letter of 1 November 1894 after the death of Drumlanrig, knew there was more to the issue than just Drumlanrig's peerage. Queensberry's hysterical attack on "Montgomerys, the Snob Queers like Rosebery and certainly Christian hypocrite Gladstone . . . that cur and Jew friend (?) Liar Rosebery. . ." showed that it was not an English peerage that was on his mind. Given Queensberry's attacks on Rosebery, Alfred Montgomery must have passed this on to his friends in the Liberal hierarchy. Thus, even had the rumours about Queensberry's attacks on Rosebery not circulated in the London clubs, the Liberals could have done little to avoid prosecuting Wilde a second time. Queensberry had publicly threatened to horsewhip Rosebery when Foreign Secretary. He would not stop at attacking Rosebery even though he was now Prime Minister.

A mysterious episode took place two days before Wilde was released on bail. This was when Queensberry visited Holloway prison. *Reynolds's News* reported that "the object of the visit . . . has not transpired, but he had an interview with the chief prison officials. Oscar Wilde and Taylor apparently knew nothing of the visit of his lordship, who did not remain at the prison long".[32] Asquith as Home Secretary presumably knew about it, and probably passed the news to Rosebery. The Prime Minister was suffering from one of his mysterious ailments during the Wilde trials. Early in March, two days after Queensberry's second appearance at Marlborough Street, when the names of "exalted personages" were first mentioned, Rosebery was afflicted while attending Queen Victoria. He became dizzy, the Queen insisted he sat down, but the problem persisted. Rosebery's doctor considered the illness "obstinate and puzzling" and thought it might be digestive, despite the soundness of Rosebery's appetite. The most obvious symptom was lack of sleep – Rosebery could only manage three or four hours a night – and nervous debility. On 13 May, Rosebery went on a sea cruise in an Admiralty yacht. He was somewhere off the sourthern coast of England when the second trial of Wilde and Taylor opened.

While the prosecution assembled its case, Wilde floundered, assailed by contradictory advice on what he should do. He was in very poor shape, physically and mentally, particularly while staying with Willie and his mother. Both were determined Oscar should stay, stand trial, and suffer a glorious martyrdom. His stay at the family home in Oakley Street made Wilde deeply depressed and he turned to drink. Robert Sherard discovered him lying on a camp bed with a flushed and swollen face, his voice broken and other signs of heavy drinking. Oscar asked why he had not brought him poison? Wilde was rescued from this misery by Ada Leverson, who put him up in the children's nursery at her home in Courtfield Gardens. There, he received more well-meaning entreaties to skip the country. Percy told Headlam that he would stand surety for all the money if he would flee – testimony to the good nature of at least one of the Queensberry family. Constance Wilde came to Courtfield Gardens and pleaded with her husband to flee, and Ada Leverson added her voice to hers. Oscar was obdurate. He had a very private reason for not fleeing, to which Frank Harris now became privy.

Harris took Oscar to dinner and outlined his idea for a victory strategy. He wanted to draw a plan of the Savoy Hotel, show that the maids could not have seen Wilde in bed with a boy, and thus destroy the strongest evidence against him. But the maids had seen a man in bed with a boy, and that man was Bosie. . . . At this, Oscar refused point-blank, also declining to embark on the steam yacht that Harris claimed to have ready to sail for the continent.[33] On 20 May, the day the third trial opened, Oscar wrote passionately to Bosie: "Love me always, love me always. You have been the supreme, the perfect love of my life; there can be no other. I decided that it was nobler and more beautiful to stay. We could not have been together. I did not want to be called a coward or a deserter. A false name, a disguise, a hunted life, all that is not for me, to whom you have been revealed on that high hill where beautiful things are transfigured."[34]

Despite the melodramatic note, these were noble sentiments which had a profound effect on Bosie. They were to destroy Wilde utterly.

As the trial came on, the letters passing between Oscar and Bosie became more fraught in their declarations of love. Bosie recalled in his *Autobiography* that "the emotion of the great crisis fanned the waning fires of our devotion to each other".[35] Whether the devotion had been waning is unknowable: certainly, the fires now glowed ever brighter. Bosie wrote in intimate terms shortly before the trial, urging Wilde to keep up his spirits and that he continued to think of him night and day, signing himself loving and devoted – simple but heartfelt sentiments.[36] Wilde was far more eloquent. In his letter of 20 May his usual controlled diction broke down into something close to bathos, as he faced the reality that his chances of acquittal were near zero. Part of the letter reads:

> It is perhaps in prison that I am going to test the power of love. I am going to see if I cannot make the bitter waters sweet by the intensity of the love I bear you. I have had moments when I thought it would be wiser to separate. Ah! moments of weakness and madness! Now I see that it would have mutilated my life, ruined my art, broken the musical chords which make a perfect soul. Even covered in mud I will praise you, from the deepest abysses I will cry to you. In my solitude you will be with me. I am determined not to revolt but to accept every outrage through devotion to love, to let my body be dishonoured so long as my soul may always keep the image of you. From your silken hair to your delicate feet you are perfection to me. Pleasure hides love from us but pain reveals it in its essence. . . .[37]

This was a comforting illusion. Wilde was soon to discover that pain did not reveal love, and that bitter waters could not be made sweet by emotion.

* * *

On 20 May, Oscar and Alfred Taylor were put on trial again at the Old Bailey. Sir Edward Clarke applied for separate trials, as there were now no conspiracy charges against the two men, and won that point. Alas, the prosecution then applied for the trial of Alfred Taylor to be heard first, and the judge, Mr Justice Wills, overruled Clarke's justified complaint that this would leave Oscar Wilde in an exposed position. Taylor's guilt was easily established, and in two days he was convicted of indecency, though the jury could not agree on the charges of procuring – technically, the only ones linking Taylor to the Wilde case. The judge decided to postpone sentence until after the Wilde case had been heard, and also decided to have a fresh jury to hear the evidence against Wilde.

Queensberry was delighted by the verdict against Taylor. He had been in court to hear the jury's decision, and went to the post office at the bottom of St James' Street to send a telegram to his daughter-in-law. For some time he had given up insulting Percy, choosing to goad Minnie as a way of getting at the now hated son who had bailed Oscar Wilde and attended the Old Bailey in his support. The telegram bore the crudely offensive message: "Must congratulate on verdict. Cannot on Percy's appearance. Looked like a dug up corpse. Fear too much madness of kissing. Taylor guilty. Wilde's turn to-morrow".[38]

Hardly had this malicious message been transmitted than Queensberry, marching up St James' Street, spotted Percy walking some one hundred yards away. What happened next made the front page of every popular paper in London. Queensberry claimed Percy charged at him, pushing him up against a shop window and shouting at the top of his voice. Percy claimed he walked up to his father and respectfully asked him to stop sending offensive material to his wife. Queensberry did not reply except to blow a raspberry. A moment later the two were fighting: a magistrate subsequently decided that the Marquis struck the first blow. A crowd collected, a PC Morrell separated them, but the two aristocrats continued their fight across the road and other police arrived to arrest them. The following day, the two men were bound over at Great Marlborough Street to keep the peace for six months. The Queensberry family had again demonstrated their capacity for bizarre behaviour.[39]

For Queensberry, however, the barroom brawler, this was merely an interlude in the serious business of bringing down Oscar Wilde. This entered its final stage the following day, 22 May 1895, when Wilde appeared alone in the dock at the Old Bailey. The trial followed the course of the first one. It became clear that the two main prosecution witnesses, the brothers Parker, were being maintained at Chiswick under the care of a Crown detective. It also appears that all the witnesses had been receiving £5 per week from the beginning of Wilde's prosecution of Queensberry.[40] The radical paper *Reynolds's News*, which had heard of the payments from police officers, was alone in being sympathetic to Wilde: all other papers were hostile, the *National Observer* branding Wilde "the High Priest of the Decadents".

The case briefly swung towards Wilde when the major Crown witness, Edward Shelley, was ruled out by the judge as an accomplice whose evidence was not tenable unless corroborated.[41] As Shelley was the only major witness testifying to indecency who was not a renter or blackmailer, this was a victory. But in the absence of a strategy to discredit the other, more credible witnesses, the servants, it was only a temporary reprieve. Clarke attacked the testimony of the Savoy witnesses, notably Jane Cotter, the maid, who had to admit she was shortsighted and could not be sure who had been in the bed with whom, but while this created doubt it did not discredit the servants' testimony. Above all, he could not deal with the intensity of Lockwood's attack, which ruthlessly dragged up every piece of evidence against Wilde. On the crucial testimony of the Savoy witnesses, for instance, he asked why, if there was no boy in Wilde's bed, Lord Alfred Douglas had not been called to testify as he had had the adjoining room?[42] This made a clear impression on the jury. Lockwood may well have realised there was no chance of Bosie appearing, but it was an effective blow against Wilde. Bosie, it must be emphasised, had wished to give precisely the testimony Lockwood referred to, but Oscar Wilde and his defence team were adamant this would not be allowed.

Lockwood had no scruples and was perfectly willing to put the letters from Wilde to Douglas, and the relationship itself, into the account against Wilde. As he did not, it is frequently assumed that the Crown had done a deal with Queensberry to shield Bosie. Gill, in the first trial, had certainly behaved as if this was so. He had consulted Hamilton Cuffe, the Director of Public Prosecutions, and wrote on 19 April:

> I have considered the question as to whether a prosecution ought to be instituted against Lord Alfred Douglas . . . and have come to the conclusion that no proceedings should be taken upon the evidence we have in the statements of the different witnesses. Having regard to the fact that Douglas was an undergraduate at Oxford when Wilde made his acquaintance – the difference in their ages – and the strong influence that Wilde has obviously exercised over Douglas since that time, I think that Douglas, if guilty, may fairly be regarded as one of Wilde's victims. . . . Comments will no doubt be made as to Douglas not being prosecuted, but these comments are made by people who do not understand or appreciate the difficulties of proving such a case.[43]

While Gill felt that Douglas was beyond prosecution and largely kept him out of the second trial, whether by arrangement with Queensberry or not, Lockwood had no compunction about using the connection to blacken Wilde's character. Bosie's name repeatedly occurs in this trial. Alfred Wood affirmed it was Bosie who introduced him to Wilde and the now notorious letters from Wilde to Bosie were raked over thoroughly. Jane Cotter deposed that Wilde and Douglas had occupied adjacent rooms at the Savoy, 361 and 362. Lockwood cross-examined Wilde mercilessly on his relationship with Douglas and the letters between them.[44] During this cross-examination Queensberry stood at the back of the court, staring at Wilde in the dock and increasing his sense of nightmare: the Scarlet Marquis had never been far from his thoughts and was a lowering, menacing presence. "Even when he was not there, or was out of sight", Wilde was to write in *De Profundis*, "I used to feel conscious of his presence, and the blank dreary walls of the courtroom . . . seemed to me at times to be hung with multitudinous masks of that great apelike face".[45] The presence re-occurred on the following day, Saturday 25 May, the final day of the trial. Queensberry had come to savour his victory.

Lockwood was in devastating form in his final address to the jury. On the Hyathincus letter, he commented: "I contend that such a letter found in the possession of a woman from a man would be open to but one interpretation. How much worse is the inference to be drawn where such a letter is written from one man to another."[46] He dismissed the argument that blackmailers were not to be believed by arguing that unless there were men prepared to pay for the services of renters, there could be no blackmail. He denied that "Mr Russell, Lord Queensberry's solicitor, or any of the representatives of the Crown, had given fee or reward to the youth who gave evidence", though he admitted to precautions against witness tampering.[47] It was an impressive performance, and in its handling of the relationship between Wilde and Douglas it was exceedingly ominous. The references to Bosie Douglas were so pointed that, in his summing-up, the judge was forced to refer to them. He argued in terms that were dangerously double-edged:

> It was impossible in dealing with Wood's case . . . to avoid dealing also with Lord Alfred Douglas. Lord Alfred was not present, and was not a party to those proceedings. . . . Anything which his lordship [*the judge*] would have to say to Lord Alfred Douglas's prejudice

Oscar Wilde, about 1890. Photographer unknown. (By kind permission of Merlin Holland)

Three Punch *cartoons satirising Wilde:*

The Six-Mark Tea-Pot: "Aesthetic Bridegroom" exclaims "It is quite consummate, is it not?" to which "Intense Bride" replies: "It is indeed! Oh, Algernon, let us live up to it!"

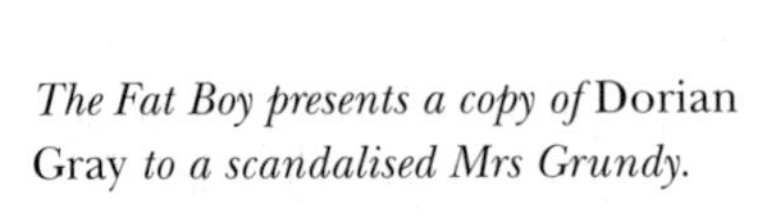

The Fat Boy presents a copy of Dorian Gray *to a scandalised Mrs Grundy.*

Maudle on the Choice of a Profession: "How consummately lovely your son is, Mrs Brown!"
The dialogue concludes with a near-libellous double entendre: *"Mrs Brown determines that at all events her Son shall not study Art under Maudle."*

Lord Alfred Bruce Douglas. Bosie, photographed by George Beresford. (National Portrait Gallery)

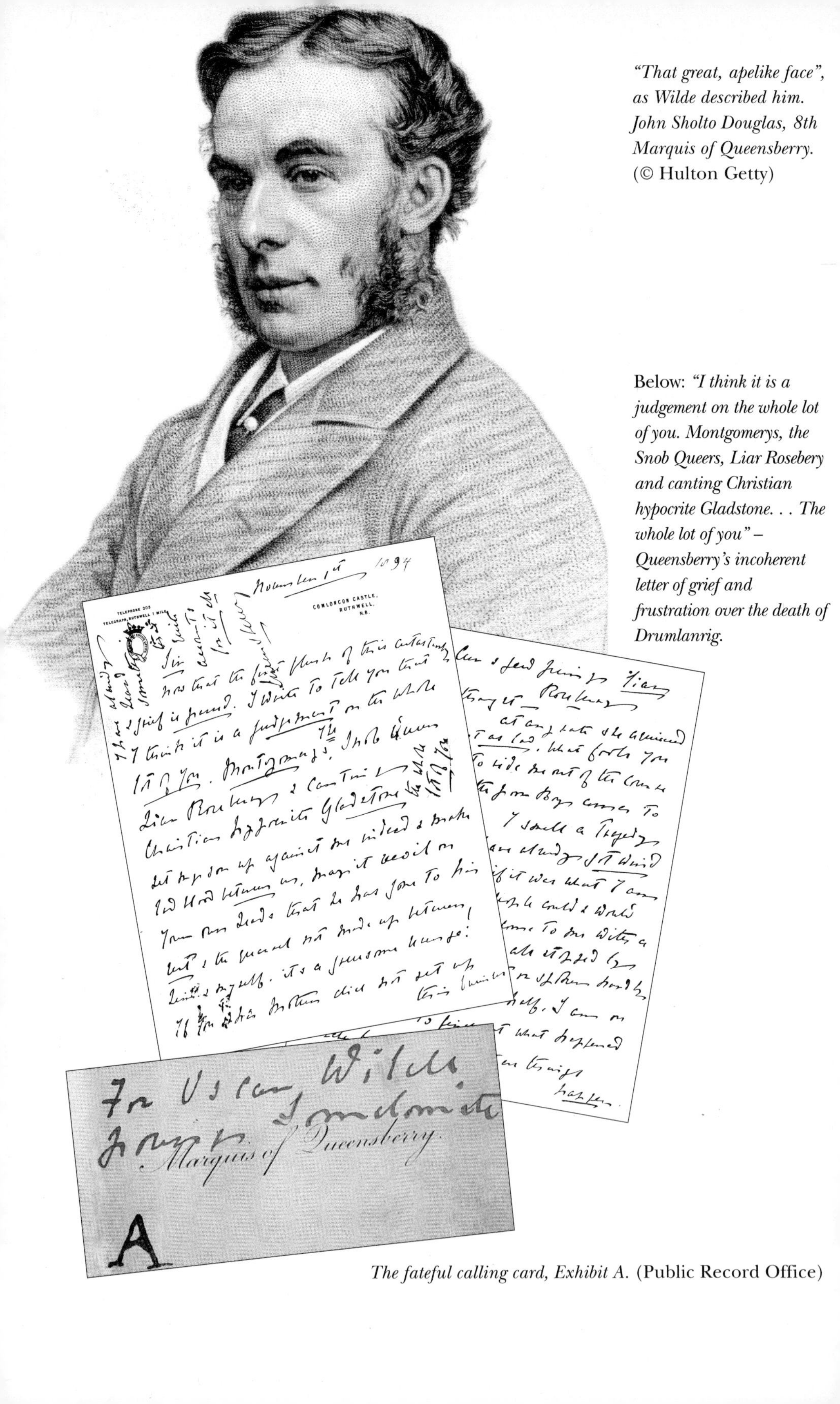

"That great, apelike face", as Wilde described him. John Sholto Douglas, 8th Marquis of Queensberry. (© Hulton Getty)

Below: *"I think it is a judgement on the whole lot of you. Montgomerys, the Snob Queers, Liar Rosebery and canting Christian hypocrite Gladstone. . . The whole lot of you" – Queensberry's incoherent letter of grief and frustration over the death of Drumlanrig.*

The fateful calling card, Exhibit A. (Public Record Office)

Constance Wilde with Cyril. (By kind permission of Merlin Holland)

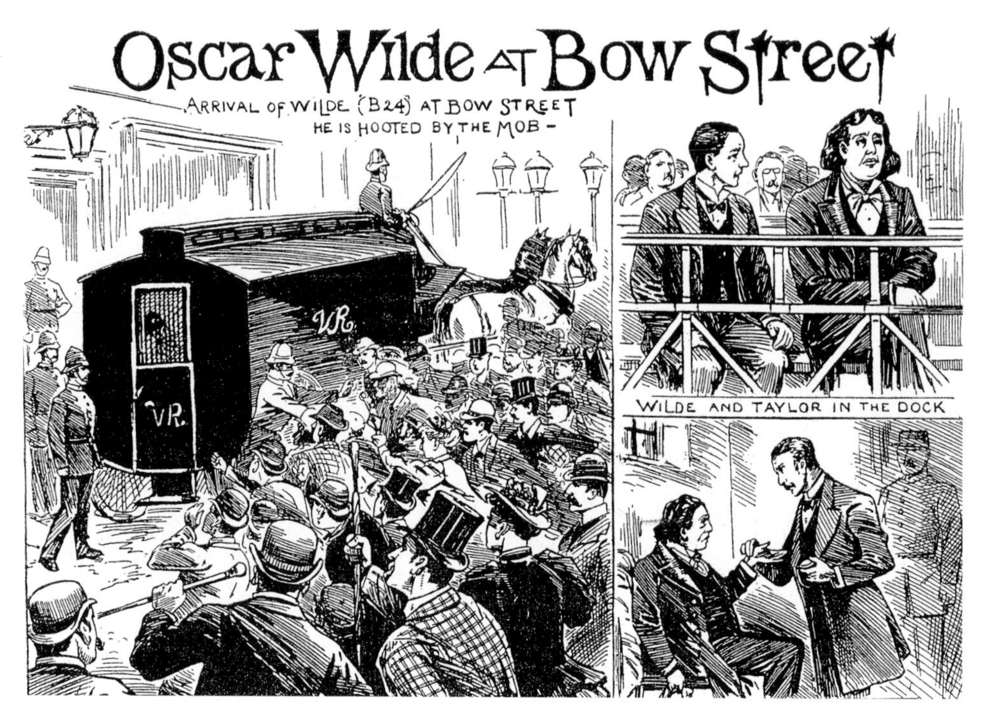

Two cartoons from Police News, Law Courts *and* Weekly Record, *20 April 1895, showing the arrival at Bow Street, Wilde and Taylor in the dock and Wilde ill in prison, and the famous punch-up between Queensberry and his son, Percy, following which the duelling aristocrats were bound over to keep the peace, 1 June 1895.*

Even the worldly Frank Harris was equally blind to the reality of Wilde's sexuality, until the trials disabused him. (© Corbis)

Arthur Ransome and companion outside the Old Bailey, April 1913. (© Corbis)

Lady Asquith. Margot Tennant, a Wilde supporter, was suspected of having Decadent tendencies of her own. (© Corbis)

"Liberal" reformer and author of the Blackmailers' Charter, Henry Labouchère MP. Wilde listed him as one of his "three heroes". (Punch)

Alfred Taylor. Thumbnail sketch from the court report in Reynolds's Newspaper, *21 April 1895.*

The Hotel d'Alsace, Paris. Not quite the style Oscar was accustomed to, but the proprietor, M. Jean Dupoirier, was kind to him during his last weeks. (© Corbis)

> would arise simply out of facts which had transpired in the course of the evidence. He was anxious, too, to say nothing in the case of a young man like this, who was just on the threshhold of life, which might to a great extent blast his career. His family seemed to be a house divided against itself. But even if there was nothing but hatred between father and son, what father would not try to save his son from the associations suggested by the two letters from the prisoner to Lord Alfred Douglas? His lordship would avoid saying whether those letters seemed to point to actual criminal conduct or not. . . . In itself, the letter produced by the prosecution might be consistent with perfect innocence, and it was not safe to rely upon the letter alone. . . .[48]

This was so inconclusive that, before the jury retired, the following exchange took place between the foreman and the judge:

Foreman: In view of the intimacy between Lord Alfred Douglas and Wilde, was a warrant ever issued for the apprehension of Lord Alfred Douglas?
Judge: I should think not. We have not heard of it.
Foreman: Was it ever contemplated?
Judge: Not to my knowledge. A warrant would in any case not be issued without evidence of some fact, of something more than intimacy. I cannot tell, nor need we discuss that, *because Lord Alfred Douglas may yet have to answer a charge*. He was not called. There may be a thousand considerations of which we may know nothing that might prevent his appearance in the witness box. I think you should deal with the matter upon the evidence before you.
Foreman: But it seems to us that if we are to consider these letters as evidence of guilt, and if we adduce any guilt from these letters, it applies as much to Lord Alfred Douglas as to the defendant.
Judge: Quite so. But how does that relieve the defendant? Our present enquiry is whether guilt is brought home to the man in the dock. We have got the testimony of his guilt to deal with now. *I believe that to be the recipient of such letters and to continue the intimacy is as fatal to the reputation of the recipient as to the sender*, but you have really nothing to do with that at present. [*Author's emphasis*]

The court then adjourned for lunch. Immediately after lunch the judge returned to the subject, commenting:

> There is a natural disposition to ask, "Why should this man stand in the dock, and not Lord Alfred Douglas?" But the supposition that Lord Alfred Douglas will be spared because he is Lord Alfred Douglas is one of the wildest injustice – the thing is utterly and hopelessly impossible. I must remind you that anything that can be said for or against Lord Alfred Douglas must not be allowed to prejudice the prisoner; and you must remember that no prosecution would be possible on the mere production of Wilde's letters to Lord Alfred Douglas. Lord Alfred Douglas, as you all know, went to Paris at the request of the defendant, and there he has stayed, and I know absolutely nothing more about him. I am as ignorant in this respect as you are. It may be that there is no evidence against Lord Alfred Douglas – but even about that I know nothing. It is a thing we cannot discuss, and to entertain any such consideration as I have mentioned would be a prejudice of the worst possible kind.[49]

After these comments in open court, Bosie's reputation was fixed. Forever after, Bosie Douglas would be linked in the eyes of the world as Oscar's boy. While at the time he devoutly wished this to be so, he would come to regret it before finally accepting it in later life. If there had been any attempt to save Bosie in the first two trials, it was not evident in the third. Lockwood was out for victory, and using Bosie to besmirch Wilde was a weapon he used implacably. His anxiety that he might lose lasted till the end.

The judge summed up with reasonable objectivity, under all the circumstances, casting doubt on the witnesses at the Savoy, and Lockwood remained in an agony of doubt. His fears were groundless. This time the conduct of the case had directed so much evidence against Wilde, albeit often tainted or circumstantial, that the result could not be in doubt. The jury found Wilde guilty on all counts save those relating to Shelley, where they were directed by the judge to find him not guilty because "that hysterical young man" had been so unreliable in the witness box. The judge called Taylor up to stand beside Wilde for sentence, and the judge treated the two men identically, despite the fact that they had been tried separately. He commented:

> People who can do these things must be dead to all sense of shame, and one cannot hope to produce any effect upon them. It is the worst case that I have ever tried. That you, Taylor, kept a kind of

> male brothel it is impossible to doubt. And that you, Wilde, have been the centre of a circle of extensive corruption of the most hideous kind among young men, it is equally impossible to doubt. I shall, under such circumstances, be expected to pass the severest sentence that the law allows. In my judgement it is totally inadequate for such a case as this. The sentence of this court is that each of you be imprisoned and kept to hard labour for two years.[50]

The severity of the sentence and the judge's remarks shocked Wilde and his supporters in the court, but were widely welcomed both in the court and in the country beyond. The *Daily Telegraph* of Monday 27 May, in a long article castigating "art for art's sake", attacked Wilde beyond measure and concluded: "Let us hope that his removal will serve to clear the poisoned air, and make it cleaner for all healthy and unvitiated lungs". This was the general view of newspapers of the time. Queensberry had won his victory. That night the Scarlet Marquis dined with the actors Charles Brookfield and Charles Hawtrey to celebrate their victory. Oscar Wilde sat in his prison cell and contemplated what two years' hard labour might mean.

EIGHT

Separation and Bitterness

Oscar Wilde was transferred from the courtroom to Holloway prison on Monday 27 May to begin serving two years with hard labour. This was a savage punishment for any man to endure. Hardened lags preferred three years' penal servitude, which was at least served in the open air with some chance of remission. Hard labour involved the prisoner in six hours' work on the treadmill every day for the first month, after which he would be put to work on menial tasks such as picking oakum, post-bag making or tailoring. Wilde wore the traditional prison uniform with broad stripes, even when being transferred between prisons, a penance that led to another terrible public humiliation. When not working, prisoners were kept in solitary confinement for 23 hours a day, with one hour's exercise in silence walking in single file round the prison yard. Until three months of the sentence were over he could not communicate with the outside world. After that, one letter was allowed to be sent and one received. Visits were allowed once every three months for twenty minutes. In consequence, Bosie could not communicate with Wilde until late August, and even then his letters did not reach Wilde as other communications took priority. This fact was to have immense consequences.

Wilde's emotions in prison were distorted by intense suffering. He was privileged to have an exceptional visit by R.B. Haldane, the Liberal MP, on 12 June. Haldane was haunted by what Wilde must be suffering and used an official warrant which enabled him to make visits to any prison in England to see Wilde.[1] Haldane secured Wilde some books: normally only the Bible and other religious books were allowed. He could however do nothing to alter prison conditions, and these were brutal.

The conditions of cell life were designed to break the spirit. The prisoner had to sleep on a plank bed, without mattress, which inevitably led to insomnia – made worse because no clocks were allowed in the cell and time passed with painful slowness. Even worse, the prison food almost inevitably led to vomiting and diarrhoea – which, when locked in a cell overnight with only a small chamber pot, led to filthy and insanitary consequences. Prison regulations did not allow warders to open cells once locked. In fact, the night warder was not allowed a key. The inevitable mess regularly led to warders being physically sick when they opened the cell door in the morning and were hit by the resulting stench.

When Wilde began to experience life as a convict, he came to realise the nonsense of his previous idealistic belief that even in prison, a man could be free. A fellow convict whispered to him on exercise "I am sorry for you, it is harder for you than for the likes of us".[2] Such sympathy was rare. On the whole, Wilde was treated with contempt. He was physically ill, partly due to the inadequacy of the prison diet. His weight dropped from 190 to 168 pounds. The prison doctor's incompetence in not diagnosing a disease of the ear had serious consequences for Wilde after his release. All this would have been hard for him to bear under any circumstances. But his condition was made worse by brooding on his downfall, the behaviour of Bosie and his father while he was in prison, and the news that his wife was under pressure to divorce him – a threat which terrified Wilde and meant that his correspondence with Constance and the lawyers had to take priority over Bosie's attempts to communicate.

Bosie's letters were rejected in favour of letters to Constance and to his solicitor. This was entirely understandable – except to Bosie – and in the circumstances was entirely justifiable. But it led Wilde in his confused state to conclude that, as he did not receive letters from Bosie in the early days, and Bosie later gave up writing to him because he had no replies, the apparent lack of communication meant that Bosie had abandoned him. When he came to write *De Profundis,* this misunderstanding was to fuel enormous bitterness.

In the early months of the sentence, however, Wilde had far more to worry about than communications with Bosie. Queensberry could not be satisfied with putting Wilde in prison. He claimed he was two thousand pounds out of pocket due to the Wilde affair, and sought to squeeze the money out of Wilde. By now, Oscar had no money; this did not stop Queensberry formally driving him into bankruptcy, thus completing his ruin. The bankruptcy petition was filed on 21 June and the first meeting of creditors took place on 26 August. Wilde owed £3,591. Queensberry moved that Wilde be officially declared bankrupt and an examination of Wilde's affairs was ordered. This entailed having to go through his financial affairs in public. This brought home to Oscar just how spendthrift and irresponsible he had been, souring his attitudes to Bosie and his brother Percy. Time and again in *De Profundis,* he refers to his bankruptcy and the way he was forced to account for every penny spent in the halcyon years of 1892–5, very largely on entertaining Bosie Douglas in expensive luxury.

On 4 July, Wilde was moved from Pentonville to Wandsworth. During a visit from Wilde's solicitors, the clerk whispered a message to him: "Prince Fleur-de-Lys wishes to be remembered to you. The gentleman is abroad at present". When Wilde made the connection, he laughed with great bitterness. In *De Profundis* he addresses Bosie, complaining at the use of this absurd name: "Surely there were many real names in real history which would have suited you much better, and by which I would have had no difficulty in recognising you at once? I did not look for you behind the spangles of a tinsel visard only suitable for an amusing masquerade".[3] This was unfair. The nickname was not unfamiliar, Wilde having used it himself writing to Ada Leverson on 3 May, and Bosie could hardly have sent a message using his own name. Prison had distorted Wilde's emotional judgement.

Bosie was at least trying to contact Wilde, though the lack of letters was to tell against him. He was totally loyal to Wilde, but his psychological state meant that his attempts to help Wilde were counter-productive; and, when Wilde learnt about them, he was horrified. Bosie had been in a near-hysterical state since Queensberry had left his card. As the tragedy unfolded, Bosie began to show signs of a persecution complex rivalling that of his father. In a letter to the *Star* of 19 April, complaining at press and judicial persecution, he wrote that he felt that he was taking his life in his hands in defending Wilde, arguing that he was seen as an undutiful son who had kicked against his father instead of running away and hiding his face.[4] This self-pitying note did not help Wilde, and alienated potential supporters, as it would throughout his later life. While Bosie Douglas was experiencing chronic guilt and remorse, he was not winning supporters for the cause.

In the first months, Bosie could not communicate with Wilde, nobody could, but this did not mean retiring to consider his best course of action. Instead, he could not stop himself writing damaging letters to the press. It was at this time that Bosie was first accused of being a Judas who had betrayed Wilde at the decisive moment. Henry Labouchère, who, despite Wilde's expressed admiration for him was an implacable opponent of Wilde and his circle, made this damaging assertion in his paper *Truth* on 13 June, shortly after Wilde's conviction. Bosie immediately wrote to Labouchère's paper, asserting that he had stayed for three weeks, visiting Wilde every day and struggling to help him, and explaining why he had been forced to leave against his will. His explanations were justified, but his attempt to defend himself rebounded, Labouchère commenting that, while Bosie had the courage of his opinions, "these opinions being what they are, it is to be regretted that he is not afforded an opportunity to meditate on them in the seclusion of Pentonville".[5]

Still more recklessly, after a sympathetic editorial on Wilde by W.T. Stead in the *Review of Reviews*, Bosie wrote from Rouen on 28 June in defence of homosexuality. Stead refused to publish this letter, which would have irreparably damaged Douglas's reputation had it appeared. This letter was of a piece with Bosie's conduct in the Summer of 1895. His mother was scheming to save her son from himself, and induced a family friend, Revd Sebastian Bowden, to visit Bosie, who was now alone in France, Robert Ross's family having stopped them sharing a hotel. Bowden arrived just in time to prevent Bosie going to Florence to visit Henry Somerset. The priest wrote to More Adey: "My fears are that A.D. is at present so self-willed and blinded as to be humanly speaking beyond redemption".[6] He was correct. Bosie was wholly self-absorbed and obsessed by his prejudices. He petitioned Queen Victoria on 25 June for clemency, arguing bizarrely that Wilde was the victim not of abstract justice but the spite and cunning of the Marquis of Queensberry, his father. Queensberry's sole object had been to dishonour his son and bring more misery to his wife.[7]

Following his father's similarly introverted petition, Victoria must have wondered at the sheer oddness of the whole Douglas clan. This was a clear statement of Douglas's view that Queensberry's strategy had been designed to attack Bosie and his mother, with Wilde merely an incidental casualty, a view still popular among Douglas's supporters. It is hard to think that such a view could play any role in seeking mercy for Oscar Wilde. In the event the authorities intercepted the petition and ensured it had no effect.

Bosie then went to Le Havre where, instead of conducting himself with the prudence needed to win over respectable opinion, he provoked immediate controversy. He hired a yacht, boys and men visited the yacht, there were reports of nude bathing, and the local paper attacked him for corrupting the city's youth. Bosie defended himself in another ill-judged letter aimed at an editor, claiming self-pityingly that he was being persecuted simply because he was Oscar Wilde's friend. He declared that he would be so till his death, and beyond if God willed it.[8]

Bosie's highly charged emotional state intensified when he found he could not communicate with Oscar Wilde. When Wilde's first three months' imprisonment were up, he was permitted to receive one letter. There were two – one from Bosie and one from Otho Holland, his brother-in-law. To Bosie's consternation, Oscar chose Holland's and received the news that his wife was under pressure to divorce him. Oscar immediately elected to write the one letter he was allowed to Constance, pleading with her not to divorce him. It touched her deeply, and she attempted to see him. Although Wilde had already had one visitor – Robert Sherard – the prison authorities waived the rules and Constance saw her husband in Wandsworth on 21 September. It was a painful and humiliating meeting. Constance wrote to Sherard afterwards, "It was indeed awful . . . I could not see him and I could not touch him. I scarcely spoke . . . . He has been mad these three years, and he said that if he saw Alfred Douglas he would kill him. So he had better keep away and be satisfied with having marred a fine life. Few people can boast of so much".[9] Constance's understandable anger at Douglas led to her agreeing to impose tough financial sanctions on her husband after his release. It certainly seems to have mirrored Wilde's own mental evolution, for his feelings for Bosie Douglas were now increasingly bitter.

This was in part because it seemed to Oscar that Bosie had simply abandoned him in prison. This was deeply unfair, for Bosie had tried to contact him and had written to Ada Leverson on 13 September of his desperation at being discouraged by the prison regulations, enforced by the Governor personally. Wilde's attack on Douglas in *De Profundis* is a curious *volte face*, under the circumstances, as it would not have taken very much effort to find out the truth. His bitterness, however, was not just because he thought Bosie had not communicated with him. When Robert Sherard visited on 26 August, he brought unsettling news. He had learned from a friend on the journal *Mercure de France* that the review was about to publish an article by Alfred Douglas quoting three passionate letters from Wilde written just before the trials. Wilde was hurt and astonished that Bosie would publish intimate letters that could do his children lasting harm and prejudice his chances of obtaining a remission of his prison sentence. He remembered bitterly that it was Bosie's irresponsibility in handling previous passionate letters that had given Queensberry some of the most damaging evidence against him. In *De Profundis*, he recalled: "You had left my letters lying about for blackmailing companions to steal, for hotel servants to pilfer, for housemaids to sell. That was simply your careless want of appreciation of what I had written to you. But that you should seriously propose to publish selections from the balance was incredible to me. And which of my letters were they? I could get no information. This was my first news of you".[10]

Wilde asked Sherard to stop the letters being published. Sherard accordingly wrote to the editor of *Mercure de France* and to Douglas asking for the letters to be removed from the article. Bosie at first agreed, but six weeks later wrote to Wilde via the Governor of Wandsworth asking formally for permission to include the letters, the common law copyright of which lay with Wilde. The timing of the approach could have hardly been worse. Wilde had had to attend a public bankruptcy hearing on 24 September, going through a considerable crowd in Carey Street curious to see what Wilde looked like as a convict. Robert Ross provided a moment of relief by waiting in a dreary corridor for Wilde to pass and silently raising his hat to Wilde as he passed, handcuffed and with bowed head. It was a thoughtful gesture that touched Wilde deeply, but it did nothing to relieve his physical and mental suffering. He was ill and accused by the prison doctor of malingering. Ten days after the visit to Carey Street he fell and bruised an ear on the cell floor, then fainted in the prison chapel. Several weeks in the prison hospital followed, and it was during this period that the governor brought him the news that Bosie still wanted to publish his letters. Wilde was infuriated and refused to give permission.

Bosie however could not see anything in his conduct that had led to this rebuff. He assumed that the cause must be Robert Sherard turning Wilde against him, and he complained that Sherard's role in the affair was meddling.[11] Sherard defended his action by arguing it was vitally important to reconcile Constance to her husband. This was not an argument a traumatised lover could accept. Bosie withdrew the article but was deeply wounded. He displayed not the slightest recognition of the impossible position Oscar Wilde had placed his wife in, nor sympathy for her position. She was about to change the family name to Holland and go into exile to escape the disaster which had engulfed her family – while his whining complaints about his own suffering show that, even after all that had happened in 1895, he still could not grasp the extent of the disaster or his share of the responsibility.

Wilde's sufferings intensified. On 20 November 1895 he was moved to a country prison, Reading, to improve his physical health. He was forced to wear his convict clothing and handcuffed during the move, which involved waiting for half an hour on a platform at Clapham Station for a train. This led to a terrible humiliation, unforgettably described in *De Profundis*: "From two o'clock till half past two on that day I had to stand on the centre platform of Clapham Junction in convict dress and handcuffed, for the world to look at. Of all possible objects I was the most grotesque. When people saw me they laughed . . . that was of course before they knew who I was. As soon as they had been informed, they laughed still more. For half an hour I stood there in the grey November rain surrounded by a jeering mob. For a year after that was done to me I wept every day at the same hour and for the same space of time".[12]

According to Sherard, what happened was worse than Wilde describes. A man who had been staring at Wilde for some minutes suddenly exclaimed, "My God, that's Oscar Wilde!", then stepped up to Wilde and spat in his face.[13] This public humiliation was not yet the lowest point of Wilde's prison misery. His mother had been ill for the previous year, and it became clear in January 1896 that she was dying. She asked to see her son, but the authorities refused. Hearing this, she turned her face to the wall, said bitterly "May the prison help him", and passed away. She died on 3 February. Constance elected to travel from Italy to break the news. She saw Oscar on 19 February, only to hear him explain, to her surprise, that he already knew. Spiritually inclined as he was, he told Constance that his mother had visited him in his cell the previous night, vanishing when he spoke to her image, and that he had heard the wail of the banshee. The death of his mother brought home to him as nothing before how low he had brought his family's name. Wilde tasted a bitter shame more intense than ever before. In *De Profundis* he wrote: "She and my father had bequeathed to me a name they had made noble and honoured, not merely in Literature, Art, Archaeology, and Science, but in the public history of our country. . . . I had disgraced that name eternally. I had made it a low byword among low people. I had dragged it through the very mire. I had given it to brutes that they might make it brutal, and to fools that they might turn it into a synonym for folly. What I suffered then, and still suffer, is not for pen to write or paper to record".[14]

It would be many months before Wilde set down these thoughts on paper. The humiliation and self-contempt which drove Wilde's pen as he wrote his epic prison letter were, however, burned into his soul less than a year after his conviction. Wilde's sufferings had reached their extremity, and he projected them into an increasing contempt for Bosie Douglas. His first Winter in prison was miserable beyond belief, driving Wilde to the verge of what he felt to be insanity, while his friends did what they could to rescue something from the wreckage of his fall. Bosie, meanwhile, continued with behaviour that alienated Wilde as its echoes reached him in his prison cell. As Wilde brooded on his sufferings in Reading gaol, he too began to see Lord Alfred Douglas as the Dark Angel who had blighted his golden path.

* * *

Oscar Wilde's bitterness against Bosie Douglas was exacerbated by long hours kept in solitary confinement, when his mind ran obsessively over the details of his fall and his apparent desertion by his lover. Wilde appears not to have been aware that Bosie wished devoutly to return to England to see him in prison, but it was impossible for him to return, communications with Oscar by letter being at first forbidden and later abandoned as they upset him. Wilde's isolation meant that the prisoner had to rely on infrequent visits from others to maintain contact with the outside world, to learn what Bosie was doing, and make plans for the future. None of his visitors was sympathetic to Douglas, and all had their own pressing business to attend to. Pre-eminent among them was Constance, whose prison visits were motivated by far more than the formalities dictated by the wreckage of her marriage.

Oscar Wilde hardly deserved his wife's love and forbearance: he had hurt her unbearably. When the crash happened, poor baffled Constance had written in agony to the fortune teller, Mrs Robinson, seeking a forecast of the future: "What is to become of my husband who has so betrayed and deceived me and ruined the lives of my darling boys. . .? You told me that after this terrible shock my life was to become easier, but will there be any happiness in it, or is that dead for me? And I have had so little. My life has all been cut to pieces as my hand is by its lines. As soon as this trial is over I have to get my judicial separation, or if possible my divorce, in order to get the guardianship of the boys. What a tragedy for him who is so gifted. . .".[15]

Constance would not go through with her divorce: she still loved Oscar, despite being cuckolded by him with a succession of male lovers. Whatever he wrote to her from prison touched her deeply and she abandoned her plans for the final break. But she had to protect her children and she entered cautiously into talks with her husband. Negotiations started in a spirit of reconciliation. At their first meeting, when Constance kissed and comforted him, they talked of the children – especially Cyril, Wilde's favourite – and Oscar suggested she appoint a guardian if the burden of looking after them became too heavy. Constance later appointed her cousin, Adrian Hope, to Wilde's satisfaction. They agreed that Oscar would have an income of £200 a year on release, and a third of his life interest in her marriage settlement if he survived her. This amicable agreement was to collapse with serious consequences for both Oscar and Bosie.

Wilde's faithful friends More Adey and Robert Sherard visited him in February 1896. Three months later, Sherard brought the even more faithful Robbie Ross. Ross was deeply shocked by the effects of a year's hard labour on his friend, telling Adey afterward that this was the worst interview he had had with Oscar.[16] Ominously, Wilde hardly talked at all and his two friends had great difficulty in maintaining a cheerful attitude. There were long periods of awkward silence, with Wilde crying all the time. His few remarks were often incoherent, but Ross understood that Wilde suffered from not being allowed pencil and paper to write, from anaemia and gout, and from the doctor's incompetence and suspicion. Wilde feared madness and asked whether they thought his brain was all right?[17] Ross had important news to tell Oscar, namely that Bosie was about to publish his poems and dedicate them to Wilde. Wilde cut him short with the peremptory comment that he would rather not hear about that just now,[18] which Ross thought ended the matter. It did not. Wilde brooded, and the following day wrote Ross a savage letter referring to Bosie as "Douglas" and expressing uncompromising hostility:

> You said that Douglas was going to dedicate a volume of poems to me. Will you write at once to him and say he must not do anything of the kind. I could not accept or allow such a dedication. The proposal is revolting and grotesque. Also, he has unfortunately in his possession a number of letters of mine. I wish him to at once hand all these without exception over to you. . . . I will not have him in possession of my letters or gifts. Even if I get out of this loathesome place I know that there is nothing before me but a life of the pariah – of disgrace and penury and contempt – but at least I will have nothing to do with him nor allow him to come near me. . . . In writing to Douglas you had better quote my letter fully and frankly, so that he should have no loophole of escape. Indeed he cannot possibly refuse. He has ruined my life – that should content him. . . .[19]

Robert Ross was now the go-between in the increasingly fractious relationship between Oscar and Bosie, a role he performed faithfully, copying Wilde's uncompromising prison letter and sending it to Bosie Douglas immediately. This efficiency has been taken by some commentators to indicate that Wilde's hostility to Douglas satisfied in Ross, a deep-seated jealousy. There is no evidence to support this view. In 1896, he was seen as an honest broker by both Wilde and Douglas, and whatever was to happen a decade later, when relations broke down with appalling consequences, in 1896 Bosie saw Ross as a trustworthy and sympathetic ally. When he received Wilde's instructions he was virtually hysterical, writing to Ross on 4 June to threaten suicide once again. In a melodramatic letter which was reported back to Wilde in prison, and in *De Profundis*, Wilde commented on it; particularly the phrase "deprived of all power of thought and expression", which Wilde mentions twice, the second time to reinforce his view that Bosie had neglected him. That Bosie did not respond to Wilde baffled and enraged him. He demanded, rhetorically: "Why did you not write to me? Was it cowardice? Was it callousness? What was it. . .? I waited for a letter . . . you cannot say that you seriously thought I was obliged to receive none but business communications from members of my family. . .".[20]

It is curious that it does not seem to have occurred to Wilde, who must have known of the regulations, that Bosie's letters were simply not getting through to him. Bosie had found, however, that his attempts to communicate with Wilde in prison only created more and more trouble and he decided to abstain from communication until Wilde was released. In June 1896, Wilde was increasingly desperate, and penned a pathetic appeal for clemency to the Home Secretary. In this appeal, fear of madness was the dominant theme.[21] Wilde's state of mind was now acutely worrying his friends, and Frank Harris was approached to intercede with the authorities. He was able to secure an interview with Evelyn Ruggles Brice, head of the Prison Commission. To Harris's pleasure and surprise, Brice proved distinctly sympathetic to Wilde and ordered an investigation.[22] Harris saw Wilde in Reading gaol on 13 or 14 July, also meeting the Governor, Major Isaacson, who was hostile to Wilde and gave Harris little comfort. Fortunately, the immediate investigation carried out by Home Office officials, with clear support from Ruggles Brice, altered the situation completely.

On 25 July, Wilde was allowed more books and, infinitely more importantly, a sufficiency of writing materials. Isaacson was moved, and a far more intelligent Governor appointed in his stead. Major J.O. Nelson's first act was to go up to Wilde and tell him: "The Home Office has allowed you some books. Perhaps you would like to read this one, I have just been reading it myself". Wilde burst into tears at this unprecedented kindness. He could not accept that he would not be released before his sentence was served in full, writing another pathetic letter to the Home Secretary in November.[23] But the worst rigours that the prison service could inflict were over.

Bosie, meanwhile, was desperate to get to Reading to see Wilde. His mother, whose allowance provided his sole income, was tactfully trying to break the relationship. Sybil and Percy both visited Bosie in Paris in early 1896, and Sybil was alarmed to learn that her son wished to go to England to see Oscar. She wrote to More Adey on 27 February that her lawyer had told her: "It would be highly dangerous for Bosie to come back to either England or Scotland, he was *most emphatic* on the subject so that I am sure he has good reason for what he says and he assured me that on no account must he think of returning at present or for a long time to come, so I hope you will impress this on Bosie."[24]

Bosie nevertheless persisted in trying to get to Reading, but was persuaded by Robbie Ross that Wilde did not want him to write or visit him. Some commentators, notably H. Montgomery Hyde, have seen this as evidence that Ross was beginning the civil war which was to wreck relations between himself and Bosie, but there is no evidence of duplicity by Ross or that he was poisoning Wilde against Douglas.[25] Indeed, Ross was attempting to prevent Wilde becoming completely antipathetic to Douglas at a time when Wilde's bleak and bitter outlook made this anything but easy to do. In November 1896 Ross warned Wilde that his bitterness against Bosie was alienating friends. Wilde replied to this warning in his letter to Ross of November 1896, making it clear that Ross was not responsible for him turning against Bosie Douglas. Wilde wrote savagely: "There is a thorn however . . . it is caused by a message you wrote on a piece of paper. I mean of course what you said about the sympathies of others being estranged from me, or in danger of being so, by the deep bitterness of the feelings I expressed about Alfred Douglas. . . . When one has been for eighteen months in a prison cell, one sees things and people as they really are. . . . Do not think that I would blame *him* for my vices. He had as little to do with them as I had with his. . . . I blame him for not appreciating the man he ruined. . .".[26]

Wilde went on to make a vituperative attack on Douglas, in which he attacked his "unrestrained and coarse appetites", "his greed for money;

his incessant and violent scenes; his unimaginative selfishness". Wilde did not need Robbie Ross to poison his views about Bosie.

Bosie wintered in Rome in considerable comfort, joining Sybil and her daughter Edith at their expense. Sybil was pleased by how well Bosie was, and wrote on 31 January 1897:

> I have been so pleased to find Alfred looking so much better than I have seen him for a long time and very bright and cheerful. He tells me that Mr Ross is urging him to advertise his poems in London papers and is trying to get them reviewed even if they are to be slated. I think this would be a great mistake and from what Bosie said to me I don't think he quite likes the idea himself.
>
> I find the English people here very kind to him and he has many nice friends and I am sure it would be a great pity to bring him prominently before the public now; it would make it more difficult for him and for us all in every way. . . .[27]

Constance Wilde observed Bosie's favourable reception by English expatriates in Italy with incredulity, writing to a friend: "It may interest your husband and disgusted [*sic*] me, to hear that A.D. is received in society by the embassy at Rome and by private persons at Nice. So much it is with a bourgeois nation to be of the aristocracy".[28] Constance's poor grammar cannot detract from her acute observation. It was dangerous for Bosie to remind the population at home of his existence. But in the more liberal atmosphere abroad, Sybil's hopes for her son's rehabilitation were bearing fruit.

Under the new régime at Reading, Wilde had also begun rehabilitation. He had recovered his spirits and begun to think of others and the future. The fear of madness receded and, in a letter to More Adey of 25 September, he talked hopefully of his children not being "bred up to look on me with either hatred or contempt".[29] He generously welcomed the success in France of Pierre Louys's book *Aphrodite*, wistfully regretting that he had chosen Bosie Douglas's friendship over that of Louys, and expressing sympathy with Aubrey Beardsley. But the most telling passage of the letter was a brief but savage reference to Douglas, writing: "I am so glad you are friends with Robert Sherard: I have no doubt he is very indiscreet, but he is very true, and saved my letters from being published. I know there is nothing in them but expressions of foolish, misplaced, ill-requited affection for one of crude and callous nature, of coarse greed, and common appetites, but that is why their publication would have been so shameful. The gibbet on which I swing in history now is high enough. There is no need that he of all men should for his own vanity make it more hideous".[30]

Wilde could not leave matters in this state. For his own sense of self-worth, he had to make sense of Alfred Douglas as more than just a man of crude and common appetites, and his situation in prison as more than just the result of folly and weakness. He began to see himself as an inhabitant of something like Dante's *Inferno* – he was reading Dante in prison – and sometime after Christmas 1896 began writing a long letter to Bosie Douglas presenting his interpretation of his fall in the most dramatic terms. Already by November 1896, in the letter to Ross defending himself against the charge of alienating his friends by his bitterness against Douglas,[31] he had cast himself as an outcast "in the lowest mire of Malebolge, . . . between Gilles de Retz and the Marquis de Sade". The former, of course, was executed for debauchery, devil worship and child murder, the latter sentenced to death, commuted to life imprisonment, for the activities which gave rise to the word "sadism". Malebolge was the 8th circle of Dante's Inferno. It was in this frame of mind that he wrote the letter to Bosie Douglas, later entitled by its editor, Ross, *De Profundis.*

It is surely one of the most extraordinary letters ever published. Over 30,000 words in length, it was ostensibly designed to preach to Bosie the lessons of his overweening pride and arrogance in taking his hatred of his father to the lengths where Wilde himself was prosecuted and imprisoned – and, by implication, damned and destroyed. Wilde sees himself as suffering a Christ-like fate, offering a vision of the relationship that transferred responsibility for his downfall to Bosie, whom he sees as loving him, but hating his father more. It provides a wealth of information on the relationship between Oscar and Bosie in the years up to the disaster of the trials, and yet is deeply flawed by his desire to blame Bosie for his downfall. Moreover, the bitterness which Wilde would inevitably feel was intensified by his belief, running through the letter as its most consistent theme, that he had been abandoned by Douglas in prison. The very first sentence of the letter reads: "After long and fruitless waiting I have determined to write to you myself, as much for your sake as for mine, as I would not like to think that I had passed through two long years of imprisonment without having received a single line from you, or any news or message even, except such as gave me pain."[32]

It was certainly true that Wilde had not heard properly from Bosie and had only received news which gave him pain, particularly over the proposed publication of their letters; but the implication that Bosie had turned his back on him was simply not true. Repeated with great authority on several occasions in the letter, this accusation would do Bosie enormous damage, damage which still affects his reputation today, some six decades after his death.

De Profundis does much more to blacken Douglas's reputation. In it, Wilde paints a picture of Bosie as an overwhelmingly destructive influence in his life, which is certainly one aspect of the story; but only one. Wilde claims, for example, that while he was with Bosie he never wrote anything of consequence, a claim which is utter nonsense, since he wrote his two most successful plays at a time when, on his own admission, the two were at their most intimate. He also painted a picture of Bosie so unattractive that it is hard to see why the two men had had a relationship at all. Bosie himself, when he finally did read the letter, argued that Wilde had missed out all the laughter that had characterised their relationship. It is a fair point. If the two men had not enjoyed each other's company, they could not have stayed together. The relationship was sunshine and storms, but Wilde recorded only the storms.

De Profundis – or *Epistola in Carcere et Vinculis,* to give it the Latin title Wilde originally suggested, modelled on that of a Papal Bull – has been enormously influential despite its palpable bias. Had the letter ever been received by Bosie it would have changed the relationship fundamentally, for it is a savage reproof such as few men have ever had addressed to them by a partner. Yet, paradoxically, the history of the letter does not form part of the relationship while Wilde lived, for it is clear that Bosie could not have read it until, in 1912, he read it preparatory to the Ransome trial, at which point it became deeply destructive. This was certainly not Wilde's original intention: *De Profundis* was written between January and March 1897, at the time when Wilde was preparing to leave prison and resume some kind of life outside. The object of the letter was to set out his views on the relationship in order to bring home to Bosie the lessons of the previous five years, preparatory to meeting again, after a suitable interval of adjustment. Wilde envisaged this as happening "in some quiet foreign town like Bruges", after Bosie had received, digested and replied to the letter. Wilde clearly assumed that Bosie would take it in the corrective spirit in which it had been written, an assumption (knowing the intended recipient) that was quite unlikely to be well-founded. Wilde wrote: "As regards your letter in answer to this, it may be as long or as short as you choose. Address the envelope to 'The Governor, HM Prison, Reading'. Inside, in another, and an open, envelope, place your own letter to me: if your paper is very thin do not write on both sides as it makes it hard for others to read. I have written to you with perfect freedom. You can write to me with the same."[33]

Had this remarkable proposal been acted on by Douglas, if he had ever actually read the letter, the whole subsequent outcome would have been different: the second great "what if. . . ?" of our story. However, the prison authorities intervened again to interrupt communications between the two men. On 2 April the prison governor wrote to the Prison Commission to ask if the letter might be sent out. Four days later, the Commission wrote back saying that this was impossible, but that Wilde could take the letter with him when he left on 19 May. This he did, having decided to pass the poisoned chalice to Robbie Ross.

Those final months in prison were also a time when Oscar Wilde was settling his affairs with Constance. Two issues dominated the negotiations, money and the care of the children. The financial settlement allowed him £150 per year from his wife, but this was contingent on Wilde doing nothing that would entitle his wife to a divorce or a judicial separation. The crucial clause required him not to "notoriously consort with evil or disreputable persons". This was aimed partly at Wilde's homosexual promiscuity in general but more specifically at a future relationship with Bosie Douglas. On 17 May 1897, two days before his release, the papers were brought to Reading gaol for Wilde to sign. The Deed of Arrangement was brought to the Solicitors' Room and Wilde signed it, deeply agitated, in the presence of his solicitor, Hansell. It dealt with the financial settlement only, the situation with the children having been settled by the Court. Constance and Oscar could never be together again, and even if they became friends and lived together voluntarily, Oscar would lose his £150 per year. In this way, the separation of Oscar and Constance was legally regulated. Any future relationship of Oscar and Bosie would be financially prohibitive. In case Oscar Wilde did not understand this implication of the agreement, Constance's solicitor wrote to More Adey on 10 May to underline "how absolutely fatal to him any further intercourse with Lord Alfred Douglas will be: apart from the fact that Lord Alfred Douglas is a 'notoriously disreputable companion', Lord Queensberry has made arrangement for being informed if his son joins Mr Wilde and has expressed his intention of shooting one or both.

A threat of this kind from most people could be more or less disregarded, but there is no doubt that Lord Queensberry, as he has shown before, will carry out any threat he makes to the best of his ability".[34] The Scarlet Marquis, armed and dangerous, still watched balefully from the sidelines.

Wilde now had to make arrangements for the prison letter. He knew that if he sent the letter direct to Bosie it was likely to be destroyed in an explosion of rage, and he wanted a copy made first. On 1 April, before he knew the decision of the prison authorities, Wilde wrote explicit instructions to Robbie Ross, naming him as his literary executor and writing:

> I send you, in a roll separate from this, my letter to Alfred Douglas, which I hope will arrive safe. As soon as you, and of course More Adey whom I always include with you, have read it, I want you to to have it carefully copied for me. There are many reasons why I want this to be done. One will suffice. I want you to be my literary executor in case of my death, and to have complete control over my plays, books and papers. . . .
>
> Well, if you are my literary executor, you must be in possession of the only document that really gives any explanation of my extraordinary behaviour with regard to Queensberry and Alfred Douglas. When you read the letter you will see the psychological explanation of a course of conduct that from the outside seems a combination of absolute idiocy with vulgar bravado. Some day the truth will have to be known: not neccessarily in my lifetime or Douglas's: but I am not prepared to sit in the grotesque pillory they put me into, for all time: for the simple reason that I inherited from my father and my mother a name of high distinction in literature and art, and I cannot, for eternity, allow that name to be the shield and the catspaw of the Queensberrys. I don't defend my conduct: I explain it.[35]

Wilde here gave very clear instructions that typewritten copies were to be made before the original was sent to Douglas: at some point, however, these were altered and the handwritten original remained with Ross and was placed in the British Museum, where it resides in the manuscript section of the British Library to this day. Whether Ross ever sent a copy of the letter to Bosie remains controversial. Ross certainly did not follow

Wilde's suggestion for a title, renaming it *De Profundis.* He did, however, obey Wilde's mischievous suggestion that Bosie not be told that a copy had been made, unless he complained of misrepresentation.[36] Bosie Douglas knew that Wilde was writing a letter to him, for More Adey had told him, and though no-one knew what the contents were Douglas feared the worst, having fully understood Wilde's bitterness towards him. On 8 February he wrote to Adey submissively, that if Wilde was going to abuse him he would rather not see the letter.[37] It is significant that Douglas stated that he would rather not read abuse: this supports the theory that he was indeed sent the letter by Ross later in the year, but having seen that it was abusive promptly destroyed it without reading it. He certainly did not read it until 1912, when its contents were to be revealed to him in a most unpleasant manner.

When Wilde was moved from Reading gaol, he had the manuscript of the letter in his hand. The prison authorities had refused to allow him to send it to Robbie Ross, but they let him take it with him on 18 May. He kept it for the next few days, while Ross was still in France. Taken to Pentonville, he was discharged from there on 19 May 1897. Alfred Douglas had never been far from his thoughts. In prison, Oscar had dwelt on the rending apart of his relationship with Bosie, and blamed him for his downfall. But, once he was free again, a separation from Douglas would prove increasingly difficult to maintain. A prudent man might have destroyed the prison letter as having fulfilled an immediate purpose, that of purging his soul of bitterness towards Bosie Douglas. But Wilde was not a prudent man. He left the letter intact, while apparently washing his hands of the implications of having it sent to Bosie – if indeed his instructions were followed.

Wilde now had to pick his way through the wreckage of his fortunes and the few remaining friendships Fate had allowed him. Pre-eminent among them would be that of Bosie Douglas.

NINE

Spirits Abroad

When Oscar Wilde left prison, the future of his relationship with Bosie Douglas was cloudy. It may not even have concerned him: whoever's fault it was, there had been no contact for two years and only increasing bitterness on Wilde's part. Bosie, although he had been briefed by friends on Oscar's feelings, had not heard directly from him and never deviated for a moment from his objective of resuming a close friendship. For Oscar Wilde and those of his friends who had read his bitter prison correspondence, this appeared the least likely outcome. Ross and the others had read letters expressing a savagery towards Douglas that rendered any resumption of the relationship unthinkable, and laid plans accordingly. Wilde himself had only the vaguest plans for his life after prison. He thought to go into a religious retreat but did not take the elementary step of contacting any religious order and convincing them of his sincerity. His friends laid more concrete plans for him to go into exile in France, living on funds Robbie Ross had collected for him. Reggie Turner had procured baggage for him marked with his assumed name, Sebastian Melmoth. It appeared that a new life, in which Bosie Douglas would play no part, was about to begin.

On his release, Wilde was exultant. Taken from Reading on 18 May to catch a train to London, he greeted the foliage on Twyford station with outspread arms, crying out: "Oh beautiful world! Oh beautiful world!" One of the warders escorting him implored him to stop: "Now, Mr Wilde, you mustn't give yourself away like that. You're the only man in England who would talk like that in a railway station".[1] It seemed to his friends that Wilde had recovered all his old spirits. When he was finally released from Pentonville at 6.15 the following morning, More Adey and Stewart Headlam were waiting to take him in a cab to Headlam's house in Bloomsbury. A small group of loyal friends then appeared. Ada Leverson was pleasantly surprised to find Wilde elated and gracious. She records that he arrived with the dignity of a king returning from exile, talking, laughing, smoking a cigarette, with waved hair and a flower in his buttonhole.[2]

One reason for Wilde's good spirits was that he foresaw spending the next six months or so in a Catholic retreat. This would have been the ideal way to gain time to adjust to life outside prison, and he duly sent a letter to a local Jesuit seminary with high expectations. While he awaited a reply, he talked airily of the prison governor and his wife, and of reading the *Daily Chronicle*. Then the reply came from the Jesuits: Oscar Wilde could not just be accepted on the impulse of the moment, the matter must be thought over for at least a year. Wilde had made no attempt to ingratiate himself with the Catholic church, apparently thinking in his childish fashion that he had only to request entrance to receive succour. This was never likely to happen, and when the letter brought home to him the fact of his continuing isolation, even, it seemed, from God, he broke down and sobbed bitterly.[3] However, he soon recovered his spirits and spent so much time talking to friends and wellwishers that his plan to go into exile in France was delayed. It was not until that evening that he and More Adey caught the boat train to Dieppe, where Robbie Ross and Reggie Turner had taken rooms.

It was at this point that the manuscript of the prison letter made its first public appearance. When Wilde stepped off the steamer in the dawn of 20 May, he was holding a large, sealed envelope, which he handed to Ross. "This, my dear Bobbie, is the great manuscript about which you know. More has behaved very badly about my luggage and was anxious to deprive me of the blessed bag which Reggie gave me". As far as Wilde was concerned, his having handed over responsibility now pushed the prison letter and the bitter thoughts it contained into the background. He seems simply to have assumed that Ross would somehow deal with it, and that was an end to it.

It may have been at this point that Wilde changed his instructions to Ross over the prison letter, requiring him to send the original to Bosie. In all events, Ross hung on to the manuscript, which was to end up in the keeping of the British Museum, but later claimed he had sent a typed copy to Bosie. In Ross's version of events, however, he could not get the letter typed and sent until August. He held firm to this story, but Douglas for his part always denied ever receiving a copy and he certainly did not read it while Wilde was alive. Wilde never asked what had happened to it after he gave it to Ross in Dieppe. By the time Wilde had settled in Dieppe, he had virtually forgotten about it, and it clearly played no part in the dramas of that Summer and Autumn.

For the next few days Wilde was still euphoric over his freedom, chaffing Reggie Turner in a way which Ross described as "childish spirits" over luggage he had bought for Wilde. The childish spirits were manifested in more irresponsible ways. Following Wilde's hysterical prison correspondence over his wasted financial prospects, Ross had exerted himself to raise £800, which he now gave to Wilde. Oscar immediately began to fritter this away, buying perfumes and other luxuries. Ross was furious, but Oscar airily waved away his anxieties to Reggie Turner with the disingenuous comment: "I have already spent my entire income for two years . . . it seemed to me cruel not to fill with rose petals the little caskets shaped so cunningly in the form of a rose".[4] Wilde would soon discover the deeper cruelty of wasting the little that was left of his fortune and talent in such frivolous self-indulgence.

More constructively, he remembered those who had stood by him in prison, writing effusive letters to them, but he did not attempt to contact Bosie Douglas. He quickly discovered that, outside his immediate circle, his reception in Dieppe, particularly from English tourists, was painfully cold. He was spurned by the artists Walter Sickert, Charles Condor and Aubrey Beardsley, the latter's rejection being a particularly hard cross for Wilde to bear. Wilde could never understand that his behaviour to Beardsley over *Salomé* had been intolerable. The illustrator, in any case, had only a short time left to live. More worryingly, Queensberry had sent a private detective to watch for any meeting between Wilde and Bosie. Wilde was so disturbed by his visibility to prying eyes in Dieppe that, on 27 May, he and Ross moved to a hotel at Berneval-sur-Mer, five miles down the coast, where Ross left him alone for six weeks while he dealt with his own business in England. Wilde alone now had no choice but to confront the emotional dilemmas that had been pushed to the back of his mind on his release.

His relationship with Constance was the immediate issue. Wilde had written to her contritely a day or two after reaching Dieppe, longing for a meeting with her and their children. Constance was touched and tempted, but her advisers were wary. She therefore replied, neither agreeing nor disagreeing, promising to meet him twice a year and offering the possibility of a meeting with the children. This was not what Wilde wanted to hear. He needed immediate emotional sustenance, his hunger for company growing as the weeks passed. In July, Wilde asked her to come to Dieppe with the children, and proposed living together. Constance prevaricated, arguing that she was not settled in her own exile in Italy. There was more to this than emotional turmoil. In late July, Wilde learned from a mutual friend, Carlos Blacker, that Constance was seriously ill with spinal paralysis after falling in Tite Street. One operation had failed to find a solution and a second was considered essential, though dangerous.

Wilde wrote to Blacker on 29 July that he was distressed to hear about Constance – he had not realised her condition was so serious. Since she could obviously not come to see Wilde, he offered to visit her in mid-August. Wilde commented: "For myself, I really am heartbroken. Nemesis seems endless".[5] Wilde was undoubtedly feeling sorrier for himself, offering little but empty phrases. He wrote that, when he thought of Constance, he wanted to kill himself. His life was spilt on the sand, "and the sand drinks it because it is thirsty. . . . I was made for destruction. My cradle was rocked by the Fates. Only in the mire can I know peace. Ever yours. . .".[6] These were empty phrases even applied to himself, and for Constance there was little real emotion. This was partly because he was hearing more seductive calls from Bosie in Italy, calls which now drove his wife and children from his thoughts.

Bosie had written to him on his arrival in France, an act which upset Oscar greatly. Bosie's attitudes were fixed on a resumption of the relationship, based on the notion that he had earned it by his devotion to Wilde. To Oscar Wilde, the idea was incredible. On 28 May, when Wilde was left alone for the first time, he wrote Robbie Ross a letter that showed Bosie Douglas still frightened and repelled him. Wilde had read Bosie's letter again before retiring and it had disturbed his sleep:

> I hardly had any sleep last night. Bosie's revolting letter was in the room and foolishly I had read it again and left it by my bedside. My dream was that my mother was speaking to me with some sternness, and that she was in trouble. I quite see that whenever I am in danger she will in some way warn me. I have a real terror now of that unfortunate ungrateful young man with his unimaginative selfishness and his entire lack of sensitiveness to what in others is good or kind or trying to be so. I feel him as an evil influence, poor fellow. To be with him would be to return to the hell from which I think I have been released. I hope never to see him again.[7]

Wilde's emotions appear unambiguous. The following day, he sounded the same note in a letter to Ross: "I am terrified about Bosie: More writes to me that he has been practically interviewed about me! It is awful. More, desiring to spare me pain, I suppose, did not send me the paper, so I have had a wretched night. Bosie can almost ruin me. I earnestly beg that some entreaty be made to him not to do so a second time. His letters to me are infamous".[8] This panic was groundless, for the article was uncontroversial, and when Wilde saw it his terror of Bosie was replaced by sympathy, then curiosity. By 2 June, he had come to regard the interview as harmless. He now wrote to Bosie cordially as "My dear boy", and warned him against fighting a duel over the article.[9] His view of Bosie was changing as the old attraction exerted itself. He could not but be flattered that Bosie wanted to see him, while Constance was reluctant. As he was isolated and in need of emotional support, Bosie's loyalty was magnetic. Oscar's memories of the traumas that had accompanied the earlier relationship faded into insignificance.

Wilde's attitudes now underwent a complete reversal, affection replacing hatred with a speed that suggests neither emotion was much more than skin-deep. On 4 June, Oscar wrote to Bosie proclaiming his love, but the impossibility of meeting, with the unambiguous words "Don't think I don't love you. Of course I love you more than anything else. But our lives are irreparably severed, as far as meeting goes. What is left to us is the knowledge that we love each other, and every day I think of you, and I know you are a poet, and that makes you doubly dear and wonderful . . .".[10] On 12 June Wilde changed again, and invited Bosie to visit him – an invitation confirmed in eager letters of 15 and 16 June for Saturday 19 June.[11] This was not to be. Wilde's solicitor caught wind of the meeting and immediately resigned. On the Thursday Wilde wrote in panic to Bosie Douglas that Queensberry was the cause of the solicitor's actions – and certainly the prospect of the Marquis descending on Dieppe with a revolver was not one a lawyer could relish. Wilde postponed the meeting indefinitely, with the words: "I think of you always, and love you always, but chasms of moonless night divide us. We cannot cross it [*sic*] without hideous and nameless peril".[12] Robert Ross has been suspected of having tipped off the solicitor. The interregnum between the postponed meeting in June and the eventual reconciliation in August was a breathing space which Wilde used to write his last great work, his long poetic commentary on prison life, *The Ballad of Reading Gaol.*

Bosie was incensed that the meeting had been cancelled, particularly when he discovered the clause in the agreement with Constance, cutting off Wilde's allowance. He wrote a furious letter to More Adey blaming him for the clause being inserted. Ross replied, taking the responsibility, but arguing that there had been no choice and, in any case, Douglas had the means to replace the money if Constance cut off the allowance, either directly or by getting Percy to fulfil his promises of finance. Bosie replied haughtily that he had no money, but in any case as an aristocrat he had the right to be impecunious while Ross as a commoner had to live within his means: Ross should take all responsibility for looking after Wilde and his finances, he himself was above such petty considerations.

Ross and Douglas had fallen out for the first time, with Wilde unequivocally taking Ross's side. On 6 July, he claimed he had sent Douglas a twelve-sided, foolscap letter defending Ross for his work in looking after Wilde's interests, and chiding him for "calling himself a grand seigneur in comparison to a dear sweet wonderful friend like you, his superior in all fine things. I told him how grotesque, ridiculous and vulgar such an attempt was".[13] Ross may have concluded that Wilde was closer to him than he was to Douglas, but there could be no contest in an emotional tug of war between Ross and Douglas over Wilde. The old attraction was asserting itself. Through July, Oscar and Bosie negotiated about meeting, with Bosie offering a flat in Paris. Oscar did not feel strong enough to go to Paris, and invited Bosie to Rouen. Bosie now became difficult, partly because he could not afford the fare to Rouen. For some weeks the spat meant that the letters ceased; then, on 21 August, Bosie wrote to Percy from the Villa Casa in Capri where he was spending the Summer that he was tired of being alone, inviting visitors who never came.[14]

At this point, Sybil Queensberry invited Bosie to stay with her, perhaps to get him out of the way of Wilde. If this was the case, she was clutching at straws. Nothing she could do would prevent Wilde and Bosie meeting, and in late August the two men finally arranged a reconciliation. Too late, Constance recognised what was going on and offered to meet Oscar, but refused to allow him to see the boys. According to More Adey, she wrote that she could now see Wilde, as she had "got their children out of the way", feeling that their lives could only be "yet more ruined" by seeing him.[15] Wilde regarded this as grossly insensitive, wrote that he was lonely and worn out by procrastination, and that he would therefore go back to the only person who offered him companionship – Bosie Douglas. This news was apparently a shattering revelation to Constance, who was unaware Douglas was back in her husband's affections. Vyvyan recalled to Frank Harris many years later, "I remember my mother's joy when he was supposed to be coming back, and I remember her misery when she found he had other claims upon his time".[16] Bosie would blame Constance for the failure of her attempts at reconciliation.

The die was cast. On 24 August, Wilde wrote to Bosie, agreeing to see him. They met, almost certainly on 28 August at Rouen station, and re-enacted their reunion of 1894, this time with Wilde shedding the tears. They stayed together overnight on affectionate terms and parted the closest of friends. Bosie recalled in his *Autobiography* that: "The meeting was a great success. I have often thought that if he or I had died directly after that, our friendship would have ended in a beautiful and romantic way".[17] The meeting was indeed the romantic high point of their relationship. All had been forgiven. They were once again the best of friends. It would have been a golden moment at which to part forever, but the meeting could not be an ending. On 31 August, Wilde sent a telegram to Bosie: "I feel my only hope of again doing beautiful work in art is being with you. It was not so in old days, but now it is different, and you can really recreate in me that energy and sense of joyous power on which art depends. Everyone is furious with me for going back to you, but they don't understand us. I feel that it is only with you that I can do anything at all. Do remake my ruined life for me, and then our friendship and love will have a different meaning to the world."[18]

In under four months, Bosie had gone from being the ruination of Wilde's life to being the only person who could remake Wilde's ruined life! Oscar had returned to the one option that seemed to offer a real chance of emotional satisfaction and artistic recovery – life with Bosie Douglas. The two men would attempt to revive their relationship for one last time, in circumstances where all those most intimately concerned with their lives were implacably opposed. That Bosie had achieved this outcome was a tribute to his steadfast devotion to Wilde, in no wise evidence of that betrayal of which he has so frequently been accused. Bosie never wavered in his pursuit of Wilde, and Oscar had been won over. The old flame burned brightly again.

TEN

A Touching Reunion

At the point where Richard Ellmann's biography of Wilde reaches the meeting at Rouen, he sums up his view of the road Wilde had taken by quoting Ovid's aphorism, *video meliora proboque: detiora sequor,* meaning "I see the good and value it: I follow the bad".[1] This view is widely held among Wilde's supporters, but it is too simple an assessment. In the *De Profundis* letter, Wilde had carefully constructed a picture of Bosie as the Dark Angel who had lured him to destruction. This is the view into which he would fall once more in the immediate aftermath of the Naples episode. Yet it cannot be anything like the truth, for Wilde clearly found great pleasure in Bosie's attraction to him, and he reciprocated. Oscar was not a masochist enjoying suffering, nor was Bosie Douglas a devil leading Wilde to destruction. They were complementary characters, whose flaws meant they could never sustain an intimate relationship. Nevertheless, they were deeply attracted to one another, and the attraction was based in similar, pleasure-loving traits. They revelled in similar tastes for easy and luxurious living, aesthetics and the arts. Above all, they enjoyed each other's company. No other reading of the relationship is possible. It is this that took Wilde back to Bosie. This was certainly Wilde's view at the time. On 21 September he wrote to Robbie Ross a telling self-justification, arguing:

> my going back to Bosie was psychologically inevitable: and, setting aside the interior life of the soul, with its passion for self-realisation at all costs, the world forced it upon me. I cannot live without the atmosphere of love: I must love and be loved, whatever price I pay for it. I could have lived all my life with you, but you have other claims on you – claims you are too sweet a fellow to disregard – and all you could give me was a week of companionship . . . for the last month at Berneval I was so lonely I was on the brink of killing myself. The world shuts its gateway against me, and the door of Love lies open. . . . Of course I shall often be unhappy, but still I love him: the mere fact that he wrecked my life makes me love him.[2]

Oscar had no interior resources to survive on without constant companionship; worship, even. Berneval had hardly failed Wilde. He had loved the village in the Summer sunshine and planned to make it his home. He even speculated on building a house with the meagre capital he had left. It never seemed to occur to him that lack of companionship would be a serious problem for one of his nature. But when August brought rain and fog from the English Channel, Wilde suddenly found Berneval intolerable. His mercurial nature immediately turned to thoughts of perpetual sunshine, to be enjoyed along with the company of Bosie Douglas. His friends had done all they could, and Robbie deserved more than the cool assessment of his usefulness Wilde offered him in his letter. His friends did much by visiting and writing letters, and Robbie Ross did more. But even Ross had to return home to attend to business, leaving Wilde suffering the old *ennui* with no resources to combat the condition. He seemed unable to accept that the days when he was the magnetic centre of a crowd of adoring young men were over, and looked for a substitute.

This immediately turned out to be Bosie, whose unqualified desire to see Oscar took on great importance for Wilde when left by himself. Bosie's letters may have been siren songs, but Bosie was not a bad influence leading Oscar away from the good. Wilde knew all about his faults, and recognised openly Bosie's ability to damage his life. But the prospect of a return to the old ways was overpowering. Harris has Wilde saying "Every day I heard his voice calling, 'Come, come, to sunshine and me. Come to Naples with its wonderful museum of bronzes and Pompeii and Paestum, the city of Poseidon; I am waiting to welcome you. Come'. Who could resist it, Frank? love calling, calling with outstretched arms; who could stay in bleak Berneval and watch the sheets of rain falling, falling – and the grey mist shrouding the grey sea. . . . I resisted as long as I could, but when chill October came and Bosie came to Rouen for me, I gave up the struggle and yielded".[3] Harris's recollection is, as always, suspiciously precise, and the date is clearly wrong, but the essence rings true.

Bosie certainly offered the prospect of a romantic future in an evocative location, while resuming the relationship appealed to much that was deeply embedded within each man's psychology. They hoped to turn the clock back to 1894. Cold rationality suggested that the odds against this working were astronomical. But cold rationality had little part to play in bringing about the reunion. Bosie may have been less enthusiastic than Oscar. He took up his mother's invitation to got to Aix-les-Bains and spent five weeks with her and his sister "having a most delightful time".[4]

Wilde was desperate to meet Bosie and begin his exile anew. His letters in early September – to Ross, Will Rothenstein, and Carlos Blacker – are full of complaints about the weather, and his depression. To Blacker, who was a friend of both Oscar and Constance, Wilde wrote on 6 September that he was raising money to go to Italy, making the offhand comment that: "I am greatly disappointed that Constance has not asked me to come and see the children. I don't suppose now I will ever see them".[5] And with this remark Wilde ended his attempts at fatherhood.

Oscar's ability to square his desire to live with Bosie with the attacks in *De Profundis* is hard to explain. It is abundantly clear that Bosie had not read the letter or he might not have contemplated living with Wilde. Bosie later claimed that Ross had never sent the letter, but the truth is more likely that Ross did send a copy but Bosie tore it up without reading it.[6] Wilde might have assumed Bosie had read the letter and was referring to it when Bosie tried to discuss something else relating to prison matters. Wilde refused to respond, arguing that, when he was in prison, he had been "starving and half-mad"[7] and the matter was let drop. *De Profundis* never entered into the relationship again, and it would be fifteen years before anyone apart from Wilde and Ross knew what Wilde had said about Douglas in that dark night of the soul.

On 15 September 1897, Wilde left Dieppe heading south. Wilde was chronically short of money and after arriving in Paris applied his consummate intelligence to extracting cash from a sympathiser, choosing the novelist Vincent O'Sullivan. Wilde wrote to O'Sullivan, asking to meet for lunch. Oscar was in good form, telling O'Sullivan a favourite story of the time his friend Strong heard that the poet Verlaine was dying. Wishing to report this but disliking the mean street and squalid conditions in which Verlaine lived, Strong sent his manservant, a well-trained, imperturbable butler of the English school. The valet returned, inscrutable. "Well?" asked Strong. "I saw the gentleman, sir, and he died immediately". This anecdote created a pleasant mood in which O'Sullivan was receptive to Wilde's message, which was that, while his friends wished him to go to a mountain retreat, he himself favoured Italy. Having gained O'Sullivan's sympathy, Wilde declared: "I shall go to Italy to-night. Or, rather, I would go, but I am in an absurd position. I have no money". O'Sullivan immediately volunteered to supply the deficit, and the two men took a cab to a bank where the cash was procured.

O'Sullivan never regretted his action, writing in his memoir of Wilde: "It is one of the few things I look back on with satisfaction. It is not every day that one has the chance of relieving the anxiety of a genius and a hero".[8]

The assignation in Naples was now in train, Bosie having left his mother in Aix-les-Bains without informing her what he intended to do. In Naples, they stayed at the Hotel Royal, Bosie running up a bill which was left unpaid at the end of the fortnight's stay: the manager foolishly assumed that all English milords were millionaires, a view which Bosie was happy to leave uncorrected. In his *Autobiography* he commented: "in the year 1897 I still lived under the pleasing illusion that life more or less belonged to me, and that money was not a thing to take seriously".[9] Wilde still had much of his literary reputation intact, and he managed to persuade the composer Dalhousie Young to put up £100 advance for the libretto of a proposed opera on Daphnis and Chlöe, money which arrived on 22 September. This allowed the couple to take a villa in the town of Posillipo, near Naples, which they occupied on 1 October. Though he specified that Bosie would provide some of the lyrics, it is unlikely that either man intended that the opera would be produced and neither seems to have devoted serious attention to it. Eventually, Young realised that he would never see the libretto or his money again.

Life was very comfortable. The villa had a piano, on which Bosie played Bach, Chopin and Mozart. A young poet named Rocco, who wished to translate *Dorian Gray* into Italian, gave Wilde lessons in the language. They had a cook, Carmine, a maid, Maria, and two houseboys, Peppino and Michele, who waited on them at table. With servants costing little more than their keep in the 1890s, Bosie reckoned the weekly cost of the household was so inexpensive they could just about manage on the combination of the £3 per week allowance Oscar had from Constance, and his own £6 a week from Sybil. Rats infested the villa but were expelled with the aid of a local witch. Oscar added several verses to *The Ballad of Reading Gaol*, while hoping that he could secure a local production of *Salomé* which would revive his reputation. On 10 December he wrote to Leonard Smithers that the opera diva Eleanora Duse was reading for the part. Nothing came of it. Meanwhile, Bosie worked at sonnets. He wrote four which were to be included in his 1899 collection *The City of the Soul*, including the title poem itself.

Bosie also wrote a sonnet inspired by Mozart's *Don Giovanni*, which he sent to Stanley Makower, editor of a magazine called the *Musician*, on 2 October with a covering letter noting that Oscar had suggested he submit it.[10] Makower rejected the poem and Bosie forgot about it – it was not published in his lifetime – but Wilde was affronted and wrote to Makower, complaining that he had snubbed Bosie, who was "quite in the front of all the young poets of England".[11] Oscar was now elevating Bosie's literary reputation with the adoring eyes of a lover.

Wilde had to defend far more than Bosie's literary reputation. The elopement had caused fury among his friends. The most furious was Robbie Ross, who had been shattered by the news. As late as 24 August, Wilde had written him, apropos Bosie's refusal to visit him in Rouen, "Since Bosie wrote that he could not afford the forty francs to come to see me, he has never written. Nor have I. I am greatly hurt by his meanness and lack of imagination".[12] A month after this latest scathing attack on Bosie, Oscar and Bosie were living together in Italy. Ross could hardly understand Oscar's latest turnround, and was understandably traumatised. He realised that whatever he had hoped for his own relationship with Wilde – perhaps he envisaged a discreet *ménage à trois* involving the myopic Constance – nothing could survive Wilde's return to Bosie. Two days later, Wilde justified his behaviour in a letter to Carlos Blacker, attacking Constance. "I must remake my maimed life on my own lines. Had Constance allowed me to see my boys, my life would, I think, have been quite different. But this she would not do. I don't in any way venture to blame her for her action, but every action has its consequences. . . . My friends in England are greatly distressed. Still, they are good friends to me: and will remain so, most of them at any rate. You must remain so too".[13] Blacker was repelled by this attitude, but Wilde seemed oblivious.

In fact, Oscar seemed to have no idea of the way he alienated his friends. On 23 September he was justifying himself to Robbie Ross, and having satisfied himself that he had disposed of Ross's anger, on the 25th he dropped an inane postcard to him asking for the loan of a copy of *Salomé*. Ross did not respond, while Constance was goaded beyond endurance. Wilde received an uncharacteristically angry letter from his wife at the end of the month in which she railed: "I *forbid* you to see Lord Alfred Douglas. I forbid you to return to your filthy, insane life. I forbid you to live at Naples. I will not allow you to come to Genoa".[14] Wilde now attempted to dismiss Constance from his thoughts. On 3 October, he wrote to Robbie Ross complaining: "How can she really imagine that she can influence or control my life? She might just as well influence and control my art. So I suppose she will now try to deprive me of my wretched

£3 a week. Women are so petty and Constance has no imagination. I wish to goodness she would leave me alone. I don't meddle with her life. I accept the separation from the children: I acquiesce. Why does she want to go on bothering me, and trying to ruin me?"[15]

Wilde displayed no understanding of the situation he had created for his family, and indeed very little insight into his own situation. In the same letter he noted in puzzlement: "It is very curious that none of the English colony here have left cards on us. Fortunately we have a few simple friends amongst the poorer classes".[16] While the tolerant expatriate English in Italy had accepted Bosie Douglas without a qualm, they drew the line at Oscar Wilde. He did not understand why. On 16 November he complained to Ross that he had not written to him for ages "except about the worrying business of my unsaleable poem".[17] Bosie and he were "terribly isolated". The isolation was less immediately damaging than the news he imparted to Ross that the financial blow he had long expected from Constance had finally fallen. His solicitor had written to say that he would be deprived of his allowance of £3 per week. Wilde had no other income at all to live on. Bosie had £25 per month allowance from his mother, and Wilde wrote to Ada Leverson that this was not enough even for Bosie's own wants.[18]

The financial situation at the villa was now desperate. A petty sum from Smithers of £10 was so badly needed that Wilde went to Thomas Cook's office in Naples twice a day to see if it had arrived. Wilde's correspondence with Ross and Smithers over the *Ballad* was now laced with acid oversensitivity about his personal life. On the key issue of the stopping of the allowance his reactions were savage. He abused his friend More Adey, when he discovered how Adey and Ross had agreed that Bosie Douglas was "a disreputable person" within the terms of the agreement they had negotiated on his behalf. Adey, astonishingly faithful despite Wilde's abusive letters, wrote that all he and Ross was done was to agree that Bosie and Wilde were living together, which triggered the clause in the agreement that Constance had deliberately inserted.[19] Wilde had walked with his eyes open into a trap his neglected and patronised wife had artlessly laid. He melodramatically claimed he was contemplating suicide, but did nothing so drastic. He realised that if he was to continue living, he had to compromise. With a humiliating swallowing of pride, Wilde was forced to turn to Robbie Ross to seek an accommodation.

On 23 November, he wrote to Robbie, as he had not heard from Hansell, his solicitor, or Adrian Hope as guardian of his children, offering the compromise of a pledge that he would not live with Bosie in the same house again. He attacked his wife. He attacked Ernest Leverson in a continuing dispute over what happened on the last day of his last trial, then rambled on about the proofs of the *Ballad*, local prospects of staging *Salomé*, and the difficulty of getting his books out of the Neapolitan port system as he had no money.[20] The letter mixed serious and trivial issues in a way that suggests he had lost any perspective on what mattered and how his friends were reacting. By now he was losing room for manoeuvre. On the 27th he wrote to Adey shamefacedly offering the compromise he had offered Ross. The following day he wrote a confused letter to Smithers, partly about the poem, but also about the iniquity of a situation in which he was being offered the choice of dying of starvation or "to blow my brains out in a Naples urinal".[21] The threat was ignored by those who had power over Wilde: nothing less than complete separation would do. He had now fallen out badly with Robbie Ross, who told Leonard Smithers he no longer had Wilde's confidence in business matters and wished no longer to be connected with Wilde's affairs. Ross has been cast as the villain of the piece, but it is clear that Ross and Adey attempted to do what they could to rescue the situation; they could do little, given the wholehearted hostility of those who had control of the finances of Oscar Wilde and Bosie Douglas.

Oscar and Bosie seem to have enjoyed themselves in the Neapolitan Autumn, money worries apart. Bosie recalled in his *Autobiography* that "Oscar and I were fairly happy at Naples, though we had several quarrels".[22] A quarrel with Bosie was rarely a light matter, but the disagreements do not appear to have been serious. Bosie could not recall life at the villa at all clearly, remembering only the infestation of rats dispelled by the local witch.[23] Wilde does not appear to have left any memories of the weeks together either, but there is no reason to think they were anything but pleasant, despite Bosie imagining later that Wilde tired of him because he was losing his youthful good looks.[24] When Smithers's cheque for £10 arrived they went to Capri for three days, and when the Swedish Dr Axel Munthe invited Bosie to dinner, he ensured that Oscar was included in the invitation. Superficially, life was civilised.

But, behind the scenes, Nemesis was waiting in the wings. Para-doxically, it was not the hated Scarlet Marquis who would finally prise Oscar and Bosie apart, but the two neglected women in the drama. Constance Wilde saw Bosie as her husband's evil genius. Sybil Montgomery regarded Wilde as the corrupter of her son. They now made common cause to end the relationship. On 13 November, Sybil wrote to More Adey, cast again as intermediary, making her views clear; stating that the struggle to live in Naples was over, as Oscar's allowance was now cut off and, though the rent was paid till the end of January, the two men did not have enough to live on. They would be forced to separate – at least for the present.[25]

Sybil was now proposing a tough settlement, to continue Bosie's allowance only on the strict understanding that the two men would no longer live together, and would sunder their relationship completely. On top of that, she offered generously to make a one-time, ex-gratia payment to Wilde of £200 to settle his debts.

The news arrived in Prosillipo towards the end of November, two months after the couple had arrived at the Villa, with predictably depressing results. Bosie went so far as to complain to friends that he and Oscar were having to write around, begging for money, and had pawned personal items in order to survive. He painted a desolate picture, in which his mother had already cut off his allowance; while Oscar's family had also drawn the purse strings firmly shut, on the grounds that he had broken his agreement with Constance. If it weren't for the fact that the couple had paid a quarter's rent in advance, it is likely that they would have faced the uncertain indignity of eviction, sooner or later – although Oscar's talent for wheedling money out of the barest acquaintances might possibly have kept things going a while longer. However, there is no doubt that two Aesthetes with a love of good living were facing a desperate time. Ultimately there was no choice but to cave in, whether permanently or just for form's sake, until the financial situation improved.

Within two days, Bosie wrote that he and Oscar would give Sybil the written assurance she required, and left for Rome on 2 December. The next day, he wrote to Sybil that he was miserable without Wilde, and defended his actions on the ground that he could not have said to Wilde that he would not live with him because his fortunes had changed.[26] But this mood changed. Four days later, having had time to reflect on the previous two months, he wrote to Sybil saying that he was glad to have got away. He had passionately wanted to live with Oscar, but once he had achieved this he was miserable and stayed only out of a sense of honour.[27]

This has the ring of truth. Bosie had wanted to go to Oscar, found the experience disappointing, but had not been able to escape until his mother and Constance forced the issue. The two months in Naples appear to have killed the longing for Oscar in Bosie's heart and this made parting for him much easier. Whether his love for Wilde was dying before the trials and had been sustained by the disasters of 1895 and his imprisonment it is impossible to tell. But it is abundantly clear that Bosie had a desire for Wilde's company before the experience in Naples that was no longer there afterwards. He would continue to be a friend of Wilde's. He would never again be his lover.

Whether or not Oscar wanted Bosie to leave is a question clouded by Wilde's deliberate myth making. Frank Harris records Wilde telling him the following year that life with Bosie had been intolerable, a repeat of 1894. According to Harris, he recalled the quarrels with Bosie as being far more serious and troubling than Bosie would ever concede:

> When I had money I gave it to him without counting, so when I could not pay I thought Bosie would pay, and I was content. But at once I discovered that he expected me to find the money. I did what I could; but when my means were exhausted the evil days began. He expected me to write plays and get money for us both as in the past; but I couldn't; I simply could not. When we were dunned his temper went to pieces. . . . As soon as the means of life were straightened, he became sullen and began reproaching me; why didn't I write? Why didn't I earn money? What was the good of me? As if I could write under such conditions. . . .
>
> At last there was a washing bill to be paid: Bosie was dunned for it, and when I came in, he raged and whipped me with his tongue. It was appalling: I had done everything for him, given him everything, lost everything, and I now I could only stand and see love turn to hate. . . . Then he left me, Frank, and now there is no hope for me. . . .[28]

Wilde first made these accusations, without the detail, in a celebrated and controversial letter to Robbie Ross of 2 March 1898, regarding his desertion by Bosie, as he saw it, "the most bitter experience of a bitter life".[29] The pity of it was that, while Oscar Wilde made his complaints to Harris and Ross, he never made them to Bosie. Douglas remained blissfully ignorant of Wilde's belief that he had been badly treated – just as Wilde remained ignorant of Bosie's exultation at having freed himself from the relationship. Money also remained a running sore blighting the friendship. Bosie secured the £200 from his mother to pay Wilde's debts and believed this wiped out the Queensberry family's debt of honour to Wilde. Wilde remained convinced he had been promised £500 which never materialised. These conflicts of understanding provided undercurrents of bad feeling that would poison relationships long after Wilde was dead.

The immediately important issue was that a decisive step had been taken: Bosie had gone, leaving Wilde in sole possession of the Villa Giudice. It made no difference to Wilde's parlous financial state. He wrote to Smithers, probably on 10 December, complaining that he had written to Arthur Clifton, a friend of his and Constance's, and to Adrian Hope, asking for his allowance to be restored, but had been ignored. In fact, Constance was moving towards restoring the allowance, though she was so much distracted by pain that she could not be expected to act rapidly. She also had to be sure that, when Bosie left, he had gone for good. Bosie's departure did however trigger Sybil's money payments. Wilde received the first of two payments of £100 via More Adey on 13 December. His immediate money worries were relieved, but he was left stranded by the failure of the Neapolitan idyll. Both men knew that they would never live together again.

ELEVEN

Parisian Intermezzo

Oscar Wilde remained in Naples alone and without purpose. He was to tell Robbie Ross that the collapse of the relationship was "the most bitter experience of a bitter life",[1] yet the devastation which might have been expected to follow Bosie's departure did not happen. The collapse of the Naples episode did not affect his extraordinary self-belief. Some days after Bosie had left, Oscar was visited by Vincent O'Sullivan, who later testified to Wilde's mental resilience. O'Sullivan was struck by how little the disasters of the last three years had affected Wilde, commenting: "Other men from such an experience would have emerged stupefied and crushed. Wilde was not crushed at all. He had to a very unusual degree the gift of putting away from him by a turn of the imagination what his physical organisation revolted against".[2]

Oscar told O'Sullivan that he had contemplated suicide but turned away from the idea, remarking that it had never had any real appeal to him:

> "There is a garden here at Naples", he said one evening, "a garden where those who have determined to kill themselves go. A short time, after Bosie had gone away, I was so cast down by the boredom of leaving the villa at Posillipo, and by the annoyance that some absurd friends were giving me, that I felt I could bear no more. . . . But one night when there were no stars I went down to that garden. As I sat there absolutely alone in the darkness, I heard a rustling noise, and sighing: and misty cloudlike things came round me. And I realised that they were the little souls of those who had killed themselves in that place, condemned to linger there ever after. . . . And when I thought that such would be the fate of my soul too, the temptation to kill myself left me and has never come back".[3]

Wilde was spinning a fairy tale here as he had done for his children, with his imagined insights into the spirit world of the Irish sheanachie, but the essence of what he said rings true. He had too much resilience to be crushed by his fall, even when he was deserted by Bosie and left without money in exile in a city he hardly knew. Above all, he had to deal with the fracturing of his two closest friendships, those with Bosie Douglas and Robbie Ross. On 9 February 1898, Wilde wrote to Leonard Smithers from Naples with a list of people to be sent a copy of *The Ballad of Reading Gaol*, including Ross and Bosie. He noted sadly in a postscript: "I don't know Robbie Ross's address – it used to be Phillimore Gardens – but it is three months since he last wrote to me, so perhaps he has left. Kindly show this postscript to Robbie".[4]

Wilde's hints to Smithers that he should make amends on his behalf with Ross bore fruit immediately. The two men resumed an intimate correspondence. On the 18th Wilde was writing to Robbie defending homosexuality – "Uranian love" as he called it – with the comment: "It is very unfair of people being horrid to me about Bosie and Naples. A patriot put in prison for loving his country loves his country, and a poet in prison for loving boys loves boys. To have altered my life would have been to have admitted that Uranian love is ignoble. I hold it to be noble – more noble than other loves".[5]

Both Bosie and Wilde were still practising homosexuals at this time. Bosie would abandon and condemn his homosexuality after the turn of the century. Wilde never abandoned or condemned anything about his life, and left no sign that he ever would have done. He had however been mortified to discover that he was being cited as an example of the new pathological category of "homosexual" by Max Nordau and his school of German sociologists. He had written to Smithers on 11 December: "My life cannot be patched up. There is a doom on it. Neither to myself, nor to others, am I any longer a joy. I am now simply a pauper of a rather low order; the fact that I am also a pathological problem in the eyes of German scientists is only interesting to German scientists; and even in their works I am tabulated, and come under the law of averages! *Quantum mutatis!*"[6] [*Original emphasis*]

Wilde used *The Ballad of Reading Goal* to repair his fractured friendships, asking Smithers to send a copy to Bosie at the Hotel Bellevue at Menton in France,[7] showing that he did not harbour bitterness over the events at Naples. Constance also showed she was not wholly alienated from her husband, writing to her brother on 19 February praising the "wonderful poem", commenting: "It is frightfully tragic and makes one cry".[8] Wilde wrote a generous letter to Frank Harris, commenting: "I have never forgotten your kindness to me when I was in prison and I hope you will accept from me a copy of *The Ballad of Reading Gaol* as a slight sign of recognition on my part".[9] Wilde never forgot the loyalty Robbie Ross and Frank Harris had shown him. When he came to publish the texts of *The Importance of Being Earnest* and *An Ideal Husband* in 1898, he dedicated the former "To Robert Baldwin Ross, in appreciation, in affection", and the latter "To Frank Harris, A Slight Tribute to his Power and Distinction as an artist, His chivalry and nobility as a friend".

The poem was a great success, going through seven printings by 1899, but doing nothing for his parlous financial position. At the end of February he claimed only 22 francs were left to him. It was imperative that Constance be induced to restore his allowance, and he had written to Ross on 21 February asking him to intervene with Constance to this end: "I am going to write to Constance to say that really now my income, such as it is, must be restored. Bosie and I are irrevocably parted – we can never be together again – and it is absurd to leave me to starve. Will you suggest this to her, if you write?"[10] Robbie Ross did indeed write, acting as go-between for husband and wife with momentous consequences. In order to convince Constance that the breach with Bosie was irrevocable, Ross asked Wilde for a description of the relationship with Bosie in Naples. Wilde replied, probably on 2 March, with a mischievous and inaccurate description of events, which was later used to tarnish Douglas as a Judas figure:

> The facts of Naples are very bald and brief. Bosie, for four months, by endless letters, offered me a "home". He offered me love, affection and care, and promised that I should never want for anything. After four months I accepted his offer, but when we met at Aix on our way to Naples I found that he had no money, no plans and had forgotten all his promises. His one idea was that I should raise money for us both. I did so, to the extent of £120. On this, Bosie lived quite happily. When it came to his having, of course, to repay his own share, he became terrible, unkind, mean and penurious, except where his own pleasures were concerned, and when my allowance ceased, he left.
>
> With regard to the £500, which he said was a "debt of honour", etc., he has written to me to say that he admits that it is a debt of honour, but that "lots of gentlemen don't pay their debts of honour", that it is "quite a common thing" and that no-one thinks anything the worse of them.
>
> I don't know what you said to Constance, but the bald fact is that I accepted the offer of a "home" and found that I was expected to

provide the money, and that when I could no longer do so, I was left to my own devices.

It is, of course, the most bitter experience of a bitter life: it is a blow quite awful and paralysing, but it had to come, and I know it is better that I should never see him again. I don't want to. He fills me with horror. Ever yours. . ."[11]

This melodramatic and self-serving letter became evidence for the Judas myth which blames Bosie Douglas for the collapse of the Naples experiment, and which has been endlessly recycled for over a century.[12] It was elaborated in the passage to Frank Harris already quoted, and yet was a distortion of the truth. Despite Wilde's references to Bosie's financial irresponsibility, Bosie cannot have expected to live off Wilde. Bosie's £6 per week was at least more than Wilde's £3 per week, and Bosie knew Wilde was bankrupt. A return to 1894 was impossible, and Bosie must have paid his share of the costs. The spinner of fairy tales was here spinning a most unpleasantly inaccurate version of the truth. It had very serious consequences in 1912 when Bosie sued Arthur Ransome for libel over allegations made by Ransome against him, for the letter was key evidence supporting the view that Bosie had betrayed Wilde in Naples.

Equally seriously, Wilde conceals – there is no other word – the arrangement that Bosie made with Sybil to provide £200 for Wilde to pay his debts and allow him a few weeks' grace. The impression that Bosie cared only for himself is wholly fallacious. Egotistical though Bosie was, he had done what he could to save Wilde from the worst results of the cul-de-sac they found themselves in. Wilde provided a dangerously one-sided view of the collapse of the relationship, presumably to salve the conscience of Ross and Constance Wilde, who were allowed to see the breakdown of the Naples affair as wholly Bosie's fault. Ross was sufficiently astute to allow Wilde to back himself into a corner. Having heard that Sybil had paid Wilde £200 to break off the relationship, he queried Wilde's view of the matter and Wilde replied with pure sophistry, arguing: "It is quite untrue that I received £200 from Lady Q on condition of not living with Bosie. Bosie owed me £500. He admitted this a debt of honour, and got his brother to formally guarantee it, etc. He paid me £200 of this, but I have had no communication with that mischievous foolish woman; I simply received less than half of what Bosie owes me. I know that Bosie made terms with his mother, but that cannot concern me. In paying debts of honour people cannot make terms.

So pray tell my wife that it is quite untrue, or that you know nothing about it. The former statement would be the true one."[13]

Wilde was in no position to make statements about the truth. The idea that he had not received £200 from Lady Queensberry is untenable. While he had had no direct communication with Sybil, More Adey had sent him the £200 and made it clear that it came from Sybil, not from Bosie. On 9 December 1897, Adey had written: "I enclose a cheque for £100, the amount I have just received from Lady Queensberry. She says she will pay the second hundred to me in a week or ten days. I write in great haste to catch the post. . .".[14]

Wilde's mendacious view of the breakdown in Naples had serious consequences after his death. It is a sad comment on Wilde's nature and state of mind in 1898 that he could pen a letter that Bosie later described, with understandable hyperbole, as "one of the most astonishing products that the history of literature has ever recorded".[15] Wilde may have had reasons for penning the letter in the depressed circumstances of February 1898, desperately trying to persuade his wife that the affair with Bosie was over and he should have his allowance restored. But he never attempted to have the letter destroyed.

However, Wilde's comments to Ross made no difference to his behaviour. Wilde resumed friendly relations almost immediately with the man who "filled him with horror". As soon as he had denounced Bosie as someone he should never see again, and that Bosie filled him with horror, he simply forgot what he had written. Nor did Robbie Ross enlighten him. Bosie was blissfully unaware of the poisonous letters Ross had in his possession and remained on good terms with both men. In his *Autobiography*, he recalled, *vis à vis* Wilde:

> During the next two years I saw Oscar constantly in Paris, where I was living in a small flat in the Avenue Kleber. I was still very hard up, but, out of what little I had, I did what I could for him. As a matter of fact, during that time he really had far more money than I had, for, though he had no regular income except his £3 a week, he was helped by a great number of people, including Frank Harris. . . . I could mention a dozen other persons who gave him money, including Ernest Leverson, Dal Young and Claude Lowther. He also got a good lot from Smithers . . . and he sold the scenario of the play, *Mr and Mrs Daventry* . . . to at least half-a-dozen different people.[16]

This is fair comment. The dispute with Frank Harris over the scenario mentioned was savage enough to cloud his last weeks of life. And, despite later arguments over finance, there can be little doubt that Bosie did help Oscar with money, and in his better moments Wilde acknowledged this – as in the letter to Robbie Ross of 11 May 1898, when Wilde claimed: "As regards Bosie, he has been very nice to me . . . when he had money he was very hospitable and generous in paying for things when we were together. Of course the difficulty is that Bosie when he asks me to dinner will always insist on going to a very expensive place and ordering champagne, spending about sixty francs in the whole evening. I would be quite content with a three franc dinner, but he hates it".[17] Douglas, though poor, still had expectations of an inheritance from his father that would allow him to live in luxury, so he saw no need to adjust his standard of living.

Wilde had nothing to look forward to and was very poor in the last years of his life, despite occasional handouts from friends and acquaintances. With those who were prepared to accept his indigent and aimless existence, he could still sparkle. With those who could not, or were embarrassed by his poverty, relations died. One such was André Gide. Gide met Wilde by accident, being called over to him as Oscar sat in a pavement cafe. Gide preferred to sit with his back to the passers-by, facing Wilde, to avoid being noticed, but Wilde insisted they sit side by side. Gide gave him some money, they parted on uneasy terms, and never met again.[18] However, despite his poverty, many people commented that Oscar's brilliant flow of conversation remained undimmed to the end.[19]

* * *

Wilde was now at peace with himself sexually, partly because he no longer pursued ideals like beauty and paradox, but simply accepted life and lived from day to day. Sexual experience was no longer dressed up with a sense of sin or the dramatic pursuit of Greek eroticism, but simply as matter-of-fact pleasure. In this, he and Bosie and their circle found a commonality of experience. For Bosie, homosexuality had always been mainly a physical pleasure; and, while he sometimes had a sentimental attachment to brief encounters, the names of his lovers were never recorded, for they had no lasting place in his life. Where his love for Oscar was concerned, this was mainly an emotional attachment, though as he remembered – and Wilde did not – there had been a physical side to it. This was now history. Love had passed from their relationship, but the relationship between the two men was maintained in part through their common pursuit of sexual encounters. Bosie later became ambivalent, but Oscar made no attempt to conceal his pursuit of "Uranian love". His most enduring relationship was with a young soldier in the marine infantry, Maurice Gilbert, whom he was seen embracing by the journalist, Jacques Durell of *L'Echo de Paris.*[20] Maurice became one of the intimates of Wilde's circle, which, as in 1893–4, did not value sexual fidelity. They cruised the boulevards, Bosie prominent among them. Writing to Ross in late April 1898, Wilde commented: "Bosie is very angelic and quiet. It did him a great deal of good being trampled on by Maurice".[21] The meaning of this is obscure, but suggests that Wilde and Bosie shared relations with Maurice. Wilde's activities were in no way affected by the sudden and tragic news that Constance had died, after a second dangerous spinal operation, on 7 April, at the age of 40. On paper, Wilde was grief-stricken, especially in letters to Carlos Blacker. When his friends met him, the grief was not so evident. His feelings for Constance had died many years earlier.

Soliciting sex, however, remained an emotional neccessity. Writing to Ross from Rome in the Spring of 1900, alluding in passing to his odd obsession with religion, he summed up his failure as a husband and the choices this left him in a telling phrase. "How evil it is to buy love, and evil to sell it! And yet what purple hours one can snatch from that grey, slowly-moving thing we call Time! My mouth is twisted with kissing, and I feed on fevers. The Cloister or the Café – there is my future. I tried the hearth, but it was a failure".[22] Yet on 1 May he found that his failed embrace of the hearth provided lasting support. Constance had willed him his allowance in perpetuity.

Bosie meanwhile was showing a keen interest in the "brigands" on the boulevard. On 11 May, Wilde wrote to Reggie Turner that: "He is devoted to a dreadful little ruffian aged 14, who he loves because at night, in the scanty intervals he can steal from the pursuit of an arduous criminal profession, he sells bunches of purple violets in front of the Café la Paix. Also every time he goes home with Bosie he tries to rent him. This, of course, adds to his terrible fascination. We call him 'Florifer', a lovely name. He also keeps another boy, aged twelve! who Bosie wishes to know, but the wise Florifer declines".[23] Bosie was living recklessly as usual. In May, he crossed swords with the proprietor of his apartment in the Rue Tronchet, who objected to Maurice staying with him. He also objected to Bosie's visitors arriving with him at midnight and leaving at 3.15 a.m.[24]

Wilde was now physically a shell of the man he had been, while Bosie lived the inconsequential life of a remittance man. Robbie and Reggie Turner visited Europe that August, but pointedly avoided Paris, which hurt Oscar. Bosie returned from Aix with £30 from Sybil to go to Venice: he promptly lost it at the Casino and had to pawn his cufflinks to get back to Paris. This was a sad life for both men, but unlike Oscar, Bosie had dreams of re-establishing himself in British society.[25] Rightly, he could see no future in a life of exile and, throughout that Summer of 1898, pursued the prospects of a return. He was anxious to oversee the publication of his poems, both a collection of nonsense rhymes for children and his collected adult poems, *The City of the Soul*. Bosie returned to London in November. He stayed in his mother's house in Cadogan Place until March 1899, and was so preoccupied with his poems that he dropped out of Oscar's life altogether. On 26 November, Wilde wrote pathetically to Reggie Turner asking for information: "Is he happy to be back? And are people kind to him? How is he behaving? He has only written to me once – a brief scrawl – not very charming".[26] Wilde was desperately short of money and tried to extort cash from Robbie Ross that November by claiming that the innkeeper at Nogent was threatening to pawn his clothes. He had to apologise as he had already told this lie once before.

In early June, however, Bosie was back in Paris, dining with Oscar at the Avenue Kleber, and received news of a good review of *The City of the Soul*, apparently while dining with Wilde.[27] Bosie returned home in the Autumn of 1899 to oversee the publication of a nonsense poem, "The Duke of Berwick", illustrated by Anthony Ludovici. His return to London saw the final act of his troubled relationship with his father. Hearing that Queensberry was ill, he visited him at Bailey's Hotel in Kensington. The Marquis embraced his son, wept copiously, called him his darling boy, promised to restore his allowance, and wrote to his cousin, Arthur Douglas, who managed his affairs, to this effect. The reconciliation lasted a week before Queensberry reverted to type. He wrote Bosie an abusive letter saying he would not give him a penny until he knew what his relations were with "that beast Wilde" – something Bosie had already done in a letter to his cousin Algie Bourke, who had shown the letter to the Marquis before the meeting at Bailey's Hotel. Bosie immediately reverted to type and wrote back an abusive letter. This ended the reconciliation.

Bosie never spoke to his father again, and saw him only once. This was a glimpse from a cab, when Bosie noted his father looked "wild and haggard". He discovered from his brother-in-law, Sir George Fox-Pitt, that Queensberry believed his son hated him and was responsible for the imaginary troubles from which he was suffering. He believed he was being persecuted by what he called "Oscar Wilders" who had driven him from various hotels by shouting abusive epithets at him at night.[28] Queensberry was displaying the same symptoms of serious mental illness that his brother Jim had suffered. Towards the end of 1899 he had a stroke at the Raleigh Club which left him partly paralysed and scarcely conscious. Sybil visited him and there was a tearful reconciliation. Queensberry told her she was the only woman he had ever loved. However, when Percy went to visit his father, the prematurely aged Marquis showed that he had not mellowed. When his son and heir entered the room, Queensberry sat up in bed and spat in his face.[29] Queensberry died on 31 January 1900, aged 55.

Despite his animus against his eldest sons, the Marquis had not cut them out of his will and Percy and Bosie now came into their inheritance. Bosie received some £8,000 immediately, with a possible £20,000 in total. This was wealth in 1900, and Bosie may well have felt that he could now live the life of the aristocratic literary gentleman, as he believed was his due. Oscar Wilde recorded wryly in a letter to George Ives shortly after Queensberry's funeral, "Bosie is over here, with his brother. They are in deep mourning and the highest spirits. The English are like that".[30] However, Bosie was never to live the life he believed he deserved; and not just because, with typical profligacy, he managed to waste his inheritance, largely on racehorses. He had already received a snub when he sent a copy of his poems to Sir Herbert Warren, President of Magdalen and a notorious social weathervane. Warren sent it back by return of post with a curt letter saying he could not accept the volume. This could be dismissed as the prejudice of an individual, for the poems had sold well. However, when Bosie issued a second edition under his own name, sales dried up. And if Bosie was inclined to put this down to the limits of public interest in poetry, the British Army made his position unmistakably clear.

The early disasters of the Boer War in 1899 had awakened Bosie's latent patriotism. He tried to enlist and was directed to the Duke of Cambridge's Corps, a volunteer cavalry unit, recruited by Lord Arthur Hill, composed entirely of gentlemen prepared to pay for their horses and equipment.

Bosie went to the depot and, after passing the riding, shooting and medical tests, was told he was accepted and left a cheque for £250 to cover initial equipment costs. Shortly afterwards, his cheque was returned to him, with a curt note to the effect that his services were not required. Bosie wrote to Hill, uncle of another of his childhood friends, Artie Downshire, telling him in typical Queensberry fashion what he thought of his rejection. It did no good, Bosie remained firmly out of the Army.

He then went back to France, where he spent the money from his inheritance on setting up a racing stable. It was at this point that the final, ferocious row between Oscar and Bosie took place. Again, it was over money, which had played such an important role in the tragedy. Robbie Ross thought it was time that he finally discharged his financial obligation to Oscar, and made a proposal. Ross suggested to Wilde that he propose to Bosie that he set up an annuity of £2,000 from his estate, which would give Oscar a regular income of £140 per annum. In the civil war between the Douglas and Ross factions that would break out after the Ransome libel case, this was interpreted as a deliberate attempt by Ross to stir up trouble by persuading Oscar to make an unreasonable demand which he knew Bosie would reject. Bosie's supporters point out that he made a number of generous donations to Wilde once he had received his money, and Bosie in his *Autobiography* lists sums paid to Oscar Wilde from his bank account, in the name of Melmott, Melmoth, or Melnotte, between 12 February and 15 November 1900, totalling £332, plus a payment of £20 to Robbie Ross on 30 April 1901.[31]

These facts are undeniable, but do not prove that what Ross was suggesting was mischievous or unreasonable. Gifts, however generous, remained charity, and subject to the whim of the giver. They provided no security for Wilde, even if the giver had not been the evil-tempered, capricious – and financially unstable – Lord Alfred Douglas. It was perfectly reasonable to suggest that a lump sum should be settled on Wilde to secure his future and, coming from Ross, who had struggled for four years to keep Wilde in funds, the suggestion was eminently understandable. Nor need it have cost Bosie a penny, as Wilde would have been unable to touch the capital. However logical the proposal was, it set off a characteristic Douglas explosion. After the dust cleared, Oscar reported sadly to Ross:

> I asked Bosie what you suggested – without naming any sum at all – after dinner. He had just won £400 at the races, and £800 a few days before, so he was in high spirits. When I spoke to him he went into

> paroxysms of rage, followed by satirical laughter, and said it was the most monstrous suggestion he had ever heard, that he would do nothing of the kind, that he was astounded at my suggesting such a thing, that he did not recognise that I had any claim of any kind on him. He was really revolting: I was quite disgusted. I told Frank Harris about it, and he was greatly surprised: but made the wise observation "One should never ask for anything; it is always a mistake." He said I should have got someone to sound Bosie, and ask him for me. I had also the same idea, but you did not seem to like the prospect of a correspondence with Bosie where money was concerned, and I am not surprised.[32]

Bosie's view of the incident was more measured, referring in his *Autobiography* to Wilde's view in this letter as follows:

> On the occasion to which he refers . . . he had asked me for £2,000, and I had told him that up to that time I had received only £8,000 from my father's estate, and could not expect to get more than another £6,000 as my whole inheritance, and that this was all the money which I had any expectation of getting for the rest of my life, I could not possibly give him such a large sum all at once.
>
> Before he asked me for the modest sum of £2,000 I had already given him, a few moments before, 2,000 francs (£80). In fact it was my gift to him of this sum which had started his begging, or rather demanding, more money. What he said in effect was "I am much obliged for this two thousand francs, but does it not occur to you that now that you have come into all this money you ought to do something substantial for me? I think you ought to give me at least a couple of thousand pounds."
>
> I was taken aback by his impudence, and I told him frankly that I thought his suggestion was outrageous, that I did not see any reason why he had a right, as he seemed to think he had, to look to me for financial support, but that I was, all the same, ready, as his friend, to help him, in reason, whenever I could, as I had already done. At the time when this incident occurred I had already given him at least £200 that year.[33]

Douglas is being economical with the truth; clearly, he completely lost his temper. The breathless language of this extract, particularly the third paragraph, suggests that Bosie was struggling to control himself writing about the incident even thirty years after it happened. On the night, he was even more savage than Wilde could bring himself to record to Ross. Frank Harris recounted Bosie's view of the quarrel on the lines suggested by Wilde. When Bosie invited Harris to see his horses at Chantilly, he could not stop himself talking about the quarrel. Harris noted "the strained white face I had seen before at the Café Royal", which others had noted when Bosie was in a temper – and the comment: "'I don't see that there is any claim at all. . . . He could earn all the money he wants if he would only write; but he won't do anything. He is lazy, and getting lazier and lazier every day . . . he is intolerable. I thought when he kept asking me for that money tonight, he was like an old prostitute . . . he was just like an old fat prostitute', and he gloated over the word, 'and I told him so'".[34]

It is possible that Wilde had misunderstood or failed clearly to explain the idea of an annuity, as it would have cost Douglas nothing, but tied up a little capital for a year or two. The fact that Bosie recalled the precise figure of £2,000 suggests that the request was made, despite Wilde's assertion that no figure was mentioned. Bosie, however, undoubtedly produced this contemptuous dismissal of his friend. He attempted to defend his use of the word "prostitute" in a letter to Harris, which Harris published at the start of the Corici Friede edition of his book, which Douglas succeeded in getting banned in Britain.[35] Bosie's view of Oscar Wilde at this point was stunningly dismissive. The quarrel did not, however, permanently damage relations between the two men: quarrels never did. Wilde would meet and dine with Bosie again, but their relationship was clearly tenuous at best.

Wilde's health was now giving rise to concern. He had been seriously ill in February 1900 but recovered. He was well enough to visit southern Italy in April, securing a blessing from the Pope, but remained concerned about his health throughout the Summer. Bosie and Percy were due to attend the grouse shooting at Strathpeffer in the Scottish Highlands on the Glorious 12th, but before going entertained Oscar at a dinner in Paris. Before the end of the dinner Oscar became depressed and told Bosie he thought he would not live to see the start of the twentieth century. "If another century began, and I was still alive", he said, "it really would be more than the English could stand".[36] Bosie pooh-poohed this depression, and promised to send Oscar a cheque from Scotland. He did so on 16 August.

Bosie would not see Oscar Wilde alive again. By September, Wilde was in bed, tormented by pain in the ear from the wound caused by the prison fall, which was now part of a more serious illness. It had not initially been related to the accident, having shown itself in a serious rash which covered large parts of his body and led to incessant scratching, that he put down to food poisoning from eating mussels. He consulted doctors, and one diagnosed neurasthenia, a depressive condition. His actual disease remains a mystery; but, though syphilis has been suspected, notably by Wilde's biographer Richard Ellmann, Ellmann himself notes that syphilitic rashes do not itch.[37] The embassy doctor visited for the first time on 27 September. He advised an operation on the ear, and Wilde borrowed money to have it done on 10 October. This increased his money worries, intensifying his quarrel with Harris over the play *Mr and Mrs Daventry*, which he accused Harris of having stolen from him. Right up until 20 November, with only ten days to live, he was writing long, accusatory letters to Harris.[38]

After the operation Wilde was very ill and, as always when in difficulties, he turned to the faithful Ross. After Brighton, Bosie was never an option where illness was concerned. Wilde telegraphed Ross on 11 and 12 October and he arrived on the morning of the 17th. Wilde had recovered sufficiently to go out, walking with difficulty and disobeying his doctors' orders not to drink, absinthe especially being prohibited (it was later made illegal). When Ross objected to Wilde drinking, Wilde killed it with the bitter comment: "And what have I got to live for, Bobbie?"

The doctor did not see Wilde's condition as particularly grave, but on 3 November the nurse who dressed Oscar's wounds each day told Ross that Wilde could live only three or four months longer unless he changed his lifestyle. Oscar was now convinced he was going to die but Ross thought he was exaggerating and, although he wrote to Bosie in Scotland, Ross did not stress the real threat, telling Douglas only that worry over debt was retarding Oscar's recovery – could he help? Douglas promptly sent some money. The idea that Bosie knew Wilde was terminally ill and chose not to visit him is false. Ross himself did not realise that Oscar was terminally ill. The same day, Reggie Turner turned up and Oscar told him he had dreamed he had been supping with the dead. Turner commented, "My dear Oscar, you were probably the life and soul of the party"[39] and Oscar became high-spirited for a time. This improvement convinced Ross that the immediate crisis had passed, so he decided to leave on 12 November to see his mother on the Riviera, a decision that upset Wilde greatly. He told Turner and the nurse to leave the room as he wanted to bid goodbye to Ross, which he did with many tears. Ross was stern, thinking him merely hysterical. He regretted this later, for these were the last articulate words Wilde spoke to him. Bosie had not been told how the illness was developing, for neither Ross nor Turner thought the situation was critical.[40]

Reggie Turner kept Ross informed on the situation in Paris and came to the conclusion that they had been too optimistic. On the 27th, Ross was alarmed to hear from Turner that Wilde was deteriorating rapidly. A telegram soon after read briefly "Almost hopeless" and Ross started back for Paris at once. When Ross reached the hotel room, Wilde was livid in appearance, breathing heavily and only able to raise his hand when spoken to. Ross decided to secure the services of a priest, and one was found with difficulty to administer baptism and extreme unction. Wilde had at last been accepted uncritically into the Church. Ross then sent wires to Frank Harris and Bosie Douglas. Bosie immediately set out to travel from Scotland. Turner and Ross stayed overnight at the hotel on 29/30 November. The nurse called twice to announce Wilde was dying, and at 5.30 the death rattle began. Foam and blood came from Wilde's mouth and had to be continually wiped away. Ross and Turner took turns to get lunch, but from 1 p.m. were constantly in the room together. The painful noise from Oscar's throat increased in volume and the two men tore up letters to keep from breaking down. At 1.45, the timing of his breathing altered, Ross took his hand and the pulse began to flutter. Wilde heaved a deep sigh, the limbs seemed to stretch involuntarily, and the breathing became fainter. It ceased finally at ten to two.

Ross later claimed surreally that Wilde's bodily fluids then exploded, making him so sick that he had to leave cleaning up the body to Turner. This story, repeated by Richard Ellmann, was later denied by Turner to Frank Harris as an invention by Ross to dramatise the passing of the great love of his life.[41] The passing away had been peaceful and without horror. If Ross embroidered the facts, it was out of devotion to Wilde and a desire to ensure everything about his friend was larger than life. Ross was always Wilde's most faithful friend, and would be so unquestionably in the years that followed. Turner respected this, thereby allowing one of the most unpleasant myths in the myth-ridden life of Oscar Wilde to take root.

Bosie travelled from Scotland as quickly as he could, but arrived on 2 December just in time for the funeral. He was the chief mourner, alongside Ross, Turner and Jean Dupoirier, proprietor of the Hôtel d'Alsace in which Wilde had spent his last days, and who had been immensely kind to Wilde, in the first carriage following the hearse. In this way the two great loves of Oscar's life were together at the last. Ellmann says there was an unseemly jockeying for position at the graveside and Douglas almost fell into the grave, but none of the principals ever described this happening. It was important to give some dignity to what was almost a pauper's burial. Alfred Douglas claimed he was the chief mourner, and his account of the event carries a poignancy which reflects on the whole troubled relationship he had with Wilde: "I took the part of chief mourner at the funeral, and was in consequence taken by some of those present for his son, or some other near relative. Someone (a lady) asked Ross (as he afterwards told me) who the 'youth' who acted as chief mourner was, and Ross told her that it was Lord Alfred Douglas; whereupon she said, 'but the one I mean was a mere boy, it couldn't be Lord Alfred Douglas, who must be about thirty'."[42]

* * *

Wilde's early death at the age of 46 was tragic but almost inevitable. Oscar Wilde loved youth, beauty, dandyism, luxury, talk. The contrast between what he had been at the height of his powers and what he had become in middleage could only have been traumatic. He personally had no future, while Bosie Douglas at thirty had a life of promise ahead of him. What the relationship might have become can only be speculation, but there is no doubt that the contrast between the seedy, aimless life of the literary pauper which Wilde endured, and Bosie's prospects, could only have soured their relationship further. No-one could have imagined in 1900 how Bosie would squander his prospects. As things stood in 1900, Wilde's death released both men from a quarrelsome friendship that had little future.

When the earth rattled on Oscar's coffin that December day in 1900 it buried the relationship with a finality that Bosie Douglas must have appreciated. What Bosie Douglas thought about as his friend's remains were committed to Destiny he did not record: a chapter of his life was closing for ever. He did not know that the ghost of Oscar Wilde would haunt him for the rest of his long life, and that he would come to hate and destroy the man who stood next to him at the graveside, Robbie Ross. What ended in December 1900 was an intense relationship that had held Oscar and Bosie in thrall for some eight years. The love that had brought them together was buried along with the body of Oscar Wilde.

The other passions – the destructive hatreds that drove both him and his father throughout their lives, and which had damaged Oscar Wilde so badly – would live on. Douglas was to pass through a period of intense hatred for the man he had loved before coming to a measured affection at the end of his life.

TWELVE

Curtain Call

In the months following Wilde's death, Bosie's life entered limbo, an aching loss for Oscar adding a minor key to his aimless pursuit of pleasure. Wilde's last days were now a bone of contention in the wearisome disputes which came to dominate his former circle. Douglas's critics later suggested that he had failed in his duty to attend Wilde on his deathbed, while Bosie and his supporters countered by suggesting Ross had deliberately withheld the news of Wilde's impending death. The truth is more mundane. Neither Ross nor Douglas had any idea that Wilde was dying; Ross told Douglas as soon as he knew. Bosie then headed for Paris immediately but arrived too late. He had no criticisms of Ross after Wilde had passed away. Douglas in writing to More Adey did criticise Ross's decision to have Wilde accepted by the Catholic Church on his deathbed, but this was mildly expressed and was in no way a serious attack.[1] The savagely destructive battle with Ross over Oscar Wilde's legacy was to erupt a decade later. What took place in the empty days after the funeral was mild bickering.

Life after Oscar would be markedly different from the aimless years following Naples. It was clearly a turning point, and Douglas had to face up to a future with few prospects. His inheritance had been squandered on the racing stables at Chantilly and with his money spent he returned to England for good in 1901. He now depended on his mother's allowance and, unlikely as it may seem, was contemplating marriage to an American heiress. He seemed to assume that, with Wilde buried, the lingering suspicions about his sexuality would die with his former lover. He was to be bitterly disillusioned.

Whatever may have taken place at the graveside in Paris, Bosie maintained good relations with Wilde's closest friends, particularly the men he would later quarrel with most savagely, Robbie Ross and Frank Harris. He even forgave Harris an act of serious fraud which had lost him the sum of £2,000, money he could ill afford. Shortly after starting his stable at Chantilly, Harris entertained Bosie at his hotel in Monte Carlo and persuaded him to put money into a casino venture, which he promised would return one hundred per cent. Whereas Oscar, the "prostitute", had failed to persuade Bosie to put up the same sum for a much-needed annuity, Harris, the swindler, was evidently more alluring. Douglas was too innocent in money matters even to make elementary checks on whether Harris had legal permission to run a casino – he didn't – and he never saw the money again. Nevertheless, this seems not to have prejudiced him against the man. Gratitude for Harris's support of Wilde during the prison years maintained the friendship. With his money gone, Bosie decided to travel to America to seek a marriage but, on 13 March 1901, he wrote to Harris that "lack of money" prevented him making the trip. He enclosed a poem written to Oscar Wilde, which he wanted to have printed in Harris's new journal the *Candid Friend*, showing that he still grieved for Wilde. It was later entitled "Forgetfulness", but in the original read "To O.W."[2] and was to be the last piece included in the last book Douglas ever wrote about Wilde, *Summing Up*, in 1940.

It was not America that was to provide the opportunity for Bosie's abrupt *volte face* in his sexual inclinations. Nor was Robbie Ross yet so far beyond Bosie's Pale, that he could not play a supporting role in this sudden and unexpected conversion. Shortly after returning to London in the Spring of 1901, Douglas received an admiring letter from a poetess called Olive Custance, who had been published in the *Yellow Book*, and had had her first book of poems published the previous year. Aged 27, she came from a wealthy Norfolk family and her father, Colonel Frederick Custance, was regularly among the shooting parties summoned by the King to hunt game at Sandringham. The only child of the marriage, her parents expected Olive to make a good, respectable marriage in Society. The young woman herself, however, was attracted to the Aesthetic world, and to Bosie Douglas in particular. Both contributed poems to a literary magazine entitled the *Academy*.

Douglas was flattered by the letter and arranged to meet Olive at the South Kensington Museum. They missed the rendezvous but Olive, châperoned by her maid, marched round to Bosie's lodgings and the first meeting took place. Mutual attraction was instant and a liaison began. The two needed a meeting place where they would not need a châperon, and Robbie Ross was pressed into service. Ross had taken over running the Carfax Gallery from William Rothenstein, and a backstairs room was an ideal place for discreet "aesthetic" assignations. The attachment grew, although Douglas was still hedging his bets and, in October 1901, finally raised enough money to visit America. However, he could not find his wealthy heiress, and found himself instead pining for Olive. On his return, he continued to write to Olive but gave her no encouragement that he, penniless and living off his mother's allowance, could provide her with a future. In the early Spring of 1902, Olive accepted a proposal of marriage from George Montagu, heir to the 8th Earl of Sandwich and a sizeable fortune. The news delighted the King. When Bosie heard the news, however, he was galvanised into action in true Douglas style. He rushed to meet Olive at Kettner's, persuaded her to elope with him, and obtained a special licence to marry at St George's Church, Hanover Square. Robbie Ross was party to the secret and turned up to observe the ceremony, although he was not one of the official witnesses. Inexplicably, in view of this moral support, Douglas was to argue in his *Autobiography* that: "for some extraordinary reason Ross always seemed to resent my marriage. All the same, I continued to be on good terms with him for several years after it took place, and he professed to be devoted to Olive and made every effort to ingratiate himself with her".[3]

The marriage created a storm of disapproval. The King was outraged. Colonel Custance descended on Scotland Yard, demanding to see Douglas's criminal file. Like many Victorians, he was convinced the police had a secret department devoted to tracking down homosexual activity, and he was flabbergasted on discovering that Oscar Wilde's closest friend had no police file. Queensberry's attempts to keep his son out of the maelstrom of 1895 had been entirely successful.

Custance would undoubtedly have cut his daughter off without a penny, but Olive, as his only child, was heir to the estate by an entail. He was forced to bide his time. A son, Raymond, was born to Bosie and Olive in 1902. To Bosie Douglas, it must have seemed that at long last his homosexual past and his relationship with Oscar Wilde had been laid to rest. His settling down pleased one of his Wyndham cousins, Pamela Tennant, wife of the prominent Liberal politician Edward Tennant and also a contributor to the *Academy*. She obtained for him the lease of a farmhouse near the river Avon in Somerset. The next three years were the happiest of his married life. Unfortunately for all concerned, the literary world would call him back and the shade of Oscar Wilde would return.

Ross unwittingly set free the first stone of the avalanche through his initial, cautious steps in rehabilitating Wilde. Unlike Douglas, Ross keenly felt his own responsibility for Oscar's fall and the suffering this had caused to Constance and the children. He felt guilty, too, about the appalling way Constance had been treated – apparently the only one of Wilde's circle who ever did. Others may have sniggered at her gullibility, but Ross was always chivalrous. He may have asked Bosie whether he wished to play a part in reviving Wilde's estate and discharging the bankruptcy to help Wilde's orphan sons, but, if he did so, Bosie declined. Ross had, in any case, been appointed by Wilde as his literary executor, and to his credit took responsibility for discharging the bankruptcy in the hope of enabling Wilde's children to benefit from their father's literary estate.

In ploughing this very unrewarding furrow, Ross had to combat public hostility in Britain – George Alexander's West End revival of *Earnest* in December 1901 had flopped. But in Germany, Wilde's work was received far more favourably. The Berlin première of *Salomé* was given in 1901 and ran for two hundred performances. As Wilde's reputation grew among the Teutons, interest in the author began to be channelled through Ross. Interest focussed particularly on the mysterious, unpublished letter that Wilde was known to have penned in prison, and Ross came under pressure in the Autumn of 1904 from a German scholar, Max Meyerfeld, to publish it. This forced Ross to confront the poisoned chalice of the manuscript *De Profundis,* which only he, the Governor of Reading gaol, and the typist who had copied the letter to send to Douglas, had ever read in full. Ross must have realised by now that Douglas had never read the letter, as there had been no emotional explosion; although, having sent the copy to Douglas, as he claimed, he seems to have been strangely uninterested in knowing what Douglas thought, and what had happened to it subsequently.

Ross realised that there was no way he could publish so scathing an attack on Bosie Douglas, but with Richard Strauss preparing an operatic version of *Salomé,* he felt that a suitably expurgated version would help to push along the increasingly lucrative interest in Wilde on the Continent. He drew up a carefully constructed text from the autograph manuscript he still possessed, excluding all references to Douglas. Meyerfeld translated this, and it was published in the journal *Die Neue Rundschau* in 1904. This was so warmly greeted that Ross felt an English version could do much to restore Wilde's reputation and financial viability. Methuen agreed to publish, and Ross produced his English language version of the letter, less than one third the actual length of the manuscript, on 23 February 1905. The book was widely welcomed as an authentic and welcome addition to Victorian literature.

Ross entitled his version of the letter *De Profundis,* 'From out of the depths'. This has since come to be the title of the full manuscript.

He edited it to exclude any reference to Douglas at all. Indeed, it was popularly believed to have been written to Robert Ross himself, Ross obscurely referred to the letter as having been written "to a friend". Astonishingly, Bosie Douglas himself reviewed the book in the *Motorist and Traveller* for 1 March 1905, without understanding that the letter was addressed to him. He gave it a cautious, but not unfavourable review.[4]

It is abundantly clear from this that Douglas had never read the letter Ross sent to him. He was wholly unaware that the two thirds of the letter suppressed by Ross were directly aimed at himself and constituted a personal attack almost unique in the annals of Victorian literature. Douglas may have been put out at not seeing the full manuscript, as Ross did tell him that references to himself were to be excluded. In the subsequent exchanges, Ross also apparently warned Douglas that he had other incriminating letters about or from Douglas that he could publish – the first indications of what Douglas and his supporters would later claim were threats of blackmail by Ross – but the quarrel blew over. There was nothing in the *De Profundis* of 1905, or a later, slightly extended version of 1908, to which Douglas could reasonably object. Relations between Robbie Ross and Alfred Douglas remained good and Ross did Douglas an enormous favour. Robbie Ross had high standing among the London artistic and literary élite, being particularly well regarded by the editor of the *Academy*, Harold Child. When Bosie wrote to Robbie early in 1907 that he was bored, aimless and lacked money, Robbie recommended that he become assistant editor to Child. This appeared a harmless occupation suiting Bosie's literary gifts, and his appointment was duly approved by Child. Ross was particularly pleased when "The Dead Poet" was published on 21 September. Bosie's work was also appreciated by Pamela Tennant.[5] Pamela had always liked Bosie and, though moving in the upper echelons of the Liberal Party through her marriage to Edward Tennant, regarded her cousin favourably as a poet while thinking him little more than a political lightweight who held somewhat romantic, diehard Tory views.

In the Autumn of 1907, Harold Child moved to *The Times*, and the *Academy* was put up for sale. Ross now suggested to Pamela Tennant that her husband should purchase the title and install Alfred Douglas as editor. Edward Tennant, an extremely rich man who was brother to Margot Tennant, wife of the then Liberal Chancellor, and future Prime Minister, Herbert Asquith, saw no problem in acceding to his wife's request and Bosie was duly installed. He took his duties seriously, moving his wife and child to London. He undoubtedly had talent as a literary editor, "discovering" both Rupert Brooke and Siegfried Sassoon. However, he could not confine himself to literature. As middle-age beckoned, the Douglas genes were asserting themselves once more, and a latent political fogeyism began to emerge in the formerly libertarian Bosie.

As editor, Douglas now came under the influence of High Church Anglicans who wanted the *Academy* to be an organ of the Tory-inclined, militant, ritualistic wing of the Church of England – a move towards religious controversy which would lead Douglas to becoming a full-blown Catholic within a few years. As the paper became noticeably more politicised, it moved towards the far right fringe of the Conservative Party. Bosie might have survived this excursion into politics unscathed, he was no polemicist, but he had filled the now-vacant role of assistant editor by appointing one Thomas William Hodgson Crosland. In true tabloid style, Crosland was a narrow-minded, fanatical, gutter journalist, nominally a Methodist. He was a bigot in most things, but particularly in sexual matters, where he had a confirmed hatred of homosexuals. Opposite poles so frequently attract, and Bosie Douglas made a most unholy alliance with this man, completing his own, remarkable conversion to Family Values, Catholicism, and reactionary High Toryism, by becoming a ranting homophobe himself.

Poor Robbie Ross now found himself no longer welcome in the pages of the *Academy*. How the quarrel began may never be known, but it is likely that Douglas resented Ross's success as Wilde's literary executor in discharging the bankruptcy and becoming friendly with Cyril and Vyvyan. When Vyvyan came of age in November 1907, Ross staged a birthday party. Douglas was not invited. This did not go unnoticed, and Bosie Douglas added this rebuff to the other slights to which he now reacted with supersensitivity. The major cause of the growing rift between Ross and Douglas was, however, the homosexuality which Bosie had abandoned but which Ross was still openly practising. Douglas and Crosland were infuriated that Wilde's sons should associate with a man engaged in what they regarded as un-Christian vice. Their responses displayed the very opposite of Christian charity, but that is the role of the bigot.

Edward and Pamela Tennant were becoming worried by the right-wing tone of the paper, which the Liberal Tennant was subsidising to the tune of £2,000 per annum but, after an altercation with Crosland, Tennant swallowed his objections in the interests of freedom of speech. Relations with Ross continued to deteriorate. On 1 December 1908, Reggie Turner and others organised a dinner for Ross to celebrate his achievements in discharging Wilde's bankruptcy and bringing out Wilde's *Collected Works.* To the bulk of Wilde's friends, Ross was an admirable figure who had proved himself a true friend, and Frank Harris made a particularly witty speech setting out the general feeling towards him. Alfred Douglas was not present, although he had been invited by Reggie Turner, and his absence was ominous.

Douglas was at this point still more or less civil to Ross, but the atmosphere between them was becoming so strained that Ross felt he could no longer visit the Douglases, and he explained to Olive why this was no longer possible in a letter the following February. Olive had been hurt by Ross's rebuff, and with characteristic politeness and concern for her feelings he wrote to her that he had no hostile feelings, as he knew Bosie too well, but he simply did not want to be friendly with him any more. It was an unwise move. Douglas saw the letter and blew up, responding with a letter on 1 March that ranks with any he had yet written for viciousness. Ross now decided to break off relations completely in the hope that Bosie's behaviour would soon moderate, as it always had following his manic outbursts. However, it was to be three years before the two men corresponded again, and it would be an even more acrimonious exchange over the Ransome biography.

If Ross thought he could simply avoid Douglas, he had underestimated his man. Douglas was now on a "high", a bigoted crusader in the manner of his father. The difference was that he had a respectable platform for his views. He attacked Asquith for suppressing a Catholic demonstration in such strong terms that Edward Tennant was forced to give up his ownership of the *Academy*. Tennant gave the journal to Douglas with a nominal sum of £500 towards expenses.

Douglas found himself in even deeper waters when a Christian publisher, Manners Sutton, sued Crosland for libel. The case came up in February 1910 after the campaigning journalist had attacking Manners Sutton, claiming that he posed as a public moralist while publishing salacious material in a different guise. Bosie stood by his colleague, testifying as to Crosland's good character. The prosecuting counsel tried to blacken Bosie's character by asking questions about his relationship with Wilde, but Bosie had now learnt how to handle cross-examination. When asked: "Was there ever anything to be ashamed of in your relationship with (Wilde)?" Bosie answered simply "No, there was not", and emerged without a stain on his character. Ross, who was in court watching, assumed that this was a denial of his homosexuality and his relationship with Wilde and was incensed. Bosie's answer was literally justified, owing to the ambiguity of the question, but there is little doubt that, psychologically, he was in a state of denial as regards his own past. Ross's dislike of Douglas was now turning to hatred.

Bosie pursued his crusades with more fervour than intelligence. In June 1910, he sued a nonconformist minister and the *Daily News* for an article which alleged the *Academy* had become a Roman Catholic paper. It was a foolish move, for while he was nominally a High Church Anglican, his paper was so militant in the Roman Catholic cause that the jurors could not see how it was not committed to the faith. He lost the case and the costs of the action drove the *Academy* to the wall. Lords de Walden and Fitzwilliam bought the title off Bosie and from July 1910 there was a new editor. Douglas thus lost his platform and his somewhat tenuous position in polite Society. This merely intensified his siege mentality. Incandescent with a sense of mission, he converted to Catholicism. He was now to prove the truth of the proverb that there is no believer more fervent than a convert, for his hatred of Robbie Ross was on the verge of erupting from smouldering feud to open warfare.

Douglas's decision, in May 1911, to enter the Roman Catholic church horrified his two most implacable opponents: Robbie Ross, who, as a Catholic himself, could not accept that the conversion was sincere, and the peppery Colonel Custance, whose Protestant hatred of Catholicism made him determined to save his grandson from the clutches of Rome. Douglas was embroiled in savage feuds with both men, the family quarrel with Custance having the more serious consequences. Backed by his solicitor, George Lewis – who was also Robert Ross's solicitor, a fact which encouraged Douglas to believe there was a plot against him – Custance told his daughter that, unless Raymond was handed over to him, he would stop her allowance and cease paying the fees for Raymond's preparatory school. Poor Olive was caught in the crossfire, and her son was the military objective. Douglas fought with the only weapons he knew, those which his father had used against Wilde. He began a campaign of letter writing to Custance designed to force him to go to court. When the Colonel threw the letters away unopened, Douglas resorted to telegrams and postcards. When Bosie threatened to write to his bank, clubs and the tenants of his Norfolk estate in Weston Longville, Custance finally instructed George Lewis to issue a summons for criminal libel. Bosie appeared at the Old Bailey for full trial on 24 April 1913. While this was extremely serious for Douglas, it was the lesser of two battles which he was fighting that Spring. The unexploded bomb which *De Profundis* constituted had finally detonated.

De Profundis had been on Ross's mind after the publication of the *Collected Works* in 1908. This had contained an expurgated version not mentioning Douglas, as Ross realised that it could never be published in full during Douglas's lifetime. He had then sought to have the original manuscript preserved in a way that would allow it to be consulted by scholars after all those connected with the affair – principally Bosie Douglas – were dead. He offered it to the British Museum with the proviso that it be kept incognito for fifty years and not made available until 1960. The Museum accepted the offer with this condition on 13 November 1909. Had Ross stuck to the agreement, the manuscript would have become no more than a literary curiosity and Wilde's bitter attack on his former lover would have been of little but historical interest.

Ross was, however, approached by a young author preparing a biography of Wilde. Arthur Ransome, later to become famous for his children's stories, was fishing for insights into Wilde's life. Ross was so helpful that Ransome dedicated the book to him, and his assistance had indeed been considerable. Ross decided to show Ransome his typescript copy of the *De Profundis* letter in full, together with letters written to him from Naples in 1898, the latter setting out Wilde's assertion that Douglas had lived off him and then deserted him when his money ran out.

There is no easy explanation of why Ross took this extraordinarily careless step. His relations with Douglas were undoubtedly strained, but there was no open conflict between them at the time. Ross must have known that Douglas was unaware of the full contents of the letter. For Bosie to read about it for the first time in the pages of a published work could only be viewed as the most savage provocation. This would trigger open warfare, which, given Douglas's combative nature, would be wholly unrestrained. It is possible Ross thought he was briefing Ransome "off the record". Nevertheless, he decided to show him the material, and, while he insisted Douglas should not be named, he could hardly have been unaware that Douglas would not realise who was being referred to.

It is normally believed by Douglas's supporters that Ross was motivated by jealousy over Douglas's supplanting him in Wilde's affections. Yet there had been no real sign of this during the previous twenty years; the trigger for Ross's actions, if they were malicious, can only have been more recent developments, notably Bosie's growing antipathy towards the homosexual community and the rift that had developed with Olive. Whatever the reason, Ross had let the cat out of the bag, and it would be interpreted, possibly not without justification, as an attack on Douglas. Accident or not, the responsibility for this lies entirely with Robert Ross.

Once he had read the Ransome volume, Douglas wrote to Ross on 6 March 1912 challenging Ross to reveal whether he was the "friend" referred to.

Ross had behaved indefensibly, first by (apparently) concealing the letters from Douglas and then by making them available to Ransome. Ross's earlier decision could be justified if the material had been put away and only made available to posterity. But to allow Ransome sight of the letters when Douglas was ignorant of their existence, knowing that Ransome would put them in the public domain, cannot be seen as anything other than blatant provocation. There could be no satisfactory answer from Ross to Douglas's questions, and it is not surprising that Douglas chose to sue Ransome and the Times Book Club (the distributors of the book) on a charge of criminal libel. It was a foolish decision, with hindsight, putting him firmly in the spotlight. Ransome's discreet references to "a man to whom Wilde felt that he owed some, at least, of the circumstances of his public disgrace" might have gone unremarked. By challenging Ransome in law Bosie ensured that, if he lost, he would be publicly identified forever as the man Wilde blamed. As with Oscar Wilde's suit against his father in 1895, the decision to sue Ransome was only logical if Douglas thought he would win; in other words, if he did not know what Wilde had actually said about him in the letters. He was soon to be enlightened.

The trial began on 17 April 1913, before Mr Justice Darling, in most inauspicious circumstances for Douglas. He was undergoing bankruptcy proceedings after a moneylender had foreclosed on a loan. His other libel trial against Custance was going badly, and he was emotionally devastated as his wife had just left him: Olive had taken her father's side against him in the libel action. These misfortunes paled into insignificance, however, before the disaster that now overwhelmed him in his action against Ransome.

Even without the family connection, the trial had curious echoes of the Queensberry libel case of 1895. Ransome was nominally the man on trial, but, like Wilde, it was Bosie Douglas who found himself transformed by legal process from plaintiff to accused. During his uncomfortable period in the witness box it was he, and not Ransome or Ross, who was to have his reputation shredded.

Douglas's complaint centred on two points: that Ransome had accused him of "being responsible for the public disgrace and infamy" of Oscar Wilde and that his book had claimed that, after Oscar Wilde came out of prison in 1897, "the plaintiff went to live with him in Naples and when there lived on him, only staying with him for mercenary motives, abandoning him when Oscar Wilde's allowance was stopped, leaving him penniless".[6] The main focus of the trial, however, was *De Profundis*, with the allegations about Naples overshadowed by the sensational attack made from prison by Wilde on his closest friend.

Early in the trial, Douglas admitted that Ross had handed him a copy of the manuscript that purported to come from Wilde, but that he had destroyed it unread, thus undermining his own credibility. The defence was prepared to support its case by having sections of the letter only read out; but Douglas's counsel, a friend called Cecil Hayes, who was deeply committed to the cause but woefully inexperienced, made the serious mistake of demanding the whole letter be read out, being presumably unaware of how damaging this was. The letter was then read verbatim, with devastating consequences. By the time counsel intoned the words "you forced me to stay, to brazen it out if possible, by absurd and silly lies",[7] Douglas asked to be allowed to sit down. The judge allowed this. When he asked if he could leave the witness box, however, Mr Justice Darling asked if he were ill? and, on Douglas agreeing that he was not, forced him to stay on and listen to Wilde's ghastly words, destroying his character like tiny, precise hammer blows from beyond the grave.

The reading continued on day two, but the judge stopped it after twenty minutes when he suddenly realised that the plaintiff was not in court. Bosie was called for, and, having no excuse for not occupying the witness box, as he was being cross-examined, he was forced to stand and listen to the rest. It was a most terrible experience and, after hearing several minutes more of the sustained, articulate cataloguing of all Wilde's bitterness against his former lover, even the jury declared they had heard enough. The judge intervened and the reading ceased.

Bosie still had to endure a searching cross-examination on all this, in the course of which he made damaging admissions. When asked if Wilde had said "your leaving him when his allowance ceased was 'the most bitter experience of a bitter life'?", he replied briefly, "Yes"; he also admitted writing, after visiting the Wildes in Tite Street in 1894, "I had great fun, though the strain of being a bone of contention between Oscar and Mrs Oscar began to make itself felt". Hayes did his best, but on the central issue there could only be one result. After an hour and fifty-five minutes, the jury returned a verdict that the Ransome book contained words which were a libel, but which were true. The Times Book Club was also acquitted and costs were given against Douglas as a final turn of the screw. Like Queensberry in 1895, Arthur Ransome left the court in triumph while his bankrupt attacker slunk away in ignominy, his reputation as a moral crusader blown to bits.

Ross's friends congratulated him on the verdict, believing him to have been the true victor in the trial. Cyril Holland wrote to him from an expedition in Tibet – he had joined the Army and was based in India – to express his congratulations.[8] Cyril and his brother Vyvyan owed much to Robbie Ross, and they would henceforth always side with him in the feud with Douglas which had now developed.

The humiliation of hearing Wilde's letter read out in court shattered Bosie Douglas, magnifying his sense that he was the victim of a persecution organised by Robert Ross, with whom he now coupled Oscar Wilde. He was so demoralised that he abandoned the Custance case, admitting libel on 24 April. Further disaster followed. While Douglas and his son went to visit his sister, Lady Edith Fox-Pitt, Olive had stripped their home of her half of the furniture. Douglas returned to a half-empty home and contemplated the ruin of all the hopes of the previous dozen years. His hatred of Robert Ross had already grown to massive proportions. He hated Wilde, whose unforgiving words in *De Profundis* were burned into his soul. Hatred now turned to thoughts of revenge.

Douglas was easily persuaded by the publisher John Long to write a book on Wilde, which would capitalise on the sensations of the Ransome trial. Douglas desperately needed the money and, even more desperately, the chance to put his side of the affair, but he was psychologically exhausted and he handed over the actual writing of the book to Crosland. Crosland used the book, *Oscar Wilde and Myself* (1914) to express his deep-seated hatred of Wilde and, as Douglas could not admit to his sexual misdemeanours of the 1890s without risking prosecution, the book is worthless as historical evidence of the relationship.

In his *Autobiography* he admitted: "At the time I wrote or endorsed that book I had really persuaded myself that it presented a true picture of me. In truth it merely presented a picture of what at that time I wished to be supposed to be"[9] – which was a lifelong heterosexual who had been wholly unaware of Oscar Wilde's homosexuality! The text of this insignificant book does not demand detailed analysis here, its only importance was that it intensified the split between Douglas and the Wilde circle. Wilde's friends tended to support Robert Ross, only Reggie Turner supporting Douglas. The bitter disputes between Wilde's friends turned savage. Robert Sherard responded to Douglas/Crosland's book with *The Real Oscar Wilde*, a work as misleadingly favourable to Wilde as Douglas's book was misleadingly hostile. Polemic was now overwhelming any rational understanding of the Wilde–Douglas relationship.

Douglas's denials of any improper relationship with Wilde were too far-fetched to be taken seriously, particularly when he allowed Crosland to indulge in outrageous falsehoods. In *De Profundis*, Wilde alleged that he had "paid for the sins of another" – the reference being to the evidence of witnesses at the Savoy to a man in bed with a boy, the man being described as Wilde. Wilde's reference to taking the blame for what a friend had done clearly indicated that he felt Douglas was the guilty party. The book was at pains to pour scorn on the idea that Wilde could have so acted, yet he knew perfectly well that Wilde had risen to just this height of altruism, for there was no-one else who could be the person concerned, other than himself. Yet he could neither admit to this truth nor leave it alone. It was a tragic sign of the manner in which the friendship had degenerated. There was still worse to come. Ross had been wrong to allow Ransome access to Wilde's letters. Douglas now responded with a venomous campaign of hate.

THIRTEEN

The Final Encore

Once they had digested the Ransome book, Crosland and Douglas began serious harassment of Robbie Ross without waiting for the long-drawn-out legal action to come to court. Douglas was apparently supported financially by Pamela Tennant, who shared Douglas's loathing of Ross and provided the bankrupt Douglas with the wherewithal to pursue his campaign. Early in December 1912, Ross noticed he was being followed. In January he confronted one of the men and discovered he was a private detective who had been watching him intermittently since the Summer, and also a man he was living with, Freddie Smith. Ross was told that a report had been sent to Scotland Yard, alleging among other offences that Ross had seduced pupils at St Paul's School. Ross was deeply alarmed in August 1913 by a visit from a former student at St Paul's, Norman Farr, who claimed he had been approached by a barrister working for Douglas, who had offered him money if he would testify that Ross had seduced him. Sir Charles Matthews, Director of Public Prosecutions, was investigating the claims relating to the St Paul's pupils and considered prosecution, but decided against this at the end of the month. The intervention of Ross's friend, Margot Asquith, who visited Matthews, may have influenced this decision. Douglas certainly considered Ross's close friendship with the Asquiths to be proof of corruption in High Places.[1]

The police net was now spreading closer to Robbie Ross as surveillance of friends began to take an ominous turn. His secretary, Christopher Sclater Millard (who, as Stuart Mason, carried out important bibliographical work on Wilde) was an overt homosexual who had already been imprisoned for gross indecency. Making Millard his secretary was a foolish act on Ross's part, more foolish in the light of Millard's utter indiscretion in conducting his affairs. In September 1913 a rent boy, Charles Garrett, was arrested leaving his flat. Ross's sense of paranoia increased, becoming acute as Douglas took to stalking him. Using Queensberry's loathsome tactics, Douglas had become an immediate, nightmarish presence, even moving into the apartment block in which Ross lived – he was evicted after trying to persuade a porter to steal papers from Ross's flat. Douglas and Crosland saw this as only a temporary defeat, a view strengthened when Garrett was convicted in February 1914 of importuning and sentenced to six months' hard labour. Crosland assumed it was a matter of time before Ross could be convicted of offences against Garrett and joined Douglas in sending Ross abusive and libellous letters. This was persecution. Robbie Ross was now desperate, seeking any opportunity to silence Crosland and Douglas. That Spring, an opportunity to do just this seemed to present itself.

Douglas was due in court to face fresh judgement from the Custance case but, fearing imprisonment, fled to France, where he was joined by Crosland. Ross concluded that with Douglas and Crosland abroad he could sue the pair and with luck neither would return to England to face the charges. Accordingly, on 24 March he issued writs against Douglas for criminal libel, and against Douglas and Crosland for criminal conspiracy and perjury, both suits centring on allegations of improper conduct with Garrett. To his horror, Crosland immediately returned home on 14 April to face the charges. In the carousel of legal actions which features so heavily in this narrative, one lesson which stands out is that libel actions rarely benefit those who stage them. This was abundantly demonstrated by the Crosland case. Ross was innocent of having sexual relations with Garrett, but was in the position of having to demonstrate this fact, an almost impossible task.

The case came down to the word of Crosland, a bluff Yorkshireman apparently upholding the highest moral standards, against that of Ross, an Aesthete who could not convincingly pose as being innocent of the activities most of his society condemned. As the trial wore on, the judge became increasingly critical of Ross's failure to express outrage that anyone should accuse him of being homosexual. Moreover, Ross's friendship with Wilde was brought up against him, even *Dorian Gray* making an appearance. In the judge's summing up, he commented prejudicially that anyone who had associated with Wilde might reasonably be suspected of sharing the same sexual tendencies, unless vigorously and systematically denied. It was inevitable that the jury would find Crosland not guilty, and when they did so there was applause in the courtroom.

Douglas had been heartened by Crosland's successful defence and decided to return home to face his accusers. On arriving at Folkestone he was arrested, not over the Custance affair but to face Ross's writs. He spent five days in Wormwood Scrubs, an experience which momentarily brought sympathy for Wilde's sufferings in prison but really only intensified his passion to see Robert Ross defeated. Douglas was well aware that while Crosland had been acquitted, he had failed to prove that Ross had committed indecency with Garratt, and his solicitor advised him that to avoid conviction for conspiracy and perjury he had to discover hard evidence of Ross's homosexual activity. Douglas could no longer afford private detectives and began a thankless search for evidence. This he found, in a manner he attributed to divine intervention.

He discovered the brother of a soldier, now dead, who had had a liaison with Ross. The brother had been offered money by Ross to keep quiet about the affair and offered to testify to this in court. Douglas also called an Inspector from Scotland Yard to allege that Ross associated with homosexuals, and accused Ross of attending a New Year's Eve party where twenty or thirty men danced together. It was all circumstantial evidence, countered by evidence of good character by literary witnesses, but it impressed the judge. Mr Justice Coleridge was appalled that Ross did not condemn homosexuality, and told the jury so. Nevertheless, the jury could not agree and the judge ordered a re-trial.

Ross viewed the proceedings with foreboding. He realised that a tactical retreat was his only option, and his solicitors obtained a judgement of *nolle prosequi*, that is abandonment of the prosecution. Ross withdrew from the action, agreeing to pay all Douglas's costs. The two men signed an agreement on 8 December that both withdraw from the action. This was victory for Douglas, allowing the libels to stand and in theory to be repeated and leaving Ross in a very precarious legal position. The papers in the case were sent to the Department of Public Prosecutions, but to Ross's relief he did not follow Wilde into the dock. Douglas, meanwhile, found his victory diminished by press silence. The First World War had broken out on 4 August and neither the government nor the press were anxious to broadcast a sensational trial about homosexuality. This was the root cause of the press blackout that rendered the case almost invisible.

Douglas, typically, suspected an Establishment cover-up and this belief fuelled his growing mania against Ross, the Asquiths and the British press. He now developed a complex conspiracy theory about homosexual corruption in High Places. This centred on Ross's friendship with Herbert and Margot Asquith. On 21 February 1915, Douglas wrote to Asquith threatening that, if he did not stop entertaining Ross, he would make his association with a man Douglas regarded as a pervert an issue with the Conservative press. Asquith made no response, but the threat was passed to the Department of Public Prosecutions and to the Home Secretary, who advised no action over what he described as a "horrible letter".[2]

Ross's friends reacted to his defeat with an impressive show of public support, in the form of a testimonial of a remarkable kind. A committee of literary notables collected around 300 signatures to a statement endorsing a high opinion of Ross as a man of letters. The Asquiths signed, as did a number of peers, an Anglican bishop and a raft of writers including Shaw, H.G. Wells, Beerbohm Tree, Lady Ottoline Morrell and Thomas Hardy. From the Wilde circle, Ada Leverson, More Adey and Robert Sherard signed. Douglas could not understand why such distinguished people could support a man he regarded as a deceiver and blackmailer. He was unable to grasp the point Bernard Shaw made to him in 1931, that "Ross did not get his testimonial for nothing. Only a good deal of good nature on his part could have won over that distinguished and very normal list of names to give public support for a man who began with so very obvious a mark of the beast on him".[3] This was good advice, for Douglas in his *Autobiography* had still failed to see anything but "Ross's own villainies and unspeakable meanness. . . . I had to prove that in addition to being a votary of Wilde's vices, he was also a blackmailer. I proved the one thing as I proved the other".[4] Douglas took no notice of Shaw's wise words.

So, Douglas protested vehemently to the press, but only one paper printed his complaints. This was the *Globe*, edited by Charles Palmer, which printed a letter from Douglas on 30 March which led to more scandalous publicity. A few months later the *Globe* was officially suppressed for a fortnight, on the pretext that it had falsely reported that the unpopular Kitchener had resigned, and a new editor was appointed. Douglas took this as yet another indication that the Establishment was out to close ranks on what he saw as a scandal.[5]

He spent the rest of the year writing a verse pamphlet setting out his views on the Establishment conspiracy. Provocatively entitled "The Rossiad", the poem embodied a highly dangerous view in which early British failure in the war was inextricably linked to the presence in Government of a nexus of vice and corruption. It was a vicious cocktail of prejudice and blame making, particularly dangerous in 1916 as the British experienced the failures of the Navy at Jutland and the Army on the Somme. The pamphlet went through four editions and sold thousands of copies.

But Douglas lacked the leadership and propaganda skills to take this conspiracy theory any further; and as, in 1916, there was no political movement he could relate to, he retired to a lonely and marginal life in the country. This was now the bitterest period of Bosie's life. He had lost even Crosland's support after an argument. Long estranged from his wife, in 1915 he lost contact with his son after a family quarrel in which Raymond sided with his mother and grandfather. He would not see him again for ten years. By January 1917, Douglas was living with his mother and sister Edith in Sussex, profoundly lonely and dependent emotionally and financially on Sybil's unquestioning support. He could not find the opportunity he craved to demonstrate his deep hatred for the memory of Oscar Wilde and the activities of Robert Ross but, after a year of isolation, Fate suddenly turned its malign spotlight once again on his fantastic theories.

As 1918 opened, the British people were war weary, the bloodletting on the Western Front appearing to have become an endless nightmare. On the political far right, explanations for British failure were centred on a vicious conspiracy theory that owed much to Alfred Douglas's postulating. The extremist paper, the *Imperialist*, edited by the Independent MP Noel Pemberton Billing, pandered to Jingoistic views about Britain's failure, notably those of Arnold White. White saw everywhere, an international homosexual conspiracy, led by Germans. In mid-January, he published an article ranting that German homosexuals, or *urnings*, were plotting to undermine Britain. On 26 January, the paper ran a story claiming that 47,000 homosexuals had been discovered by German spies operating in the British Establishment, from the Privy Council and the Cabinet downward, and that a Black Book containing their names was in the possession of a German prince who was using the information to blackmail the British government. Male and female homosexuality were alleged, but no names were mentioned.

Lord Beaverbrook, the press magnate who had been financing the paper, understandably refused to continue sponsoring such dangerous rubbish, at which point the *Imperialist* was renamed the *Vigilante*, adding anti-Semitism to its poisonous concoctions. Lord Beaverbrook, family name Aitken, was himself Jewish. It did not go down well.

None of this directly affected Bosie Douglas or the memory of Oscar Wilde, but on 10 February the *Sunday Times* carried a short notice that two private performances of *Salomé* were to be given in London, on 7 and 14 April. This appearance of Wilde's most decadent play, at the height of the war, with the central character played by the dancer Maud Allan, seemed to be proof of Douglas's theories. Allan was well known and controversial. She had been invited to Downing Street before the war by

Margot Asquith, who, despite her marriage to Asquith, was believed by many to be a closet lesbian. The staging of *Salomé* seemed to be more than coincidence. On 16 February the *Vigilante* ran a deliberately provocative item entitled "The Cult of the Clitoris", which ran: "To be a member of Maud Allan's private performance in Oscar Wilde's *Salomé* one has to apply to a Miss Valetta, of 9 Duke Street, Adelphi, WC. If Scotland Yard were to seize the list of these members I have no doubt they would secure the names of several thousand of the first 47,000".[6]

This was libellous, and designed to provoke. The paragraph came to the attention of J.T. Grein, the producer, on 5 March and he showed it to Maud Allan. Without realising their actions would play straight into the hands of Billing and his followers, Grein and Allan initiated proceedings for obscenity and criminal libel three days later. This was utter folly. Whether or not Grein and Allan understood what the reference to "the 47,000" meant, they certainly did not grasp that, once they came to trial, the issue would not be whether Billing had libelled Maud Allan but whether Oscar Wilde, *Salomé* and an Aesthetic clique engaged in conscious decadence were exerting a baleful influence in a time of war. On this issue there could be no doubt of the outcome; Robbie Ross later claimed that he foresaw their defeat and warned Grein against starting the action.[7] Ross's permission was needed before the play could be staged, and he could have stopped the imminent disaster; but, once again displaying a fatal lack of perceptive judgement, he chose not to do so. Grein could not see the danger, having the naïve belief of an immigrant in the essential fairness of British justice. At Bow Street magistrates' court, Grein defended *Salomé* as a masterpiece containing the finest prose written in modern English.[8] These were admirable sentiments, but against Pemberton Billing they were grist to the mill.

The trial opened on 29 May against a background of further defeats in France. The German Spring offensive had broken the British Fifth Army and breached the Allied line on the Western Front. To Billing and his supporters this was proof that decadence in high places was losing the war, and he saw the libel action as his chance to destroy his opponents and reverse the tide of battle. Billing's strategy was outright attack and his star witness was Bosie Douglas. No one was better placed to aver this than the man who had translated *Salomé* from the French. It was a dangerous strategy as far as Douglas was concerned, because the very fact that he had been so close to Wilde opened him to the accusation of being perverted himself. To guard himself against this insinuation, Douglas decided to repudiate openly Oscar Wilde and all his works. The Billing trial was a highly public stage to make it clear that he loathed Wilde and all that he stood for.

Alfred Douglas appeared on the fourth day of the trial, a day when the newspapers reported that German troops were approaching the River Marne and bombarding Paris. Lloyd George rushed to Versailles to consult the French government amid growing panic. Bosie was cross-examined, firstly by Billing (who was conducting his own defence) to establish that Wilde and *Salomé* were both depraved and corrupting, then by the prosecution counsel, who sought to discredit his evidence as he had been actively involved in the Wilde culture he now condemned. Douglas was on his mettle, particularly as the judge in the case, Mr Justice Darling, had tried the Ransome case and Douglas had scores to settle.

Pemberton Billing elicited from Douglas at the outset the statement that he had translated the play from the French, and had had many conversations with Wilde about it, developing a very particular knowledge of what he meant by the play. Douglas claimed: "He intended it to be an exhibition of perverted sexual passion and excitement in a young girl, and also there are other things in it. There is one passage which is sodomitic and meant to be sodomitic."[9] This was merely the opening gambit. Billing drew from Douglas the news that Wilde had been studying Kraft-Ebbing's *Psychopathia Sexualis*, playing off xenophobic fears of foreigners with strange theories, and that, in Douglas's view, "normal minded people would be disgusted with *Salomé*, and sexual perverts would revel in it".[10] This evidence, from Wilde's closest friend and collaborator, could only have a deep impact on a stolid English jury.

In attempting to discredit Douglas, the prosecution was clearly trying to blacken his character by his association with Wilde in the 1890s. In so doing they produced the letters which had been shown at Wilde's trial and which were brought up again and again, probably from the files of Ross's solicitor Lewis. This was counter-productive. Douglas did not deny associating with Wilde but argued effectively that he had long ago abandoned Wilde and his circle. Mr Hume Williams for the plaintiffs read out the Hyathincus letter, outraging Douglas, who protested: "That letter was produced by my father in an effort to smash Wilde and to save me. It was my father trying to save his wretched son and you lawyers come here after twenty-five years and drag it up because you are paid to drag it up".[11] Bosie had by now accepted that his father had been out to smash Wilde in order to save him.

Douglas's trial testimony, very widely reported in a sensational trial which dominated the front pages, left no doubt at all that he now took his father's side in the battles of 1895. Douglas referred to the Hyacinthus letter as "a rotten, sodomitically inclined letter written by a diabolical scoundrel to a wretched, silly youth".[12] He became hysterical when the letters were produced, though not so hysterical that he could not see the dangers of a question from Counsel "When did you cease to approve of sodomy?", and on the whole his testimony was delivered in a devastatingly considered and level-headed tone of voice. This gave him additional gravitas, and there is no doubt he contributed greatly to the acquittal which the jury delivered at the end of the trial. But there was more to his evidence than merely a contribution to a sensational libel trial. Douglas was giving formal notice to the world that he was repudiating Oscar Wilde and all that he had embraced in the eighteen nineties. He made this unmistakably clear early in his cross-examination, when Billing was establishing his relation to Wilde:

Billing: Where did you meet him? – In his own house first. I was taken there by Lionel Johnson, the poet.
Billing: Do you regret it? – I regret it intensely.
The witness then claimed that Wilde had had "a most diabolical influence over others. He was the greatest force for evil in Europe for the last 350 years".
Billing: Do you refer to sexual evil? – No, he was the agent of the Devil in every possible way. It was his whole object in life to attack and sneer at virtue and undermine it by every means.[13]

Standing in the witness box at the Old Bailey in June 1918, at the age of 47, Alfred Bruce Douglas now demolished the notion that he was in any way a friend or supporter of Oscar Wilde. He had become to all intents and purposes the standard bearer and true representative on earth of John Sholto Douglas, Marquis of Queensberry, his father. His reaction to the terrible humiliation of the Ransome trial was to repudiate Wilde and his works with all the fanatical fervour with which, twenty-five years earlier, he had embraced and defended them.

* * *

J.T. Grein suffered a nervous collapse and Maud Allan left Britain for a decade; but Bosie Douglas emerged from the Old Bailey a national hero, cheered by a tumultuous mob. Billing, too, was on the crest of a wave of war-induced hysteria. Had Britain lost the war, it is not too hard to imagine that the country, impoverished and with no faith in its leaders, might have experienced similar upheavals to those that followed the formation of the Weimar Republic in Germany. Fortunately, the British and French armies stopped the German advance and, with American troops flooding onto the Western Front, the Allies reversed the tide of war. By November 1918, with starvation looming at home, it was Germany who had to sue for peace. The absurd campaign to expose "47,000 homosexuals" in Government collapsed and Douglas could find less and less of an audience for his hysterical attacks on Decadence, but he now had a taste for notoriety and public campaigning which he would indulge with increasing recklessness.

This sudden eminence of his bitterest enemy cut Robbie Ross to the quick. He was now prematurely aged, under police surveillance, his friends suffering persecution by the law, and after a decade of struggle the triumph of Douglas at the Old Bailey was a bitter reverse. Ross felt Douglas's triumphant reception after the Old Bailey trial as a personal insult. While others noted with alarm the victory of Billing and the xenophobia which greeted it, Ross could not fail to note the bitter parallels between Bosie Douglas emerging from the Old Bailey to the cheers of a hateful mob, and the emergence of Queensberry from the same door to a similar mob in 1895. Oscar Wilde had been defeated again, and all Ross's work to rehabilitate the public image of his friend seemed in pieces.

Despite continuing ill-health – or perhaps to escape London and its bitter memories – Ross planned a trip to Australia and the USA. As the time came for him to leave, he was visited by many distinguished friends whose support testified eloquently to the high regard in which he was held. Siegfried Sassoon, Edith Sitwell, Clive Bell, Lady Ottoline Morrell, Charles Scott Moncrieff and the young Noel Coward all came. They could not have known they were paying a final farewell. On Saturday afternoon, 5 October, Ross lunched with friends and then went home with indigestion and asked his maid, Nellie Burton, for tablets. She had none, but assisted him to bed. When she went to wake him for dinner, she found him dead. He was only 49. A post mortem concluded that his death was from "syncope, caused by chronic bronchitis and gastritis". A sentimentalist might conclude that he died of a broken heart.

Robbie Ross in death took on something like the martyr's crown long worn by the shade of Oscar Wilde. There can be little doubt that the battles with Douglas had hastened his end and, as Douglas had gained a mob following through his appearances at the Old Bailey, in a sense Douglas had secured victory in their feud. Yet in the long run this was not so. Wilde's reputation continued to rise, and Robbie Ross's with it. In his will, he asked to be cremated and his ashes put in Wilde's tomb in Paris. This could not be carried out until after Douglas's death in 1945 because of fears that Douglas would create a scandal but, in 1950, this instruction was carried out, with Vyvyan Holland's wife attending. Ross's reputation as Wilde's faithful friend was to gain in lustre; Douglas's was low and his public image that of an extremist. Despite his triumph at the Old Bailey he was ill-tempered and unloved. When his wife converted to Catholicism in 1917, Olive confided to the priest that when he became violently angry, she was positively terrified of him.[14] He continued in his bombastic style after the Old Bailey jury showed him how to appeal to fanaticism. His polemics and journalistic activities, intemperate and controversial, continued for nearly five years, earning Douglas a reputation as a fearsome litigator in frequent court cases. He had great good fortune in the libel court but, in 1923, made the serious mistake of attacking Winston Churchill. Douglas had sued the *Morning Post* for accusing him of anti-Semitism. He won this case on a technicality but the jury allowed him only one farthing damages and he was denied costs. This was a warning that he was going too far, but it went unheeded.

Douglas immediately set about attacking Winston Churchill. He suggested that Churchill had delayed news of the Battle of Jutland to allow Jewish financiers to make a killing on the New York stock exchange. He now extended this obsession over Churchill's alleged involvement with Jewish financiers by alleging that Jews in the British Secret Service had murdered the British C-in-C, Lord Kitchener, by blowing up the warship HMS *Hampshire* in 1916 on its way to Russia with Kitchener on board, and that Churchill was linked with this. This immensely serious libel brought the government to Churchill's defence as it involved his work for the state in wartime. Douglas found it imposssible to sustain this conspiracy theory, he lost the inevitable libel action and was fortunate to be sentenced to only six months in prison. *The Times* commented savagely – but with justice: "To those who have watched the career of the man, it will be regarded as a moderate sentence. For years, in newspapers, and in circulars and in pamphlets, he has conducted a campaign of calumny regardless of facts and intrepid of defamatory invective. At last he has been laid by the heels in quite a gentle way, but in a way which we hope –

not with great confidence – will teach him a lesson".[15] Bosie Douglas had put himself beyond the Pale of mainstream political thinking.

The leader writer was, however, wrong to say that this was a gentle way of treating Alfred Douglas. For a man of 53 and from an aristocratic background, six months in Wormwood Scrubs was a severe sentence and it damaged his health. Prison did have a salutary effect on Douglas and, in a curious echo of Wilde's case, he purged his anger with a series of sonnets later titled by him *In Excelsis* – a deliberate contrast with *De Profundis* – which allowed him to come to terms with the worst aspects of his behaviour of the previous dozen years. The Bosie Douglas who emerged from prison in May 1924 was no longer paranoically suspicious and primed to attack at the slightest obstacle. He began to attract the friendship of younger writers, notably Harford ("H") Montgomery Hyde, John Betjeman and Rupert Croft-Cook; became friendly with his wife again, and, in May 1925, made up the quarrel with his son. Above all, he began to come to terms with his relationship with Wilde and abandoned the corrosive bitterness of the period in which he had been dominated by Crosland and the circle around Pemberton Billing. Douglas also now entered a third sexual period of his life: celibacy, which, together with the strict Roman Catholicism he practised, allowed him to come to terms with the demons which had long haunted him.

Coming to terms with the legacy of Wilde and Ross was more difficult, and, where Ross was concerned, he never overcame his loathing. His old love for Wilde, however, reasserted itself, although his supersensitivity about any challenge to his interpretation of the relationship continued to the end of this life. It led to a bitter quarrel with Frank Harris. By the Spring of 1925, Harris was making strenuous attempts to contact Douglas in a bid to correct his 1916 book on Wilde, which he had based on the testimony of Robert Ross. Harris now distrusted Ross, particularly after Reggie Turner had denied the claim that Wilde's body had exploded with fluids on death. Douglas initially refused to meet Harris; but, when a friend of Harris's acted as an intermediary, Douglas fell into a characteristic pattern of wholehearted trust followed by a reversal into suspicion and hostility. On 20 March 1925, he wrote a letter to Harris in which he detailed explicitly the nature of the physical aspects of his affair with Wilde.[17] He followed this up with a longer letter on 30 April, detailing his version of the trials and subsequent events, without going into his sexual relations with Wilde, but confirming Harris's version of the Café Royal meeting in 1895. Harris produced a new version of his book, but Douglas felt this was insufficiently biased towards his version of events, and he refused to allow any copies to be sold in Britain. He successfully sued Harrods, in their capacity as a bookseller, in a high profile action designed to deter others. Harris was enraged, and the subsequent argument was still unresolved in August 1931, when Frank Harris died.

Harris had published a new version of his book in 1930. It was not on general sale, but was only available via the publishers, Covici Friede, in the USA. The 30 April letter was included, and Douglas had this work banned in Britain. Meanwhile, Douglas published in London, as a pamphlet, a draft joint preface which he and Harris had written and then abandoned because they could not agree on the wording, attaching his own commentary. The pamphlet was largely ignored because review copies were not sent out. Bosie was infuriated and decided to write a full autobiography, in which he hoped to put his relationship with Wilde in the context of his life as a whole.

Throughout the Summer of 1927 he worked on his autobiography, without the benefit of having the manuscript of *De Profundis* to hand. He attempted to obtain it from the British Museum that January on the grounds that it was addressed to him so it was legally his possession.[16] This claim started a long legal battle between Douglas and his supporters against the British Museum. It would have done Douglas little good to have the document, for he still could not write logically and objectively about Wilde's view of him, as expressed in *De Profundis*. Whenever he had to deal with the comments made about him by Wilde, Ross or Harris he was irascible to the point of hysteria. At one point, he referred to the latter as a "lying text" and the three men as comparable liars.[18] While the book is infinitely superior to *Oscar Wilde and Myself*, nevertheless the wounds caused by the Ransome trial and the many other slights he had suffered burst repeatedly through his attempts at plain storytelling. The *Autobiography* is dominated by the relationship with Wilde, which takes up half its pages and, despite outbursts of bitterness, contains real affection for Wilde. In Chapter XII, with remarkable honesty, Douglas sets out a true statement of the physical relationship and the emotional bond between them. Nevertheless, Douglas was unable even in his fifties to acknowledge the reality of the life he and Wilde had lived, and his own activities with "renters".

Bosie contended that his relationship with Wilde was cooling before the trials and that Wilde's behaviour would have destroyed what remained of it, arguing: "It is not likely that I could have gone on indefinitely keeping up a sentimental friendship with a man whose ideas of what he describes . . . as his 'Great Love' for me could yet allow him to live the kind of life of promiscuous nastiness with a dozen or more boy paramours which was revealed in his trial".[19] It would have been better for Douglas to have mentioned nothing of the rent boys, rather than make this mendacious statement, which is followed on the next page by the assertion that Wilde "concealed his infidelities as much as he could".[20] What Douglas could mean by this is impossible to fathom. Only the naïve reader could have believed that he had not known what Wilde was doing. The cognoscenti would have known immediately that he himself had taken the lead in "cruising" the homosexual underworld.

The *Autobiography* demonstrates that Douglas still saw Ross as a malevolent figure. He argues with little justification that Ross "deliberately poisoned" Wilde against him.[21] Ross had become the villain of the piece, blamed even for Douglas's intemperate destruction of the intimate letters written by Wilde to him at the time of his trials, which Douglas later bitterly regretted. He had destroyed some 150, keeping only the most colourless, claiming that this was done before the Ransome trial at the instigation of an unnamed friend of Robbie Ross.[22] But why, at that stage, given the hatred he had fomented for Ross, would Bosie Douglas have done anything at his suggestion?

Despite these remaining delusions, the *Autobiography* moves well away from the paranoid attacks on Wilde of *Oscar Wilde and Myself*, which, in Chapter XXII, Douglas repudiates, blaming the fanatical Crosland as the real author. In this chapter, Douglas even forgives Wilde for writing *De Profundis*, accepting that he ran down Wilde unfairly, and that he "entirely misrepresented the strength of my own love and devotion for him, which persisted right up to the time when I read the 'unpublished' *De Profundis* in 1913".[23] When the *Autobiography* appeared in March 1929, it showed that the worst of the Wilde-hating period was over. In 1931, Douglas spoke to the Catholic Poetry Society and repudiated his statement from the Billing trial that Wilde was "the greatest force for evil that has appeared in Europe in the last 350 years".[24] Bosie was now over sixty, and had at last come to develop a more balanced view of the relationship which had dominated his life.

FOURTEEN

Time Ends All Things

Bosie had now purged himself of the poisonous hatreds which had wrecked the middle years of his life, and, by the time he passed his sixtieth birthday, he had become good company for those who could avoid the dangerous topics which still triggered his irascible Douglas temper. H. Montgomery Hyde met him for the first time in May 1931, being one of a group of younger writers, including Hugh Kingsmill, Hesketh Pearson (who was to write a good biography of Wilde), Malcolm Muggeridge and Harold Nicolson, who visited Douglas; while he continued to enjoy a remarkable, and very revealing, correspondence with Bernard Shaw. He became friendly with the birth control pioneer, Marie Stopes, an unlikely sympathiser given the Catholic view on birth control, but it was a friendship founded on genuine respect. These exchanges did something to offset the pain caused by the death of his beloved mother in October 1935, aged 91. Sybil had shortly before been received into the Catholic church, following her favourite son with the fidelity that had marked their relationship throughout sixty-five years.

Douglas's attitude to Wilde in the last decade of his life was seemingly without rancour. In 1938, he produced a book of memoirs entitled *Without Apology*, in which Wilde was written about sympathetically, notably in a section on the trials that presented a very positive view of Wilde as a kind and charitable man of "enormous genius", whose friendship with Bosie had never been broken. It was clear from Bosie's later writings that the disastrous Ransome trial had only served to remind him of how much he had once loved Oscar Wilde. But he criticised Constance, once again quite unfairly, for setting conditions on his living with Oscar after prison, and showed no insight whatever into the suffering he had helped to cause the Wilde family. He maintained his illogical hatred of Robbie Ross, having transferred to him all the rancour he still felt over the break-up with Wilde.[1] And his attitude to his father remained confused, seeing him early on in the text as being out to destroy Bosie and hurt his wife, Bosie's mother, returning to the confused reasoning of his petition to Queen Victoria of 1895. [2]

Had this been his last word on his friendship with Wilde, and his terrible feud with his father, it might have been an appropriate note on which to sum up his troubled life. However, in the Summer of 1939, nearing seventy, Bosie Douglas was persuaded by a publisher to write a life of Wilde, which inevitably turned into an apologia for their relationship. Bosie could be honest about Wilde's homosexuality, which he regarded as a sin but not a crime. The sensible approach was that of the French Napoleonic code, which embodied this distinction. Douglas now saw Wilde as a martyr to progress because of the cruelty shown to him by the society of the time.[3]

While he had clearly forgiven Wilde, Douglas's attitude to Ross remained obdurate, his former friend being used as the scapegoat for all that had gone wrong with his relationship with Wilde. This was in part because of Douglas's deep hatred of homosexuality; for, while he could accept Wilde as a homosexual he was still, at the end of his life, still unable to be honest about how he and Wilde had been living in the 'nineties.

This continuing evasiveness had lasting consequences for Douglas's reputation, further adding fuel to the myth that he betrayed Wilde. Specifically, he could not admit that he and not Wilde had the boy in the bed at the Savoy. Thus, he could never reveal the meaning behind his offer in the first of Wilde's trials to give evidence, which could not have been limited to testimony against his father's character. In consequence, he was never able to effectively counter the charge made by Labouchère publicly, and by Wilde privately, that he was a Judas who abandoned Wilde in his hour of need. He was never able to explain what Wilde meant by the gnomic observation in *De Profundis* that "the sins of another were being placed to my account".[4]

However, his evidence of his feelings for Wilde is more authentic. The relationship was revived after Wilde left prison precisely because Bosie Douglas convinced him that he still loved him and desired to be with him above all else. It was this that was the driving force behind the reconciliation in Naples. It is abundantly clear that Wilde's later claims that Bosie wanted to live off him and abandoned him when his money ran out are a serious misrepresentation. The failure of the Naples experiment lay partly in the impossibility for either man of recreating the golden years of 1892–4 in exile, and more in the financial crisis engendered by Constance and Sybil cutting off their money. Without this, the relationship might have drifted on for some time. It was Sybil and Constance who wrecked the reconciliation; and, while Bosie relished his freedom once he had it, and reacted bitterly against Wilde's claims on his money, sentimental feeling underlay Bosie's attitudes to Wilde through to the Ransome trial, and re-emerged in the late 1920s.

Oscar Wilde: A Summing Up was virtually the last thing Bosie Douglas wrote about Wilde in the last years of his life, although he continued to write and lecture on a range of topics. He relished his image as a right-wing reactionary, seeing himself as Colonel Blimp and writing so in a sonnet. By now, his old adversary, Winston Churchill was Prime Minister of a wartime coalition, earning Douglas's unstinted admiration as he led the country with great fortitude through the dark days when Britain stood alone against the Nazis. In the Summer of 1941, Douglas wrote a sonnet praising the Prime Minister, which was published in the *Daily Mail* of 4 July. Bosie's nephew Francis, the elder of Percy's sons, sent a copy of the poem to the Prime Minister before it was published which led to a most generous reply from Churchill. Despite the enormous pressures he faced, Churchill wrote personally to Francis, "Thank you very much for the sonnet you sent me which I will keep and value. Tell him from me that 'Time Ends All Things'".[5] Churchill had forgiven the storm which had led him to have Douglas imprisoned.

The actor Donald Sinden, who became friendly with Douglas in those last years, found Douglas good and charming company, but also discovered how furious Douglas could become when reminded of the unpleasant aspects of the Wilde relationship. One day, he innocently showed him a copy of *Oscar Wilde and Myself* which he had bought in a secondhand bookshop. Douglas was immediately beside himself with rage, and Sinden later recalled:

> Bosie leaped to his feet, his whole body twitching, his face became deathly white and his eyes glared, he spluttered and mucus ran from his nose and mouth. He seemed to be choking and his eyes grew larger and sightless. "The walls seemed suddenly to reel, and the sky above my head became like a casque of scorching steel". At last he managed an intake of breath and screamed, "WHERE DID YOU GET IT? WHERE DID YOU GET IT?" I was deeply shocked but tried to explain. He snatched the book with jumping hands – for a moment I thought he was going to throw what had cost me two shillings and sixpence on the fire. I was seeing the Douglas I had read about.[6]

However, Douglas calmed down and merely wrote in the flyleaf a repudiation of the book and gave it back to Sinden. This was an uncharacteristic show of his old manic temper. When not aroused by ancient feuds he could be objective about the relationship. Sinden asked him about the Hyacinthus letter, and Bosie told him "My dear darling, you must realise that this letter was by comparison with others insignificant. I had received scores of letters from Oscar far more beautiful, far more personal than that one. I kept them locked away, but I burned them after the Ransome case". Sinden was close enough to Bosie in his last years to attend his funeral, and his overall recollection set down in his memoirs was that Bosie was "to me, a very kind old man".

Overall, Bosie Douglas remained affectionate towards Oscar Wilde and, almost at the last, was able to be objective and lucid about the relationship. When Hesketh Pearson wrote to him with two chapters of his proposed biography, Douglas wrote back a month before he died, saying that he had found it "exceedingly painful to read once more the dreadful story of cruelty and hypocrisy and humbug",[7] but rejecting once again, Oscar's claims of his meanness with money.

The end was now very near. Bosie had already suffered the death of Olive in February 1944. They had not lived together after the First World War, but met regularly, especially at Christmas. Douglas kept up a regular correspondence with Bernard Shaw almost up to his death, although curiously the only time they ever actually met in the whole of their long lives was at that fatal meeting with Wilde and Frank Harris at the Café Royal in 1895. He had become friendly with a farmer called Edward Colman who lived with his wife Sheila near Lancing on the South Coast, moving in with them on a temporary basis on 1 December 1944 for Christmas. He never left their home, being too ill to move, and after a falling out with his heir, Adrian Earle, a young man for whom he had formed a sentimental attachment, he made the Colmans his literary executors. He commented to Marie Stopes in a letter that they had "been angelic to me, dear people".[8] He realised that he was coming to the end of his life and tried to make amends for the quarrels, allowing Robert Hichens the right to re-publish *The Green Carnation* – withdrawn in 1895 when the trials began – and hoping to mend relations with Wilde's surviving son, Vyvyan Holland. Both Wilde's sons had taken Ross's side in the great feud, for entirely understandable reasons, and Bosie regretted this deeply. He had once met Vyvyan at a ball in the late 'thirties, when they "chatted on general subjects for five minutes and then parted", according to Vyvyan.[9] No reconciliation beyond this was possible; the catastrophic consequences of his relationship with Wilde would not merely live with him to the end of his life, but would gain in vigour after his death. They bedevil understanding to this day.

The friends he had made since coming out of prison, however, remained with him to the last. In the depth of the early Winter of 1945, when he was clearly dying, Bosie recieved a constant stream of letters and phone calls to the Colmans which were a comfort to him. In the early hours of Tuesday 20 March, the night nurse called the Colmans to sit with him as he was slipping away, and they held his hand through the last hours. He died around 4 a.m. and was buried three days later. His sister Edith attended the funeral with other members of the family, including Francis, Marquis of Queensberry and the Colmans, H. Montgomery Hyde, Donald Sinden and other friends. Montgomery Hyde was to write a lengthy biography of Bosie Douglas, and his comment at the end on the relationship which dominated his life and its aftermath is apposite and echoes Sinden's portrait: "The Wilde tragedy was to a great extent his own and he added to it by his action in never allowing the world to forget it. However it is now beyond dispute that he neither ruined his friend nor deserted him, as his enemies so often alleged. To those of a younger generation, like the present writer, he was an essentially kindly man".[10]

This is undoubtedly true. He had always had charm, and this was the basis of the attraction he had had for Wilde. Yet the duality of his character, displayed in obsessive behaviour and frequent violent rages, is equally undeniable. If he inherited kindliness and charm from his mother, he inherited the fatal Douglas temperament from his father. The tragedy for Wilde, Bosie and even his manic father, is that the combination of this temperament and the circumstances of the relationship with Oscar Wilde was deeply destructive.

The death of Lord Alfred Douglas, "Bosie" to his friends right to the end, broke the last link with the eighteen-nineties and the passionate relationship that had such enormous consequences. Queensberry, Constance and Lady Wilde, Oscar Wilde himself had not survived the decade. Robert Ross died in 1918, Frank Harris in 1931, More Adey, Reggie Turner and Robert Sherard in 1943. With the death of Bosie Douglas, the affair should have shaded into a cooler perspective than had been possible when the principals were alive and their relationships still living memory. The act of putting Robert Ross's ashes into Oscar Wilde's tomb in 1949 could have symbolised an attempt to end the drama that he, Oscar Wilde, Bosie Douglas and their circle had played out half a century earlier. This did not happen. The partisans for Ross and Douglas kept the quarrels alive. The publication of an almost complete version of *De Profundis* with an introduction by Vyvyan Holland in 1949 ensured that Wilde's baleful version of events would live on.

Those who had known Bosie Douglas contributed their own memoirs. In the same year, his nephew Francis Queensberry published, in conjunction with Percy Colson, a censorious view of his uncle. Francis, who was close to Winston Churchill and clearly disliked Douglas, dedicated the book to Vyvyvan Holland, "to complete the circle".[11] Douglas had his defenders, however, notably two men who knew him in his last years, H. Montgomery Hyde and Rupert Croft-Cook, and their defences ran along lines which were laid down by Bosie himself, blaming Wilde and Robert Ross for the disasters which had taken place. For over half a century after the death of Alfred Douglas, his relationship with Wilde has been examined by one or other of the two opposed camps. It is surely time to look at the relationship through eyes unblinkered by these ancient quarrels.

228-237
notes 255-

EPILOGUE

And All Men . . .

In the century since it ended, the story of Oscar and Bosie has taken on a life of its own. Much of the writing about the two men is markedly partisan, Oscar Wilde in particular has become a secular saint whose downfall has taken on mythic qualities – an outcome he himself in part constructed.[1] Bosie Douglas spent much of the last two thirds of his life attempting to come to terms with it, analysing his relationship with Wilde with a maladroitness that added new elements to the mythology. A hundred years have, if anything, served to compound the arguments and to entrench the opposing views.

The myths derive as much from the two men's own writings as from their defenders' attempts to champion their cause, but the most damaging of all, that Bosie Douglas forced Wilde to challenge his father in the courts and then abandoned him, had an independent origin. It was started by Henry Labouchère in his paper *Truth* shortly after Wilde began his sentence. Labouchère accused Douglas of cowardice. Bosie replied immediately with a letter, which Labouchère published. He had been prepared to testify in the trial of his father, had offered to testify in the first Wilde trial, but had been prevented from doing so and sent away. He was telling the truth. Wilde himself wrote to the *Evening News*: "It would have been impossible for me to have proved my case without putting Lord Alfred Douglas in the witness box against his father. Lord Alfred Douglas was extremely anxious to go into the box, but I would not let him do so".[2] Bosie defended himself effectively against the charge of cowardice; but, while he countered Labouchère's allegations, the idea that he had betrayed Wilde took root.[3] Moreover, he was to find that a far more damaging version of the charge that he played the role of Judas would be laid at his door, and by Oscar Wilde himself.

The prison letter, *De Profundis,* contains extremely damaging allegations against Douglas. The rhetorical flourish claiming "It was a case of that tyranny of the weak over the strong which in one of my plays I describe as being 'the only tyranny that lasts'"[4] is brilliant advocacy. In buttressing this argument, Wilde painted a picture of the relationship as a nightmarish period consisting of little more than a series of selfish outbursts by Bosie Douglas. There is certainly some truth in this, but as a complete explanation for Wilde's downfall it fails on several counts.

The prison letter was classic polemic, written at a time of great personal trauma for Wilde and presenting a persuasive but one-sided version of the relationship that stands suspiciously apart from Wilde's public acknowledgement of Bosie's predicament before and during the trial, and the touching reunion after his release into exile. The Naples letters provide an even more dubious version of events, powerfully reinforcing the myth that Douglas exploited Wilde and then abandoned him when he was no longer financially viable. The presentation of Wilde's letters at the Ransome trial in 1913 thus created an overwhelming impression of Bosie Douglas as a deceitful individual, a verdict that was accepted by the jury and has persisted. The disgraceful vendetta Douglas launched against Ross following the Ransome book could only cement the view that he was an unregenerate and deeply unpleasant version of his father.

Douglas was later able to combat some of the allegations made against him at the trial, but not those that had the greatest historical force. Moreover, the very shrillness of his defence weakened even those elements of his case which were valid, notably the fact that he secured £200 from his mother to support Wilde when the Naples episode ended. Both Wilde's allegations against Douglas, and Douglas's defence, need more careful scrutiny than they have conventionally been accorded.

Wilde's belief that Bosie had abandoned him in prison was at least based on ignorance. That Douglas and his father had driven Wilde to launch his disastrous legal action against Queensberry, Wilde the victim of an hereditary feud, is a more conscious construct. The idea that Wilde was driven heedlessly to sue Queensberry by Bosie Douglas acting out of malice against his father is untenable. He had been contemplating legal action against Queensberry as early as the Summer of 1894, but was dissuaded by George Wyndham. He must have discussed it with Robbie Ross, since Ross put him in touch with his solicitor Humphreys. An action for breach of the peace would have been viable in 1894 and even more certain to succeed after the attempt to disrupt the première of *Earnest*. Alas, George Alexander declined to give evidence on behalf of his star writer, understandably not wanting to court publicity. Wilde must have known that merely binding Queensberry over not to cause another disturbance of the peace would have been of limited effect. Whether he discussed any other option is not known.

It is clear then that, even before Douglas entered the frame, Wilde was contemplating legal action. Wilde's letter to Ross on the night of discovering the infamous calling card warned: "I don't see anything now but a criminal prosecution", and invited Ross to come to see him at 11.30 p.m., Bosie to attend on the following morning. Ross noted that the letter arrived at 6.40 p.m. and that, when he went up at 11.30, Bosie Douglas was already there.[5] Wilde later told More Adey, in echoes of *De Profundis*, "at that moment AD arrived, saw his father's card, and by taunts of cowardice and terror drove me to the final step. I stumbled like an ox into the shambles. . .".[6] This suggests strongly that in the time between Wilde writing to Ross in the early evening and Ross's arrival at the appointed time of 11.30 Douglas had begun putting Wilde under pressure. However, the letter to Ross indicates that this was probably only to take a decision to sue – which Wilde was already contemplating. The fact of Douglas arriving unexpectedly appears significant, but Wilde claimed Bosie was omnipresent. He had attempted to bring a boyfriend to live at Wilde's hotel and flown into a temper when Oscar refused permission for him to take such a suicidal step. He had just received an offensive letter, presumably about this quarrel. The discovery of Queensberry's card overshadowed this immediate quarrel with an infinitely larger dispute, which Douglas instantly threw himself into, but Wilde did not take the decisive decision even under Bosie's browbeating. At the meeting that evening, Ross urged Wilde to consult his solicitor before deciding, and Wilde went with Douglas to see Humphreys the following morning, 1 March. Before going, Wilde had received another letter from Douglas, which suggests that Douglas was applying the most extreme pressure on Wilde to prosecute. It was at this meeting that Wilde told lies to his solicitor, denying the truth of Queensberry's allegations, a course of action he must have known was extremely dangerous. Wilde's last attempt to escape the action of suing Queensberry, which he clearly did not want to do, was to cry poverty, but Douglas promised money for the trial and Wilde acquiesced in going to the magistrates' court to take out the warrant.

What Wilde meant by the letter of 1 March giving "the most shameful reason" for prosecuting Queensberry is not known: the letters of that Winter are not among the slim volume of letters from Bosie to Oscar that have survived. It is entirely plausible that Douglas saw the chance to destroy his father, and bent all his willpower to forcing Wilde into taking the action which would remove his father to prison. It is clear from the decisive Café Royal meeting with Wilde, Harris and Bernard Shaw that Douglas applied the most intense emotional pressure on Wilde, and must therefore take much of the blame for what then happened. He believed he could turn the libel action by testifying to his father's appalling character, not appreciating that in a libel action evidence as to character is irrelevant.[7] While Douglas's ignorance of the law played a major factor in his driving Wilde onward, it has to be conceded that he was quite prepared to expose himself to danger in so doing. He certainly did not incite Wilde to take action then run away. He was intensely anxious to appear in the witness box, seeing this not as an action that would open him to risk but the decisive act in bringing down his father. As this was his objective from the moment he saw the calling card, his whole force of character was focussed on this and he was heedless to any arguments to the contrary.

However, this does not place the responsibility for suing Queensberry on Douglas's shoulders. Wilde ultimately made the decision. He was a man of the world, more intelligent than Douglas, sixteen years older and immensely more experienced. He was advised by figures of the stature of Frank Harris and Bernard Shaw against fighting Queensberry in court. Wilde's character in other respects was conspicuously strong and heterodox; he had made a life out of defying convention. It remains a mystery why, at this decisive moment, he could not assert himself. One can only postulate some deep psychological explanation, that Wilde was in some way "programmed" to bring about his own destruction. But if the psychology of the decision is hard to fathom, one fact stands out: there was no external reason by which Oscar Wilde had to do what Douglas urged, other than his feelings for Bosie himself.

When Wilde argued, as he was to do after the event, that "(Bosie) once played dice with his father for my life and lost . . . in the whole of this law business my life has been gambled for and staked on the board with utter recklessness",[8] he slid round the crucial point which Frank Harris made – that this did not have to happen. He did not have to follow where Douglas was leading. Douglas had no hold over Wilde save an emotional one, and Wilde had plenty of opportunities to refuse. He later wrote ruefully: "All trials are trials for one's life". Given the truth of this epigram, he should not have allowed Bosie Douglas to gamble with his. Indeed, it was not Bosie Douglas who did gamble. The responsibility for casting the die was his alone. Oscar did not have the moral courage and simple instinct for survival to say No.

Wilde was not the only person who preferred to evade reality. Constance, who, despite Bosie's belief that she liked him, had always loathed her husband's friend, came to the same conclusion as her husband as to the cause of the disaster. Shortly before her untimely death she wrote to Vyvyan that he should never hate Wilde: "Try not to feel harshly about your father; remember that he is your father and that he loves you. *All his troubles arose from the hatred of a son for his father*, and whatever he has done he has suffered bitterly for it".[9] [*Author's emphasis*] Others among Wilde's friends came to this conclusion, which was well established long before *De Profundis* became known to the world. Douglas, naturally, never accepted this view and in his mad petition to Queen Victoria in June 1895 put forward his own interpretation of the fall, ascribing it to Queensberry's determination to destroy his son and further hurt his wife. This interpretation has become the polar opposite to Wilde's, but it is equally suspect. Queensberry's purpose was to save his son from Wilde by destroying Wilde, and he did so from love. Bosie finally realised this in his sixties, but never fully accepted it. Echoes of his earlier belief that he, and not Wilde, was the real target remained to the end. It is a view that surfaces tenaciously in the writings of his defenders, but it is not justified by the facts.

And, as always, one returns to the relationship. Bosie Douglas never confronted *De Profundis* head on, retreating again and again to the myth that it had been "faked up" by Robert Ross. In his final word on the subject, *Oscar Wilde: A Summing Up*, in 1939, he fell out badly with Bernard Shaw on this and other critical aspects of the biography. Shaw had an objective view of both Douglas's *bêtes noires*, Ross and Harris, and advised him that: "You must make up your mind as to whether *De Profundis* is a forgery or not. If it is, you have no grounds for complaining that Wilde attacked you and all that stuff must come out. If you accept that it is genuine, which it obviously is, you have no grounds for describing it as a fake. As nobody now remembers anything about Ross, your weakness for vulgar abuse really does him a resurrectional service".[10]

Douglas rejected Shaw's wise advice in favour of more vulgar abuse. This reinforced the view of his critics that he was evasive and unreliable in his view of the relationship. His other writings suffered from equally damaging flaws. While *Oscar Wilde and Myself* is wholly worthless, refusing to accept the homosexuality he and Wilde had experienced in the 'nineties, his later writing did accept that his relationship with Wilde had been physical. These admissions took great courage at a time when homosexuality was still illegal, but were marred by the fact that he could never admit he knew of Wilde's penchant for rent boys and working class youths. Still more damaging to his credibility, he never admitted his own. These fatal flaws have reinforced the view of Douglas's opponents that all Douglas's writings are unreliable, while his supporters have glossed over the essential need to remove the mythical elements Douglas had created about his life in the eighteen nineties to establish what is myth and what elements are valid.

There remains one more puzzling aspect to the case – why Douglas came to pardon Wilde for writing the letter, but not Ross for revealing it when, by his own admission, *he had thrown the original away unread. . .* This puzzle can only be considered as part of the wider, central issue of the relationship between Oscar Wilde and Lord Alfred Douglas, namely the bond which held the two men together and which gave Douglas so great a hold over Oscar Wilde at the two critical moments, the decision to sue Queensberry, and living together after Berneval.

The heart of the relationship is elusive, partly because of the lack of written evidence – both men destroyed most of the letters they wrote to each other – and partly because so much of the attraction for both men lay in its evanescent qualities: the pleasure of each other's company and the talk this engendered. Wilde loved to be the centre of attention, and Douglas hung on his every word. But this was the common currency of Wilde's circle. To become the great passion of Wilde's life there had to be more than a Robbie Ross or a John Gray could offer. The devotion Douglas felt for Wilde from 1892 to the end of 1897 was the expression of a deeply felt emotion. Wilde's commitment to Douglas expressed a similar emotional content. What the bond was will always remain obscure, but certain elements can be established with confidence.

It is clear that the relationship was not primarily sexual. Douglas was remarkably frank about the physical aspects in his later life, and there is no reason to disbelieve what he said. He claims to have been pursued by Wilde, and to have given in to him to please Wilde rather than for his own satisfaction. The physical aspects did not include sodomy. Wilde eventually understood that Douglas did not enjoy them and they were discontinued and not subsequently resumed. Douglas's recollections are plausible because neither man was the other's preferred sexual type, Douglas in particular valuing boys younger than himself. Wilde also fancied young men of a particularly beautiful aspect, and Douglas's astonishing youthfulness and languid good looks undoubtedly drew

Wilde to him initially. But they could not have provided the basis for the strong bond that developed.

The strength of this bond is undeniable, and Wilde was correct to argue that, by early 1895, Douglas had complete ascendancy over him. The trips to Algiers and Monaco demonstrate this conclusively. There are few more pathetic lines in Wilde's letters than in the one to Ada Leverson of 14 January: "I begged him to let me stay and rehearse, but so beautiful is his nature that he declined at once",[11] although this is matched by the bitter comment in *De Profundis*: "I had always thought that my giving up to you in small things meant nothing: that when a great moment arrived I could reassert my will-power in its natural superiority. It was not so."[12] Wilde was certainly dominated by Douglas, suggesting an element of the older lover fearing the loss of the younger – it would also account for the financial extravagance – but this is too shallow an explanation.

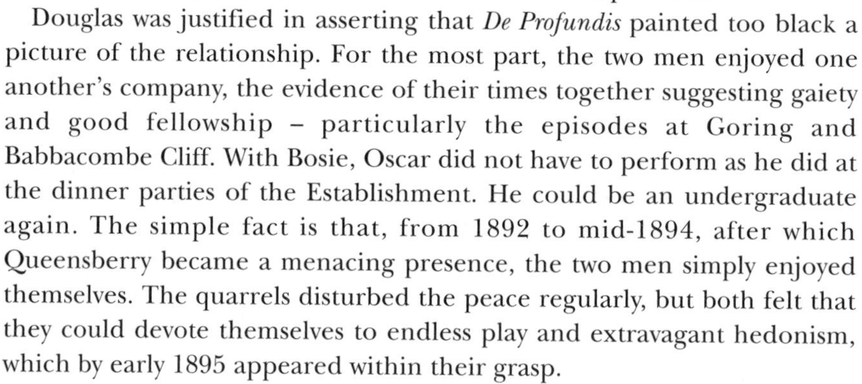

Douglas was justified in asserting that *De Profundis* painted too black a picture of the relationship. For the most part, the two men enjoyed one another's company, the evidence of their times together suggesting gaiety and good fellowship – particularly the episodes at Goring and Babbacombe Cliff. With Bosie, Oscar did not have to perform as he did at the dinner parties of the Establishment. He could be an undergraduate again. The simple fact is that, from 1892 to mid-1894, after which Queensberry became a menacing presence, the two men simply enjoyed themselves. The quarrels disturbed the peace regularly, but both felt that they could devote themselves to endless play and extravagant hedonism, which by early 1895 appeared within their grasp.

Their commitment to pleasure was clearly an absolutely vital part of the attraction each had for the other. That Bosie was a Lord was important, with his professional-class Dublin background Wilde was always a *parvenu*, but while his title gave him a unique value for Wilde, it was more important that, like Wilde, he was committed to a life of irresponsible dissolution. Unlike Wilde, Bosie had not studied Platonism and the theories of Walter Pater, he may never have read *Marius the Epicurean*, but this was not important. The fact that he was a hedonist and an epicurean by nature, by upbringing habituated to a life of conspicuous consumption, gave him an overwhelming appeal to Wilde: Bosie was the very personification of all Wilde's intellectual aspirations, the Platonic ideal made flesh. After his fall, Wilde could rail about Bosie's materialism, ranting to Robbie Ross that: "An illiterate millionaire would have suited him better. As long as my table was red with wine and roses, what did he care? My genius, my life as an artist, . . . were nothing to him when matched with his unrestrained and coarse appetites for common profligate life: his greed for money: his incessant and violent scenes: his unimaginative selfishness. . .".[13] But Bosie needed literature, brilliant wit and incessant sparkling talk, the aesthetic adventure. Bosie needed Wilde. No one else would do.

The bond that held Wilde and Douglas together, more than anything else, was the pursuit of an idyll in which they could share a life of pleasure heedless of the consequences. Wilde was unrepentant about his hedonism, writing lubriciously even from his prison cell: "I don't regret for a moment having lived for pleasure. I did it to the full, as one should do everything that one does to the full. There was no pleasure I did not experience. I threw the pearl of my soul into a cup of wine. I went down the primrose path to the sound of flutes. I lived on honeycomb. . .".[14]

Hesketh Pearson, in many ways Wilde's most perceptive biographer, comments that there are times when it is difficult to think of Wilde as a responsible person at all, and this is central to Wilde's behaviour: the Dieppe episode is a case in point. A commitment to sensual experience on the amoral model advocated by Walter Pater could have embraced a variety of activities. But the pursuit of pleasure is the one Wilde chose unerringly, and the one to which Bosie was introduced from birth. This is the key to the attraction of Bosie to Oscar, that both men were essentially childlike in their pursuit of self-gratification. Cambridge remained a golden period, the period of his only real literary success, but childhood at Kinmount was for Bosie Douglas the lodestar by which he steered his life. His Oedipal fixation on his mother and hatred of his father are one thing: but more to the point, he loathed Queensberry for having torn him away from Kinmount, the idyll where he could be with a mother who pampered him endlessly without his having to ask for anything. This childish nature was apparent to Bernard Shaw, who was immediately irritated by it. He complained: "Why has heaven afflicted me with this infantile complex of yours which keeps you making 'a low spirited noise', like Mrs MacStinger's baby, down the ages because somebody has been unkind to you. . .?"[15]

Douglas was far from affronted by this, for he recognised its accuracy. He believed, having read Thomas à Kempis, that when a soul got to heaven it could choose what age it would remain throughout eternity. Douglas tellingly decided he would spend eternity as a child. Bernard Shaw was both perceptive and good humoured, and for the rest of their long correspondence dubbed Douglas "Childe Alfred", a nickname which carried its own message.

In the years before the trials, Wilde had achieved exactly the Camelot-like state he most desired, writing brilliantly and spending money as it came in without thought for any consequences. It was in order perhaps to preserve this idyllic state of existence that he embarked on his disastrous action against Queensberry. These traits explain the Naples experiment, too. As Wilde made clear in his letter to Douglas on 31 August 1897, he saw his only chance of regaining his literary gifts was by living with Bosie, contradicting his earlier statements that Bosie's presence killed his ability to write: "you can really recreate in me that energy and sense of joyous power on which art depends. . ."[16] Oscar saw Bosie as his Muse; Douglas saw Wilde as a father figure, perhaps a substitute for the gentle, loving father he had never had. Oscar could hardly look after Douglas's finances, he could not look after his own. Wilde's dream of returning to the creative impulse of his golden years under Bosie's influence was less obviously absurd, but both men desired a Camelot that could not be. The years before the trials could never be recaptured. Wilde could no longer write, Bosie could never hope to be dependent on Wilde, the opposition to their relationship was now implacable. Constance and Sybil ensured that this could not happen, money was the lever, and in retrospect both men realised that Camelot had been an impossible dream.

The intensity of the bond that had held them together from 1892 to the collapse of the Naples experiment died thereafter, but its after-effects were always present. There was little sign that their relationship would become legendary, and both were too preoccupied with securing the pleasures of the moment to care. By 1900 the relationship was becoming tenuous, and Oscar's death could have released Bosie to live a life where his memory was just that. In the event, Bosie could never escape the relationship that had dominated his life in his twenties, and brought Oscar Wilde's to a premature end. Their relationship had been an extraordinary one, and would have been so even had Queensberry not taken a violent dislike to it. By challenging him, Wilde transformed a private quarrel into a public catastrophe whose consequences appear more controversial a century later than ever.

At the heart of the public events were private tragedies, which, while brought on by the self-destructive, solipsistic natures of the two protagonists, remain nonetheless profoundly moving in human terms. In the final analysis, the relationship of Oscar Wilde and Lord Alfred

Douglas was a true Fatal Passion. It is time to strip away the quarrels and disputes that marked it from its inception, and see those trapped in the maelstrom, Oscar and Bosie, Constance and Lady Wilde, Cyril and Vyvyan, Robbie Ross and Alfred Taylor, the "Scarlet Marquis" and his children, as players written into a drama that could never have a happy ending. Wilde sought as his life's goal an idyll of Greek Love, as once revealed to him by a schoolmaster. His relationship with Bosie Douglas, however, produced a tragedy the Ancients would have understood.

Notes

PROLOGUE: DESTRUCTIVE PASSIONS

1 The precise date is unknown and even July is controversial. Neither man could ever remember exactly when the first meeting took place. The consensus among biographers is July, supported by the fact that at the second meeting, at the Albemarle Club, Wilde gave Bosie the inscribed copy of *Dorian Gray*. The book version had been published in April.

2 Lionel Johnson was aged 23 in July 1891. He was a pupil at Winchester and had contributed to Bosie's school paper the *Pentagram* though already at Oxford. A close friend of Bosie and his mother, he was a brilliant scholar and poet, taking a double First in classics. He came to regret introducing Bosie to Wilde. Like Bosie he became a Catholic but was a far more tortured man and took to the bottle. He died aged only 35 after falling and breaking his skull.

3 Douglas, Oscar Wilde, *A Summing Up*, 1940, p. 122.

4 Croft-Cook, *Bosie*, 1963, p. 51, states that this autographed copy was in existence when he was writing and contained just his inscription. By June 1892 Wilde was writing, in a copy of his *Poems*, "From Oscar to the gilt mailed boy at Oxford in the heart of June, Oscar Wilde". Quoted Ellmann, 1988 p. 363.

5 For the Centenary of Wilde's death, November 2000, the British Library as the holder of the manuscript, issued two facsimile editions, priced respectively £125 (for an edition of 250 copies) and £245 for a leather bound edition of 50 copies.

6 Douglas asserted this in his petition to Queen Victoria in 1895 following Wilde's conviction, and reasserted this throughout his life. The most recent statement of his position by a sympathetic commentator is Douglas Murray, Bosie 2000 p. 74, appropos of Wilde stating "He had become involved in a dispute in which the father's aim was simply to 'smash' his son and thus was a subsidiary character".

CHAPTER ONE: THE DOUGLASES AND THE WILDES

1 The line was later renumbered so that today Archibald is the 8th Marquis and John Sholto the 9th. In this book the numbering they knew in their lifetime is used.

2 *The Times*, 10 August 1858.

3 *Dumfries and Galloway Standard*, 12 August 1858.
4 *Sporting Times*, 13 June 1858.
5 Ellmann, p. 12.
6 W.B. Yeats, *Autobiographies*, pp. 137–8.
7 Robert Sherard, *The Real Oscar Wilde*, p. 32.
8 Vincent O'Sullivan, *Aspects of Wilde*, p. 63.
9 Ellmann, p15.
10 Quoted Douglas, *Oscar Wilde and Myself*, p. 34.
11 Roberts, p. 51.
12 Ellmann, p. 28.
13 Wilde, *Letters 2000 (De Profundis)*, p. 732.
14 Wilde, *Letters 2000 (De Profundis)*, p. 735.
15 Holbrook Jackson quotes this in The Eighteen Nineties as part of the revised conclusion to the edition of *The Renaissance*, of 1888 and quoted on pp. 53–? of the Pelican edition of 1939.
16 Quoted Ellmann, p. 43. Whether Wilde said it is uncertain, but Ellmann perceptively comments that no-one else could have done so.
17 Quoted in Hyde, *Trials*, p. 46. Ellmann, pp. 44–5 gives the full conversation and source.
18 Queensberry and Colson, p. 50.
19 Douglas, *Autobiography*, p. 10.
20 Ibid, p. 16.
21 Queensberry and Colson, p. 51.
22 Douglas, *Autobiography*, p. 16.
23 Ibid, p. 92.
24 *Whitehall Review*, 30 November 1882.
25 Douglas, *Autobiography*, pp. 91–2.
26 Ibid, p. 2.
27 Douglas, *Without Apology*, pp. 237–40.
28 For the suicide, *The Times*, 7 April 1891.
29 Douglas, *Autobiography*, p. 17.
30 Ibid, p. 17.
31 Ibid.
32 Ibid, p. 26.
33 Ibid, p. 2.
34 Ibid, p. 56.
35 Ibid, p. 22.
36 Ibid, pp. 9–10.
37 Ibid, pp. 48–9.
38 Douglas, *Oscar Wilde and Myself*, pp. 36–7.
39 The *Spirit Lamp*, 27 May 1892, p. 119.
40 Wilde, *Letters 2000 (De Profundis)*, p. 694.

CHAPTER TWO: A LONG AND LOVELY SUICIDE 28–44

1 Ellmann, p. 130, quotes *New York World*, 8 January 1882.
2 Hamilton, p. 95.
3 Quoted Hamilton, p. 115.
4 Quoted Sherard, *The Real Oscar Wilde*, p. 200.
5 Ellmann, p. 232.
6 Ellmann, p. 235, quotes a letter from Sherard to A.J.A. Symonds, 3 June 1937.
7 W.B. Yeats, *Autobiographies*, pp. 134–5.
8 Wilde, *Letters 2000*, 16 December 1884, pp. 241–2.
9 Amor, pp. 60–1.
10 Otho Lloyd, Constance Wilde's brother, is quoted by Ellmann as writing to Arthur Ransome on 28 February 1912 that a virtual divorce took place, presumably meaning an end of sexual activity. Ellmann cites, p. 262.
11 Wilde, *Letters 2000*, 12 December 1885, p. 272. Emphasis added.
12 Wilde, *Letters 2000*, 13 October 1888, p. 360.
13 Raffalovich, *A Willing Exile* Vol 1, p. 79.
14 Wilde, *Letters 2000*, 1 December 1890, p. 457.
15 Wilde, *Picture of Dorian Gray*, OUP ed, p. 17.
16 Wilde, *Letters 2000*, note p. 438. The editorial was not written by Henley. Wilde replied, letter 9 July 1890, pp. 438–9.
17 Wilde, *Dorian Gray*, p. 119.
18 Wilde, *Letters 2000*, p. 795, wrote to More Adey from prison that Percy Douglas, Bosie's brother "should know a little more of the mere outlines of my unfortunate acquaintance with his brother. The friendship began in May 1892 by his brother appealing to me in a very pathetic letter to help in terrible trouble with people who were blackmailing him". (Letter 7 April 1897) This is slightly different to the account given in *De Profundis*, but agrees in essentials that the intimacy – the friendship had already begun – came when Bosie revealed that he was in desperate straits. Though Wilde claimed he had only met Bosie four times, the friendship was clearly already strong. What the blackmail centred on can only be conjectured, but Douglas's known behaviour suggests homosexual activity with rent boys.
19 Douglas, *Oscar Wilde, A Summing Up*, p. 122.
20 The Latin version is in *The Complete Poems of Lionel Johnson*. English translation by Ellmann, pp. 305–6.
21 Douglas in the *Autobiography* p. 69 states he was elected a year later.
22 Further details of the Crabbett Club from Douglas, *Oscar Wilde and Myself*, pp. 78–81.
23 Elizabeth Longford, *A Pilgrimage of Passion*, pp. 289–90.
24 Ibid.
25 Ann Clark Amor, p. 105. Ms original in the Clark Library.

26 Amor, pp. 105–6.

27 Ibid.

28 Ellmann, p. 345.

29 Wilde, *Letters 2000,* to *Pall Mall Gazette,* 1 October 1894, p. 617.

30 Douglas Murray, *Bosie,* p. 33 suggests the seduction 'probably' took place in January 1892, but gives no evidence. At this first sexual encounter Douglas later claimed Wilde "sucked" him at Tite Street. Letter to Frank Harris 20 March 1925 now in Texas.

31 Douglas, *Autobiography,* p. 75.

32 Ibid, p. 76.

33 Letter to Frank Harris quoted Hyde, *Lord Alfred Douglas,* p. 28.

34 Ellmann, p. 363.

35 Quoted Wilde, *Letters 2000,* p. 530, note by Hart-Davis, emphasis added. That Wilde went to Homburg is clear, but whether Bosie accompanied him is disputed by Horst Schroeder pp. 42–3. Other biographers accept the two went together.

36 "The Portrait of Mr W.H.", alleging W.H. to be a boy actor Will Hews, appeared in Blackwood's *Edinburgh Magazine,* July 1889.

37 Quoted Hyde, *Trials,* p. 56.

38 The poem is in *Collected Poems of Lionel Johnson,* p. 94. Fletcher comments pp. xxv–xxvi that it is impossible to say whether Wilde is referred to directly, then writes as though the matter is settled.

39 According to Matthew Sturgis, *Passionate Attitudes,* p. 86.

40 See Wilde, *Album,* p. 141.

41 See Fryer, *André and Oscar,* especially pp. 24–9.

42 Douglas, *Autobiography,* pp. 138–9.

43 Sherard, *The Real Oscar Wilde,* pp. 127–8.

Chapter Three: Feasting with Panthers

1 *Letters 2000,* May–June 1892, p. 526.

2 Ibid, 19 February 1892, p. 520.

3 Ibid, June 1892, p. 528.

4 Ellmann, p. 329.

5 *Letters 2000,* 20 April 1894, p. 590.

6 *Letters 2000, De Profundis,* p. 687.

7 Douglas, *Autobiography,* pp. 98–99.

8 Ibid, p. 76.

9 Harris, p. xxxv, quoting Douglas, blames Douglas for introducing Wilde to rent boys.

10 Croft-Cook, *Bosie,* pp. 57–8.

11 Brasol, p. 412.

12 On Atkin's career as extortioner and relations with Wilde, see Hyde, *Trials*, pp. 184–93.
13 Information on stained sheets, Hyde, *Trials*, p. 188.
14 Atkins stated Schwabe was seen in bed with Wilde. Mason, p. 218.
15 Mason, p. 152.
16 *Letters 2000*, October–November 1892, p. 537.
17 Douglas, quoted in Hyde, *Lord Alfred Douglas*, p. 33. Not reprinted in the collected sonnets.
18 *Letters 2000*, ? January 1893, p. 544. This is the "Hyacinthus" letter.
19 Croft-Cook, *Bosie*, p. 65.
20 For Beerbohm Tree comments and dealings over the Hyacinthus letter, Hyde, *Trials*, pp. 66–9.
21 Croft-Cook, *Bosie*, p. 70.
22 Ellmann, p. 371.
23 Ibid.
24 Ibid.
25 Ibid, p. 372.
26 For Percy's attempts at a career, Roberts, pp. 161–5.
27 For Sholto's attempts at a career, pp. 234–42.
28 *Letters 1962* edition, Campbell Dodgson. See Hart Davis note to page 867. This letter is not given in *Letters 2000*. See note p. 556.
29 *Letters 2000*, from Campbell Dodgson to Lionel Johnson, 8 February 1893, p. 867.
30 *Letters 2000*, 8–11 February, p. 547.
31 *Letters 1962* edition, p. 868.
32 *Letters 2000*, OW to Campbell Dodgson, 23 February 1893, pp. 555–6.
33 Croft-Cook, NEL edition of Bosie, considers Dodgson's account 'most happy' on p. 66. In his book, *The Unrecorded Life of Oscar Wilde*, he records that when he met Bosie years after the event Bosie could recall the humour, which was distinctly undergraduate.
34 *Letters 2000, De Profundis*, p. 691.
35 *Letters 2000*, March 1893, pp. 559–60. The letter was read out at the first trial, but the section in brackets was left out as too obscure or obscene.
36 *Letters 2000, De Profundis* p. 688.
37 Quoted Croft-Cook, *Bosie*, p. 72.

Chapter Four: Queensberry Rules 62 - 69

1 *Letters 2000, De Profundis*, p. 760.
2 Douglas, *Oscar Wilde and Myself*, p. 34.
3 *Letters 2000*, ?June 1893, p. 566.
4 Ibid, ? May 1893, p. 565.

5 *Letters 2000, De Profundis*, p. 688.
6 Frank Harris, 1997 p. 105.
7 *Letters 2000, De Profundis*, p. 694.
8 *Letters 2000*, 9 September 1893, p. 571.
9 *Letters 2000, De Profundis*, p. 693.
10 Wilde wrote in *De Profundis* that a friend had represented it would be humiliating to send back Bosie's work like a schoolboy exercise. No name appears in the text, but Hart-Davis notes that the original name was Robbie, crossed out. This on p. 432, *Letters 1962*.
11 *Letters 2000*, 8 November 1893, p. 575.
12 *Letters 2000, De Profundis*, p. 433.
13 Beerbohm, *Letters to Reggie Turner*, p. 84.
14 Letter from Browning to Harris, 3 November 1919, quoted in Ellmann, p. 383.
15 *Letters 2000, De Profundis*, p. 686.
16 Beardsley quoted Hyde, *Lord Alfred Douglas*, p. 47. The Rothenstein quote is from Max and Will, *Laro and Beckson*, p. 343, note 46. Beardsley quote Croft-Cook, *Bosie*, 1963, p. 82.
17 Croft-Cook, *Bosie*, 1963, p. 79.
18 *Letters 2000, De Profundis*, p. 694.

CHAPTER FIVE: ROGUE ELEMENTS

1 Ensor, p. 77.
2 *Hichens Yesterdays*, cited in Croft-Cook p. 88.
3 Quoted in Croft-Cook, pp. 88–92. The date was 10 December 1893.
4 Quoted in Croft-Cook, pp. 92–5. The date was 6 January 1894.
5 Robert Hichens, *The Green Carnation*, p. 5–6.
6 Ibid, p. 24.
7 Ibid.
8 Douglas, *Autobiography*, p. 87.
9 Quoted Hyde, *Lord Alfred Douglas*, p. 54.
10 Douglas, *Autobiography*, p. 89.
11 Ibid, p. 88.
12 *Letters 2000, De Profundis*, pp. 695–6.
13 Ibid, p. 696, emphasis added. All quotes in this paragraph from this source.
14 Frank Harris, pp. 110–11.
15 *Letters 2000, De Profundis*.
16 Queensberry and Colson, p. 51. The Marquis of Queensberry is relating family legend. Drumlanrig died before he was born.
17 Roberts, p. 184.
18 Ibid.

19 Rhodes, *James*, p. xi.
20 Douglas, *Without Apology*, p. 230.
21 Paget, *In My Tower*, pp. 5–6.
22 Douglas, *Autobiography*, p. 94.
23 Mason, pp. 96–7.
24 Rhodes, *James*, p. 287.
25 Ibid.
26 Douglas, *Autobiography*, p. 95.
27 Queensberry & Colson, p. 61.
28 *Letters 2000*, 5–6 November 1894, pp. 620–1. In this letter he also proposed writing a book "How to live above one's income: for the use of the sons of the rich", jointly with Bosie.
29 Mason, pp. 94–5. Bosie's telegraphed reply is quoted on p. 85.
30 Hichens, 1961, p. 17.
31 There is often confusion between Lord Alfred Somerset, who went abroad after the Cleveland St scandal of 1889 to avoid arrest, and his elder brother Henry. Both were sons of the Duke of Beaufort, but Henry had been married and fathered a child. This marriage was ended by judicial separation and he was forced to resign his public offices. It was rumoured he had fallen in love with a young man called Henry Smith. See Hyde, *Lord Alfred Douglas*, p. 56.
32 *Letters 2000, c.* 16 April 1894, pp. 588–9.
33 Hart-Davis and Holland, Wilde, *Letters 2000*, note on p. 589.
34 *Letters 2000, De Profundis*, p. 708.
35 Frank Harris, p. 132.
36 Mason, p. 105 gives Wilde in court saying he did not take steps against Queensberry in 1894 because of strong pressure exerted by an MP linked to the family – this was Bosie's cousin George Wyndham.
37 Ellmann, p. 397.
38 Letters cited by Mason, pp. 106–7.
39 Mason, p. 96.
40 *Letters 2000, c.* 13 August 1894, p. 603.
41 Ibid, ? June 1894, p. 592.
42 Ibid, p. 593.
43 Ibid, p. 594.
44 Ibid, p. 594, note.
45 Ibid, p. 598.
46 Queensberry and Colson, p. 57.
47 *Letters 2000, De Profundis*, pp. 708–9.
48 Mason, pp. 105–6.
49 Ibid, p. 107.
50 *Letters 2000*, p. 602.
51 Ibid, p. 617.

52 Hichens, *Green Carnation*, p. 17.
53 *Letters 2000, De Profundis*, p. 698.
54 Ibid, p. 699.
55 Ibid, p. 700.
56 *The Times*, 25 October 1894.
57 Hansard, 25 June 1894, cols 106–10.
58 Roberts, pp. 182–4, *The Times*, 19 October 1894.
59 Letter in Ellman papers in Oklahoma University Library. Emphases and orthography in original. See illustration.
60 *Letters 2000, De Profundis*, p. 701.
61 Ibid, p. 701.
62 *Letters 2000*, *c.* 9 November 1894, p. 622. Wilde had dedicated his story "The Star Child" to Margot Tennant, soon to be Mrs Asquith and later to play a major role in the Ross/Douglas feud.
63 Frank Harris, p. 125.
64 Jerome K. Jerome, quoted Ellmann, p. 404.
65 *Letters 2000*, p. 625, early December 1894. It is interesting that Wilde is still calling Gray "Dorian".
66 Ibid, p. 629, *c.* 25 January 1895.
67 Ibid.
68 Amor, pp. 155–6.
69 *Letters 2000*, p. 629.
70 Hyde, *Lord Alfred Douglas*, quotes André Gide on the two exiles in Morocco, pp. 68–9.

Chapter Six: The Storm Breaks

1 *Letters 2000, De Profundis*, pp. 758–9. The reference to Atkins is probably a slip of the pen, as the blackmailer over the Hyacinthus letter was Allen. Clibborn later received a seven year sentence for blackmail. A Note on p. 759 of the letters has George Ives referring to him as a "bold, scheming and enchanting panther" (Diary entry 23 December 1893).
2 *Letters 2000*, p. 159.
3 Ibid, *c* 17 February 1895, pp. 632–3.
4 Ibid, p. 634–5.
5 Ibid.
6 *Letters 2000, De Profundis*, p. 703.
7 *Letters 2000*, February 1895, p. 633 almost certainly after the opening of *Importance*.
8 Ibid, 28 February.
9 *Letters 2000, De Profundis*, p. 759.
10 Douglas, *Autobiography*, p. 97.

11 Mason, pp. 14–15.
12 The encounters are described by Harris pp. 132–40.
13 Shaw quoted on pp. 139–40 of Harris. In the Croft-Cook 1963 edition of *Bosie* he quotes Shaw as saying "Wilde was in a curious double temper. He made no pretence either of innocence or of questioning the folly of his proceedings against Q. But he had an infatuate haughtiness as to the impossibility of his retreating". p. 115. Unfortunately not sourced anywhere else.
14 Queensberry and Colson, p. 59.
15 Harris, pp. 134–5.
16 Ellmann, p. 414.
17 Marjoribanks, p. 210.
18 See Ellmann, p. 415, Hyde *Trials*, p. 83.
19 Hyde, *Trials*, p. 90.
20 Ibid, Ellmann, p. 415, Maston, p. 27. There are discrepancies as to addresses.
21 Harris, p. 137.
22 Hyde, *Trials*, p. 87.
23 Ibid, p. 93.
24 *Letters 2000*. First wire, p. 636.
25 Hyde, *Trials*, pp. 95–6.
26 *Letters 2000*, 3 April 1895, second wire p. 636.
27 Mason, p. 58.
28 Ibid, p. 66.
29 Ibid, p. 83.
30 Ibid, p. 90.
31 Ibid, pp. 90–1.
32 Ibid, p. 99.
33 Ibid, pp. 108–9.
34 Ibid, p .110.
35 Ibid, p. 112.
36 Ibid, p. 115.
37 Ibid, p. 113.
38 Frank Harris, p. 166. Harris says he later asked Wilde many times why he did not flee, but Wilde could never explain. He concludes Wilde was "amiable, weak, of a charming dispositon – easily led in action though not in thought", p. 163.
39 Mason, p. 124.
40 *Letters 2000*, p. 637.
41 Hyde, *Trials*, pp. 149–50.
42 Queensberry quote Mason, pp. 133–4.
43 Mason, p. 129.
44 Hyde, *Trials*, pp. 152–3 for Wilde that afternoon.
45 *Letters 2000*, 5 April 1895, pp. 637–8.

CHAPTER SEVEN: THE TRIALS OF OSCAR WILDE

1 *Daily Telegraph*, 6 April 1895.

2 Hyde, *Trials*, p. 156.

3 Hyde, *Lord Alfred Douglas*, p. 85. Lady Wilde depended on Oscar. She was in considerable financial straits until her death in 1896.

4 *Letters 2000*, 9 April 1895, p. 642.

5 Ibid, 9 April 1895, p. 642.

6 Ibid, 16 April 1895 p. 644.

7 Ibid, p. 644.

8 Ibid, p. 645.

9 Ellmann, p. 433.

10 Mason, p. 171 notes that "It had been obvious from the start that the Treasury had been anxious to avoid overloading the case against the accused, rather than press the charge, which remained one of misdemeanour", and outlines the reasons for this.

11 Douglas, *Autobiography*, pp. 119–20.

12 For the magistrates hearing, Mason, pp. 139–55.

13 Ibid, p. 158.

14 Ibid, p. 159.

15 Ibid, p. 161.

16 For detailed analysis of the testimony of Wilde's male friends, Hyde, *Trials*, pp. 170–93.

17 For the servants, Hyde, *Trials*, Mrs Applegate, p. 188, Savoy servants on pp. 193–4.

18 Mason, p. 184.

19 Ibid.

20 *Letters 2000, De Profundis*, p. 714.

21 Hyde, *Trials*, p. 201, Mason, p. 257–8.

22 Ibid, p. 207.

23 Ibid, p. 212.

24 Ibid.

25 *Letters 2000*, pp. 646–7. Bosie's letters to Wilde have not survived for the most part, only three having been discovered. (Hart-Davis, *Letters 1962*, p. 396).

26 Roberts, p. 245.

27 Hyde, *Trials*, p. 222.

28 Ibid.

29 Marjoribanks, p. 230.

30 Mason, p. 96.

31 Ibid, p. 109.

32 *Reynolds's News*, 5 May 1895.

33 The key passage naming Bosie was removed from the English edition of Harris's book, and read, "It was not I they spoke about at the Savoy. It was

Bosie Douglas. I was never bold enough. I went to see Bosie in the morning in his room". This passage is given in Hyde, *Trials*, p. 225. The story was rejected by Hesketh Pearson, but is now generally accepted.

34 *Letters 2000.* p. 652. See Bosie's comment, *Autobiography*, p. 112, that "it was an insane thing not to go".

35 Douglas, *Autobiography*, p. 121.

36 Ellmann, p. 443, quotes the letter.

37 *Letters 2000*, p. 651.

38 Roberts, pp. 251–2.

39 Full description of the fight, Hyde, *Trials*, pp. 232–3.

40 Mason, p. 365 on Parkers at Chiswick, Ellmann on the payment of witnesses, pp. 446–7.

41 Mason, pp. 374–5.

42 Hyde, p. 260.

43 Goodman, *The Oscar Wilde File*, p. 95. In *Letters 2000* Gill is quoted as writing it would be "undesirable to start such a prosecution unless there was a strong possibility that it would result in a prosecution", p. 766. Source given as MS Public Record Office. Two journalists in the *Daily Telegraph* 28 December 1999 stated they had found the letter in the PRO.

44 Mason, pp. 361–4 on relations Wood, Wilde, Douglas. Lockwood cross-examined on the relation with Douglas and the letters, pp. 383–7.

45 *Letters 2000, De Profundis*, p. 758. Francis Douglas, 11th Marquis of Queensberry, did not publish this unflattering description of his grandfather in the 1949 'Complete' version of *De Profundis*, which contained many other errors as it was written from a typescript. The original could not be consulted in the British Museum till 1960.

46 Mason, p. 410.

47 Ibid, p. 414.

48 Mason, pp. 418–19.

49 *Letters 2000*, pp. 765–6.

50 Mason, p. 426.

CHAPTER EIGHT: SEPARATION AND BITTERNESS 146-162

1 Hyde, *Trials*, p. 281. Haldane had been a member of the Gladstone Home Office Commitee on penal reform.

2 *Letters 2000, De Profundis* p. 762.

3 Ibid, pp. 716–17.

4 Comment on Bridges, *Star*, 19 April 1895. Quoted *Letters 2000*, p. 711.

5 *Truth*, 13 June 1895. *Letters 2000*, p. 712.

6 Hyde, *Lord Alfred Douglas*, p. 92.

7 Ibid, pp. 91–2.

8 Ibid, p. 93.
9 Hyde, *Trials*, p. 286.
10 *Letters 2000, De Profundis* p. 716. Merlin Holland comments "Wilde's indictments of Douglas in this letter need to be approached with some caution. While some are undoubtedly valid, others . . . seem both unfair to Douglas and inaccurate if taken at face value" (p. 684). This is fair comment. Wilde's attack on Douglas for not writing is both unfair and inaccurate.
11 Ellman, p. 460.
12 *Letters 2000, De Profundis*, pp. 756–7.
13 Sherard, *Story of an Unhappy Friendship*, p. 212.
14 *Letters 2000, De Profundis*, p. 721.
15 *Letters 2000*, note p. 642.
16 Robert Ross, *Friend of Friends*, ed. Margery Ross, no date p. 39.
17 Ross, op cit p. 40.
18 Ross, op cit p. 41.
19 *Letters 2000*, pp. 654–5.
20 *Letters 2000, De Profundis*, p. 725.
21 Quoted Hyde, *Trials*, p. 345.
22 Hyde, *Trials*, p. 347.
23 *Letters 2000*, pp. 667–8.
24 Hyde, *Lord Alfred Douglas*, p. 100.
25 Ibid, pp. 100–1.
26 *Letters 2000*, pp. 669–71.
27 Hyde, *Lord Alfred Douglas*, p. 101.
28 Hyde, op cit.
29 *Letters 2000*, p. 665.
30 *Letters 2000*, p. 666.
31 *Letters 2000*, pp. 668–71.
32 First sentence of *De Profundis. Letters 2000*, p. 683.
33 *Letters 2000, De Profundis*, p. 778.
34 Quoted Hyde, *Lord Alfred Douglas*, p. 104.
35 *Letters 2000*, pp. 780–2.
36 Comment on Douglas, *Letters 2000*, p. 782.
37 Hyde, *Lord Alfred Douglas*, p. 103.

CHAPTER NINE: SPIRITS ABROAD

1 Quoted Joseph Pearce, p. 265.
2 *Letters 2000*, Reminiscences of Ada Leverson, pp. 841–2.
3 Ada Leverson, op cit.
4 *Letters 2000*, p. 855.
5 Ibid, p. 920.

6 Ibid, p. 921.
7 Ibid, p. 858.
8 Ibid, p. 865.
9 Ibid, p. 873.
10 Ibid, p. 880.
11 Ibid, p. 899.
12 Ibid, p. 902.
13 Ibid, p. 909.
14 Quoted Murray, p. 103, note 83.
15 Ellmann, p. 513.
16 Ellmann, op cit.
17 Douglas, *Autobiography*, p. 152.
18 *Letters 2000*, pp. 932–3.

Chapter Ten: A Touching Reunion 170-179

1 Ellmann, p. 513.
2 *Letters 2000*, p. 942.
3 Harris, p. 280.
4 Douglas, *Autobiography*, p. 152.
5 *Letters 2000*, p. 935.
6 In Chapter XXII of his *Autobiography*, which deals with *De Profundis*, Douglas states that he received a long letter from Ross containing remarks by Oscar Wilde, which Douglas tore up and threw into the River Marne (p. 135). This is probably the text of *De Profundis*, which Ross had had typed and which Douglas probably thought was from Ross.
7 Douglas, op cit, p. 135.
8 O'Sullivan, pp. 194–7. Quoted *Letters 2000*, pp. 941–2.
9 Hyde, *Lord Alfred Douglas*, p. 114.
10 *Letters 2000*, p. 960.
11 Ibid, p. 960.
12 Ibid, p. 930.
13 Ibid, p. 947.
14 Quoted by Wilde in a letter to Adey, *Letters 2000*, p. 994.
15 *Letters 2000*, p. 955.
16 Ibid, p. 955.
17 Ibid, p. 980.
18 Ibid, pp. 980–1.
19 *Letters 1962*, 6 January 1897, More Adey, p. 697. *Letters 2000*, pp. 1009–10.
20 *Letters 2000*, pp. 991–2.
21 Ibid, p. 996.
22 Douglas, *Autobiography*, p. 154.

23 op cit, pp. 158–9.
24 op cit, p. 138.
25 Croft-Cook, p. 165.
26 op cit, pp. 302–5.
27 op cit, p. 305.
28 Harris, pp. 299–300.
29 *Letters 2000*, p. 1029.

CHAPTER ELEVEN: PARISIAN INTERMEZZO

1 Letter to Ross, *Letters 2000*, p. 1029.
2 O'Sullivan, pp. 69–70.
3 Ibid.
4 *Letters 2000*, pp. 1012–13.
5 Ibid, p. 1019.
6 Ibid, p. 1000. Latin tag in full is *Quantum mutatis ab illo* – how changed from what he once was.
7 Ibid, p. 1012.
8 Ibid, note p. 1022. Letter of 19 February, Constance to Otho.
9 Ibid, p. 1019.
10 Ibid, p. 1023.
11 Ibid, p. 1023.
12 Most recently as *The Judas Kiss* by David Hare.
13 *Letters 2000*, p.1038.
14 *Letters 2000*, letter from Adey on Sybil's first £100. p. 1009. Note Wilde's comment to Adrian Hope, p. 1008 defending Bosie's character.
15 Douglas, *Autobiography*, p. 159.
16 op cit, p. 161.
17 *Letters 2000*, p. 1067.
18 André Gide, *Oscar Wilde*, pp. 42–5. But there was correspondence.
19 As Douglas commented in *Oscar Wilde, A Summing Up*.
20 Ellmann, p. 528.
21 *Letters 2000*, p. 1057.
22 Ibid, p. 1187.
23 Ibid, p. 1066.
24 Ibid, p. 1071.
26 Ibid, p. 1104.
27 Ibid, p. 1153.
28 Douglas, *Autobiography*, pp. 122–4.
29 Roberts, p. 270.
30 *Letters 2000*, p. 1173.
31 Douglas, *Autobiography*, pp. 322–3.

32 *Letters 2000,* pp. 1187–8.
33 Douglas, *Autobiography,* p. 320.
34 Harris, *Confessions,* p. 361.
35 Harris, *Confessions,* pp. xxxiii. Shaw tried to produce a version of Harris's book in order to raise finance for Mrs Harris, who was in severe financial straits following Harris's death. Douglas would accept some of the American version of Harris's book, but was adamant that the Chantilly episode had to be cut and Shaw had to agree.
36 Hyde, *Lord Alfred Douglas,* p. 127.
37 Ellmann, p. 545.
38 *Letters 2000,* 21 November 2000, pp. 1206–8. The last recorded letter Wilde wrote, and largely in the hand of Maurice Gilbert. For Harris's view see *Confessions,* pp. 444–57.
39 Harris, *Confessions,* p. 452. Ross's letter describing Wilde's last days is on pp. 449–57.
40 On 23 December 1900 Ross wrote a long letter to Adele Schuster describing the final days. This is on pp. 62–9 of Robert Ross, *Friend of Friends.* The doctor had told him on 1 November Wilde might have five years to live, and when Ross decided to leave he did not realise Wilde was likely to die soon. These references on p. 65.
41 Harris, *Confessions,* pp. xii–xiv.
42 Douglas, *Autobiography* p. 183.

CHAPTER TWELVE: CURTAIN CALL

1 Quoted Croft-Cook, *Bosie,* p. 190.
2 Hyde, *Lord Alfred Douglas,* p. 132.
3 Douglas, *Autobiography,* p. 198.
4 Hyde, *Oscar Wilde, The Aftermath,* Methuen 1962, p. 209. Hyde reproduces the whole article.
5 Hyde in *Lord Alfred Douglas* has Sybil taking Bosie to the house of Percy Scawen Wyndham in the summer of 1887 and meeting their daughter Mary, later Balfour's mistress, while Bosie (then 17) played a noisy rhyming game with Pamela, later to marry both Edward Tennant and Sir Edward Grey, Asquith's Foreign Secretary. Pamela as Lady Tennant would provide finance for Bosie in the decade after Wilde's death.
6 All references to the Trial from *The Times,* 18, 19, 22, 23 April 1913.
7 *The Times* reported thus. The actual sentence is "You forced me to stay to brazen it out, if possible, in the box by absurd and silly lies".
8 Robert Ross, *Friend of Friends,* p. 244. Dated 1 July 1913. Douglas's supporters tend to assume Ross was exultant over the verdict, notably Croft-Cook.
9 Douglas, *Autobiography,* p. 210.

Chapter Thirteen: The Final Encore

1 Information in this paragraph from Maureen Borland, *Wilde's Devoted Friend*, pp. 189–93 and 199–200.
2 Quoted in full in Hyde, *Lord Alfred Douglas*, pp. 214–15.
3 Bernard Shaw and Alfred Douglas, *A Correspondence*, p. 4.
4 Douglas, *Autobiography*, p. 47.
5 Borland, op cit, p. 248.
6 Kettle, *Salome's Last Veil*, pp. 18–19. Borland, p. 277, claims Douglas was behind this move.
7 Borland, p. 281, citing a Ross letter to Charles Ricketts.
8 Kettle, op cit, p. 23.
9 *The Times*, 3 June 1918, 1st column, p. 4.
10 Ibid, op cit, 2nd column, p. 4.
11 Ibid, op cit, 3rd column, p. 4.
12 Ibid, op cit, 3rd column, p. 4.
13 Quoted Murray, p. 225.
14 *The Times*, Leader, 14 December 1921.
15 Quoted Hyde, *Lord Alfred Douglas*, pp. 27–8.
16 Douglas complains with some justice of how his correspondence was treated, *Autobiography*, p. 115.
17 On p. 81 of the *Autobiography* he refers to "Deliberate lies and misrepresentations . . . in the unpublished part of *De Profundis*, and again, afterwards, by word of mouth to numerous persons . . ." On pp. 67–8 Harris is referred to as a "monumental liar and worthy in that respect to rank with Robert Ross himself".
18 Douglas, *Autobiography*, p. 121.
19 Ibid, p. 122.
20 Ibid, pp. 118–19.
21 Ibid, p. 114. Destruction of letters at alleged instigation of a friend of Ross, p. 129. A sadly self-seeking passage.
22 Douglas, *Autobiography*, p. 138.
23 Quoted Murray, p. 273.

Chapter Fourteen: Time Ends All Things

1 Douglas, *Without Apology* section on Wilde, pp. 209–33.
2 *Without Apology*, quote on seeking to ruin Bosie and harm Sybil, p. 212, "avowed object" to smash Bosie, p. 237. It was of course not Queensberry's object to smash his son, whatever may have happened as a result of the trial.
3 *Without Apology*, p. 253.
4 *Letters 2000*, p. 714.
5 Queensberry and Colson, p. 143.

6 Sinden, pp. 47–51.
7 Hyde, *Lord Alfred Douglas*, p. 337.
8 Hyde, op cit, p. 337.
9 Vyvyan Holland, *Son Of Oscar Wilde*, pp. 192–3.
10 Hyde, *Lord Alfred Douglas*, p. 339.

EPILOGUE: AND ALL MEN . . .

1 On 18 March 1898 Wilde commented in a letter to Ross that "I shall now live as the Infamous St Oscar of Oxford, Poet and Martyr". The idea of St Oscar was taken up by Terry Eagleton in a play of the same name and the idea that Wilde was a martyr is now widely accepted.
2 *Truth*, 13 June 1895. Wilde's letter to the *Evening News*, *Letters 2000*, p. 637.
3 The myth of Bosie as betrayer existed before the Ransome trial, aided by the fact that he had not been prosecuted, suggesting that a deal had been struck to keep him out of court. It was expressed with poetic skill by Aleister Crowley in his poem "A Slim Gilt Soul", in the set *A Winged Beetle* privately printed 1910. Quoted in Queensberry and Colson, pp. 145–6.
4 *Letters 2000, De Profundis*, p. 689.
5 *Letters 2000*, p. 634.
6 *Letters 2000*, p. 796.
7 It was not only Douglas who failed to appreciate that in a libel action evidence of bad character is irrelevant. Hesketh Pearson also argued that Clarke failed Wilde in not putting Queensberry's character into the account and calling Douglas into the witness box to testify against his father. In a recent commentary, Jean Graham Hall and Gordon D. Smith have commented "In our opinion Pearson failed to grasp the essential elements of the law of criminal libel. The Marquis of Queensberry's character and his motive for publishing the libel were immaterial. Whether or not his son, Lord Alfred Douglas, would have cast doubt on his father's character if he had given evidence for the prosecution was of no consequence." See *The Tragedy of Being Earnest*, p. 18.
8 *Letters 2000*, pp. 818–19.
9 In *Son Of Oscar Wilde*, Robinson edition 1999, p. 130.
10 Bernard Shaw and Alfred Douglas, *A Correspondence*, 1989, p. 121.
11 *Letters 2000*, p. 629.
12 Ibid, p. 690.
13 Ibid, p. 670.
14 *Letters 2000, De Profundis*, pp. 739–40.
15 Letter from Shaw, 4 July 1931. Shaw–Douglas Correspondence op cit, p. 18. The reference is to a child in Dickens's *Dombey and Son*.
16 *Letters 2000*, p. 933.

Select Bibliography

(All publications London except where indicated)

Amor, Ann Clark *Mrs Oscar Wilde, A Woman of Some Importance.* Sidgwick & Jackson 1983

Beerbohm, Max *Letters to Reggie Turner,* ed Rupert Hart-Davis, Hart-Davis 1964

—— *A Catalogue of Caricatures,* ed Rupert Hart-Davis, Macmillan 1972

Borland, Maureen *Wilde's Devoted Friend (Robert Ross),* Lennard 1990

Brasol, Boris *Oscar Wilde,* Williams & Norgate 1938

Callow, Simon *Oscar Wilde & His Circle,* National Portrait Gallery 2000

Calloway, Stephen *Aubrey Beardsley,* V&A Publications 1998

Calloway, Stephen & David Colvin *Oscar Wilde,* Orion 1997

Croft-Cook, Rupert *Bosie, The Story of Lord Alfred Douglas, his friends and enemies,* W.H. Allen 1963. New English Library (NEL) Four Square Books, nd.

—— *Feasting with Panthers, A New Consideration of Some Late Victorian Writers,* W.H. Allen 1967

—— *The Unrecorded Life of Oscar Wilde,* W.H. Allen 1972

d'Arch-Smith, Timothy *Love in Earnest: Some Notes on the Lives and Writings of English 'Uranian' Poets from 1889–1930,* Routledge & Kegan Paul 1970

de Bremonte, Anna (Comtesse) *Oscar Wilde and his Mother,* Everett & Co, 1914

Douglas, Lord Alfred *The Autobiography of Lord Alfred Douglas,* Martin Secker (2nd edn) October 1931

—— *Oscar Wilde, A Summing Up,* Duckworth 1940

—— *Oscar Wilde and Myself,* John Long, Haymarket 1914 (with T.W.H. Crosland)

—— *Sonnets by Lord Alfred Douglas,* Academy Publishing 1909

—— *The Spirit Lamp* (ed Alfred Douglas) Oxford 1892–93

—— *Without Apology,* Martin Secker 1938

Dowling, Linda *Hellenism & Homosexuality in Victorian Oxford,* Cornell University Press, Ithaca & London 1994

Eagleton, Terry *St Oscar and Other Plays,* Blackwell 1997

Ellmann, Richard *Oscar Wilde,* Penguin Books, 1988 (Hamish Hamilton 1987)

Fisher, Trevor *Scandal: The Sexual Politics of Late Victorian Britain,* Sutton, Stroud 1995

Freeman, William *The Life of Lord Alfred Douglas, Spoilt Child of Genius,* Herbert Joseph 1948

Foldy, Michael S. *The Trials of Oscar Wilde,* Yale 1997

Fryer, Jonathan *André and Oscar: Gide, Wilde, and the Gay Art of Loving*, Constable 1997, Alison & Busby 1999
—— *Robbie Ross, Oscar Wilde's True Love*, Constable 2000
Gaunt, William *The Aesthetic Adventure*, Jonathan Cape 1975
Gide, André *Oscar Wilde*, William Kimber 1951 (first published 1910 by Mercure de France. Expanded and translated.)
Goodman, Jonathan (ed) *The Oscar Wilde File*, W.H. Allen 1989
Hall, Jean Graham & Gordon D. Smith, *Oscar Wilde: The Tragedy of Being Earnest*, Barry Rose Law Publishers, Chichester 2001
Hare, David *The Judas Kiss* (play), Faber & Faber 1998
Harris, Frank *Oscar Wilde, His Life and Confessions*, Covici Friede, New York 1930. This text amplified the original version of 1916, notably with Douglas's letters to Harris of 1925, and for this reason Douglas went to law to prevent it being available in the UK. Bernard Shaw had to expurgate it to produce his 1938 version.
Hichens, Robert *The Green Carnation* (Anon 1894, William Heinemann), Icon Books 1961, using the text of the Unicorn edition of Martin Secker, 1949, with introduction by Hichens written in December 1948 explaining how the book came to be written in 1894 and why it was withdrawn from publication at the time of the trials, then reissued after the death of Douglas.
Hoare, Philip *Wilde's Last Stand*, Duckworth 1997
Holland, Merlin 'Biography and the Art of Lying', in: Peter Raby (ed), *The Cambridge Companion to OW*, Cambridge University Press 1997
—— *The Wilde Album*, Fourth Estate 1997
Holland, Vyvyan *Son of Oscar Wilde*, Rupert Hart-Davis 1954, reprinted by Robinson 1999, with foreword and revisions by Merlin Holland.
Holroyd, Michael *Bernard Shaw, Vol 1, 1856–1898, The Search for Love*, Penguin 1990
Hyde, Mary (ed) *Bernard Shaw and Alfred Douglas, a Correspondence*, Oxford Letters and Memoirs, Oxford University Press 1989
Hyde, Montgomery H. *Christopher Sclater Millard*, Global Academic Publishers, New York & Amsterdam 1990
—— *Lord Alfred Douglas*, Methuen 1984
—— *Oscar Wilde*, Eyre Methuen 1976
—— *Oscar Wilde: the Aftermath*, Methuen 1963
—— *The Other Love*, Heinemann 1970
—— *The Trials of Oscar Wilde*, Dover Publications Inc., New York 1973
—— *The Cleveland Street Scandal*, W.H. Allen 1976
Jackson, Holbrook *The Eighteen Nineties, A Review of Art and Ideas at the Close of the Nineteenth Century*, 1913, Pelican Books 1939
James, Robert Rhodes *Rosebery*, Weidenfeld & Nicolson 1963
Johnson, Lionel *The Complete Poems of Lionel Johnson*, ed Iain Fletcher, The Unicorn Press 1953

Kaufman, Moises *Gross Indecency: The Three Trials of Oscar Wilde* (play), Methuen Drama 1998

Kettle, Michael *Salomé's Last Veil, The Libel Case of the Century*, Granada Publishing 1977

Knox, Melissa *Oscar Wilde: A Long and Lovely Suicide*, Yale University Press 1994

Longford, Elizabeth *A Pilgrimage of Passion: The Life of Wilfred Scawen Blunt*, Weidenfeld & Nicolson 1979

Marjoribanks, Edward *Lord Carson*, Gollancz 1932

Mason, Stuart (Christopher Sclater Millard) *Three Times Tried*, Paris nd. Originally Ferrestone Press, London January 1912. Limited edition.

Mitchell, Julian *Wilde* (screenplay with introduction by Stephen Fry), Orion 1997

Morley, Sheridan *Oscar Wilde*, Pavilion 1997, original edition Weidenfeld & Nicolson 1976

Murray, Douglas *Bosie, An Autobiography of Lord Alfred Douglas*, Hodder & Stoughton 2000

Nicholls, Mark *The Importance of Being Oscar*, Robson Books 1981

O'Sullivan, Vincent *Aspects of Wilde*, Constable 1936

Page, Norman *An Oscar Wilde Chronology*, Macmillan 1991

Pearce, Joseph *The Unmasking of Oscar Wilde*, HarperCollins 2000

Pearson, Hesketh *Oscar Wilde*, MacDonald & James 1975, Methuen 1946

Pine, Richard 'Oscar Wilde', *Gill's Irish Lives*, Gill & MacMillan, Dublin 1983

Queensberry and Percy Colson *Oscar Wilde and The Black Douglas*, Hutchinson 1949

Raby, Peter (ed) *The Cambridge Companion to Oscar Wilde*, Cambridge University Press 1997

—— *Aubrey Beardsley and the 1890s*, Collins & Brown 1988

Raffalovich, André *A Willing Exile*, 2 vols, F.V. White & Co 1890

Roberts, Brian *The Mad Bad Line*, Hamish Hamilton 1981

Ross, Margery *Robert Ross, Friend of Friends* (edited letters), Jonathan Cape 1952

Schroeder, Horst *Additions and Corrections to Richard Ellmann's Oscar Wilde*, Braunschweig 1989, privately printed

Sherard, Robert Harborough *The Life of Oscar Wilde*, T. Werner Laurie 1906

—— *The Real Oscar Wilde*, T. Werner Laurie, nd (likely to be 1914, cites Douglas's comments in court in the Ransome trial April 1913)

Sinden, Donald *A Touch of the Memoirs*, Hodder & Stoughton 1982

Sinfield, Alan *The Wilde Century*, Cassell 1994

Smith, Gordon D., see Hall, Jean Graham

Stoppard, Tom *The Invention of Love* (play), Faber & Faber 1997

Sturgis, Matthew *Aubrey Beardsley*, HarperCollins 1998

—— *Passionate Attitudes: The English Decadence of the 1890s*, Macmillan 1995

Turner, Frank M. *The Greek Heritage in Victorian Britain*, Yale 1988

Wilde, Joy *Mother of Oscar*, John Murray 1994

Wilde, Oscar The only complete version of *De Profundis* is that in the *Letters of Oscar Wilde*, reprinted in the 2000 edition of the *Complete Letters*. The following two versions are important in their own right:

De Profundis (ed and with an introduction by Vyvyan Holland. Despite claim on title page this is not complete), Methuen 1949

De Profundis (ed and with an introduction by Robert Ross. This is the 1905 edition slightly expanded but with no reference to Bosie Douglas, and which did not give any offence to Douglas), Methuen 1908

—— *The Letters of Oscar Wilde*, ed Rupert Hart-Davis, RHD, 2nd edn (corrected) 1962

—— *The Complete Letters of Oscar Wilde*, ed Merlin Holland and Rupert Hart-Davis, Fourth Estate 2000

—— *The Complete Stories, Plays, Poems*, Michael O'Mara Books 1991

—— *The Picture of Dorian Gray*, 1891 ed and with an introduction by Isobel Murray, Oxford University Press 1974

—— *Plays, Prose Writings and Poems*, with an introduction by Terry Eagleton, Everyman's Library, published by David Campbell Publishers Ltd 1991

Yeats, William Butler *Memoirs*, ed Denis Donoghue, New Edition, Papermac 1988

—— *Autobiographies*, Macmillan 1955

Index

Notes: B = Bosie (Lord Alfred Douglas); OW = Oscar Wilde